Women's Rights at Work

Women's Rights at Work

Campaigns and Policy in Britain and the United States

Barbara Ehlers

Elizabeth M. Meehan

MACMILLAN

First published 1985 by
Higher and Further Education Division
MACMILLAN PUBLISHERS LTD
Houndmills, Basingstoke,
Hampshire, RG21 2XS,
and London
Companies and representatives
throughout the world

Typeset by
Wessex Typsesetters Ltd
Frome, Somerset

Printed in Hong Kong

British Library Cataloguing in Publication Data
Meehan, Elizabeth
Women's rights at work.
1. Women—Employment—Law and legislation
—Great Britain—History   2. Women—
Employment—Law and legislation—United
States—History
I. Title
344.104′14   KD3103.W6
ISBN 0–333–36125–3
ISBN 0–333–36126–1 Pbk

This book is dedicated to my parents for their unflagging support through the several changes of career that led me to the one in which I feel at home. It is also dedicated to Mrs Thatcher, whose jest that I abandon the thesis from which it is derived was an incentive to finishing it.

Contents

List of Tables

Acknowledgements

Shorter versions of a few of the ideas that are in this book have already appeared. I am grateful to the following for allowing me to incorporate them into this book:

Politics ('Importing Equal Opportunity Policies') vol. 2, no. 1, April 1982.
Political Quarterly ('The Priorities of the Equal Opportunities Commission') vol. 54, no. 1.
Women's Welfare/Women's Rights, J. Lewis (ed.) 1983. ('Equal Opportunity Policies, Some Contrasts Between Britain and US').

I also wish to thank the following who have kindly given permission for the use of copyright material:

Cambridge University Press for tables from *Occupation and Pay in Great Britain 1906–1960* by G. Routh (1965).

The Controller of Her Majesty's Stationery Office for extracts from published Crown copyright material.

National Association of Teachers in Further and Higher Education (NATFHE) for an extract from 'Education, Training and the Employment of Women and Girls' (1970).

Introduction

The 1960s and 1970s were decades of renaissance for feminism in Britain and the United States. Women were angry about their continued inequality of treatment in social, economic and public life. But, in different ways at different times in the two countries, the expression of their anger was connected to the other large issues of the time: war, civil rights and poverty. Governments of the respective countries appeared in part to be taken by surprise by the discontent and then, suddenly, willing to respond. Equal pay laws were passed, followed by laws banning discrimination at work, in education and in the provision of goods and services. In the United States things went even further. Affirmative action was introduced for racial minorities and then women because it was thought insufficient simply to remove remaining barriers to equality; if lives were to be transformed, remedial steps were necessary to eliminate the long-term effects of past discrimination. In both countries, new institutions were created to ensure that the norms embodied in new laws would have practical as well as symbolic significance.

The new laws and institutions did not escape feminist criticism in their infancy; but it was also believed that they were an important step towards a more civilised society in which the discrepancy between women's formal political equality and their social and economic subordination would eventually come to an end. In the meantime, avenues of redress were provided against transgressions of socially unacceptable practices.

In the twenty or so years since the first American Federal

reforms and the ten years or so since the British, there have
been some improvements in women's conditions of work. But,
in both countries, there is widespread disappointment that
gains have not been greater and that losses are now being
experienced. Women's earnings as a proportion of men's grew
rapidly after the British Equal Pay Act but have remained low
in the United States, despite a similar law. In recent years
British women's pay has begun to fall back. The low proportion
of American women's pay is attributable in part to success of
affirmative action in bringing women into new occupations at
entry-level salaries or wages. Occupational segregation has
indeed declined faster in the United States than in Britain but
in both countries it remains a major barrier to equal pay and
promotion prospects. Commitment to equal rights for women
among political leaders and administrators came, after a
disappointing start, to be a major factor in reinforcing general
social values about the equality of women in the United States.
But with the rise of the 'moral majority', the political climate is
now closer there to that of Britain where there is relatively little
political leadership on the subject. Some recent Commissioners
on the EOC have stood up for feminist concerns in the way that
American counterparts did in the last days of the liberal
ascendancy. But they took up their duties at the onset of
recession and at the triumph of a non-interventionist political
philosophy, the combined effects of which are to accord state
guarantees of women's socio-economic equality very low
priority – if any at all.

The story of the struggle, the hopes and the setbacks deserve
to be told and it is interesting to do so comparatively. This is
because feminist ideas in the two countries have influenced
each other in some respects and because government thinking
in Britain about women's rights at work was sharpened by
knowledge of civil rights policies in the United States. However, despite the transatlantic inspirations, and, although the
conditions of working women were relatively similar in the two
countries before the new laws, the stories are not exact parallels.
The book discusses differences in the growth of organised
pressure for legal recognition of women's rights at work and
considers why politicians in the two countries chose 'to hear'
demands for change at different times. It is argued that

capitulation was not necessarily related to beliefs that the demands were just. Other factors like business rationality, race relations, poverty and, in Britain, membership of the EEC all contributed to the timing of reforms. The book also deals with differences in implementation and enforcement, outlining the more complex set of institutions in the United States than in Britain and comparing the roles of judicial bodies. Variations in approach are explained by reference to more general differences in regulatory agencies, in attitudes to the use of the law for public purposes, in systems of accountability, in patterns of interest group representation and in ideas about groups and classes in democratic society. Taking account of different institutional emphases, it is argued, however, that in both countries it is necessary to combine use of existing or modified laws and voluntary initiatives in collective bargaining in order to decrease occupational segregation. The other main impediment to equality – unemployment – is also discussed. Resistance is called for to the use by political leaders and employers of unemployment as a reason for inaction on equality. Indeed, it is concluded that concern about unemployment must be made into an opportunity for a careful reassessment of what it means to hold a job and of the relationship between paid work and domestic responsibility – for men as well as for women.

The book could not have been written without the help of many people in public and private capacities. My thanks to them all are recorded in the Afterword.

ELIZABETH M. MEEHAN

PART ONE
The Background

PART ONE

The Background

1

Why Study Equality Policies?

The new constitutions of most modern revolutionary societies embody the idea of equal rights for women. In the last two decades or so, equal rights for working women have appeared as policy objectives in most liberal democracies too. Their introduction has often been followed by anger and frustration among feminists at their ineffectiveness. This book compares the origins and implementation of equal employment opportunity laws in two liberal democracies: Britain and the United States of America. The first aim of this introductory chapter is to show why a comparison of these countries is of interest both to those who actively seek to promote women's equality and to students of politics and comparative politics. In setting out these reasons, the plan of the book is also outlined.

It is sometimes argued that one reason for policy failure might be that there was no real problem to solve in the first place. Consequently the second aim of this chapter is to disprove such a possibility in this particular case and, in so doing, to provide the reader with some background information on the state of the labour markets in the two countries before the advent of reform.

Women's rights, civil rights and welfare

A study of the legislation in the two countries is important for historical reasons both directly and indirectly related to the

3

issue of women's rights. There are five significant aspects. First, laws about equality for working women represent a new stage, if only at the normative level, in the history of women's emancipation. Acceptance among political leaders of the rectitude of using the law to proclaim women's rights as a proper goal of civilised society is discussed in Chapter 3. The fragility of this advance is, however, evident to all and this is discussed in Chapters 4, 5 and 6. Secondly, policies on women's equality are closely connected to the politics of civil rights. In the United States the connection is a paradoxical one. In Chapter 2 it will be shown that, from the days of the anti-slavery movement, productive connections have existed between feminists and racial minority groups. Yet, as will be shown in Chapter 3, the inclusion of women in the 1964 Civil Rights Act was, in part, a result of conservative opposition to the idea of any legislative guarantees of equal treatment for anyone. In Britain, while the beginnings of such guarantees appeared in laws about race relations in 1965 and 1968, innovatory legal concepts and institutional powers which were introduced in the Sex Discrimination Act (1975) were replicated in the 1976 Race Relations Act. This is discussed in Chapter 3. The third point of historical interest is that the British Race Relations Acts, Equal Pay Act (1970) and Sex Discrimination Act mark a move away from the principles of universalism and anonymity underlying at least some of the intentions behind the Welfare State. They do so by guaranteeing specific forms of equality for groups identifiable by innate characteristics. This reflects twin concerns. On the one hand, it had become evident that welfare legislation was failing to eliminate poverty and deprivation and, on the other, anxiety was growing about inefficiencies in the use of scarce resources. In the United States, although social issues are less often though of in class terms, there was in the 1960s a comparable concern about the failures of policy delivery in the welfare field. In both countries the overlap of victims of discrimination and of welfare policy failure was noted. This is discussed in Chapter 3. Fourthly, anti-discrimination reforms were facilitated by changing attitudes in the British Parliament about the proper scope and function of the law and in the United States, despite the conservative opposition, by the belief that such measures were compatible with the values expressed in the constitution. These aspects are discussed in Chapters 2, 3 and 5. Fifthly, the elimination of sex discrimination was, in any case, becoming part of Britain's international obligations arising from expected or actual membership of the European Economic Community. Part of the planning stage of the Equal Pay Act included consideration of what obligations would be entailed by signing the Treaty of Rome. By the time that Europe was discussing an equal opportunity directive, British governments were beginning to consider a sex discrimination law. But, at the same time, it was being pointed out in the European Parliament that the only available European models were in communist states. The then Labour Home Secretary, Roy Jenkins, and his political advisers were already impressed with American race relations policies. It was, therefore, natural that they also turned to the United States for inspiration on the question of women's equality. Pressure from the EEC and specific American influences are discussed in Chapter 3.

The benefits of comparing policies

Adaptations, such as this one, of solutions devised in one political system by another are thought by some writers to be made too hastily and uncritically for whimsical reasons.[1] Goodin[2] argues, however, that the 'whims' of politicians are not arbitrary and that the timing of legislation (or failure to act) depends on the particular configuration of interest groups confronting politicians. It is argued in Chapter 3 that the configuration of policy imperatives facing American and British governments in respect of the distribution of the labour force and international obligations played a part in the timing of their respective equal pay and opportunity laws. And it is argued in Chapters 4 and 5 on enforcement, that different configurations of corporate and women's interest groups have made some difference in implementation.

Broadly speaking, the reasons for comparing policy initiation and implementation fall into two methodological categories. First, comparative analysis is sometimes undertaken as a form of experimentation in order to advocate better policy. Examples of this objective can be found in a collection of essays edited by Nagel.[3] Secondly, the operation of broadly similar policies in two countries or the presence of a policy in one and its absence in another otherwise similar system are used to explore institutions, interest groups and power relationships in the two societies. A persuasive proponent of this approach and critic of the first is Ashford.[4] Throughout this book, but particularly in Chapter 5, equal opportunity policies are used to illuminate understanding of the general comparative politics of Britain and the United States. However, the last chapter moves from strict analysis to recommendation. The suggestions for activists which arise from the whole study and which are presented in Chapter 6 may be of limited interest to those who believe that women's inequality is wholly and necessarily a consequence of a capitalist system of production. But they may be useful for American and British feminists who believe that improvements, at least, are possible and ought to be pursued.

The economics of women's work

If judgments are to be made about the effectiveness of new policies, it is necessary to demonstrate that a real problem existed in the first place. Patterns of pay and occupational distribution in the two countries are essentially similar except that, as in the case of political reform, some changes appear about ten years earlier in the United States than in Britain. A description of these patterns is followed by some of the major theoretical explanations in economics for discrimination which have implications for judgments about the new laws and for the direction of political pressure for further improvements.

Major upheavals in the employment of women in both countries accompanied the industrial revolutions, the triumph of Victorian ideas about domesticity, civil and world wars, market movements and technological changes in work processes before 1945. There were also periodic demands for equal pay and rights which will be referred to in Chapter 2. But it was particularly the state of affairs after the Second World War that finally caught the attention of governments and this is what is dealt with here.

Pay

As far as pay is concerned, the pattern was similar in both countries. Using aggregate differences within occupational groups, Routh[5] calculates the figures, given in Table 1.1, for Britain. There are some notable shifts and class differences here but, although there is some disagreement about whether the public or private sector was in the lead in better pay for middle-class women, most writers agree that figures like 75 per cent applied to about 10 per cent of working women only.[6] Routh's figures for all women show a stability that continued to 1972, when according to the Department of Employment, all full-time non-manual women earned 51 per cent of male average weekly earnings and female manual workers 51.7 per cent.[7]

TABLE 1.1   *Women's average as per cent of men's pay, Britain*

	Years		
Occupational group	*1935/6*	*1955/6*	*1960*
Higher professional	—	75	75
Lower professional	69	72	72
Managers, administrators	38	54	54
Clerks	46	57	61
Foremen	57	61	59
Skilled manual	44	51	50
Semi-skilled manual	75	57	58
Unskilled manual	57	52	53
All (current weights)	56	50	54

SOURCE   Routh, *Occupation and Pay in Great Britain 1906–1960*, p. 105.

In the United States, pre-war aggregate rates for women were, on average, between 50 per cent and 60 per cent of men's pay, social work being the rare exception where, by 1939, the gap had narrowed to 84 per cent.[8] Between 1962 and 1964,[9] the experience of different occupational categories is given in Table 1.2.

TABLE 1.2   *Women's median wages or salaries as per cent of men's; US*

	Years		
Occupational group	*1962*	*1963*	*1964*
Professional, technical	66.1	64.8	64.3
Managers, administrators	57.8	55.2	55.5
Clerical workers	68.6	67.7	66.2
Sales workers	43.6	39.0	40.4
Operatives	59.4	57.4	57.8
Service workers	51.8	57.5	53.7
All	59.5	59.6	59.6

SOURCES   United States Department of Labor, *Bulletin* 297, Table 53; 2080, Table 52.

The experience of white women deteriorated marginally in the period leading up to the Federal Equal Pay Act. The position for ethnic minority women was much worse in absolute terms although it shows some unsteady improvement in relation to white men and women and minority men (Table 1.3).

Aggregate figures exaggerate and conceal inequalities. They do not, for example, take account of longer hours worked by men (in Britain and the United States between 43 and 47 hours a week for men and 38 and 41 for women) but they also conceal the fact that when women do overtime work their shift premia are smaller. In 1973 overtime pay for British women accounted for 3 per cent of their earnings while the corresponding figure for men was 27 per cent. The average hourly earnings for all

TABLE 1.3   *Median wages or salaries of year-round full-time workers by sex and race, 1939, 1960–3; US*

Year	As per cent of white men			As per cent of minority men		As per cent of white women
	White women	*Minority women*	*Minority men*	*White women*	*Minority women*	*Minority women*
1939	60.8	23.0	45.0	135.1	51.2	37.9
1960	60.2	41.9	66.9	90.0	62.6	69.6
1961	59.2	39.5	66.0	89.6	59.9	66.8
1962	59.8	37.8	63.1	94.8	60.0	63.3
1963	59.3	37.7	65.4	90.7	57.7	63.6

SOURCE   United States Department of Labor, *Bulletin* 297, Table 57.

full-time women workers in Britain in 1972 was 64.5 per cent of men's, including overtime, and 64.6 per cent excluding it.[10]

Inequalities in pay occur either where different rates are paid for similar work or in occupations with heavy concentrations of female employees and which are low paid. A list of collective agreements for 1970 compiled by the British Office of Manpower Economics shows that 156 of 228 agreements specified lower rates or lower minima for women in similar jobs to men.[11] Equal rates were specified in occupations like mining and quarrying, notable for the absence of women! In 1971 the New Earnings Survey showed that the seven industries with the highest pay employed only $12\frac{1}{2}$ per cent of all working women, the seven lowest paid industries employed 52.2 per cent of them. In the United States a similar characteristic can be seen. Table 1.2 showed the worst rate for women as a percentage of male rates is among sales workers. At the same time, the retail section of this occupation is also notable because three-quarters of its employees are women.

Occupational distribution

Since the Second World War women and, in particular married women, have been entering the labour market in increasing numbers (Table 1.4).

TABLE 1.4 *Working women in Britain and the United States, 1950–71*

	1950–1		1970–1	
	Totals	Per cent of labour force	Totals	Per cent of labour force
United States	17.9 m	29.1	31.3 m	38.1
United Kingdom	7.0 m	31.0	9.0 m	36.5

SOURCES United States Department of Labor, *Bulletin* 297, Table 2. United Kingdom Central Statistical Office, *Social Trends*, 1 and 3.

This table shows that women substantially increased their share of the labour markets in both countries in the years after the war. Before the war, women in both countries tended to be single and young. After 1945, a spectacular increase began in the employment of older, married women. In the United States it was normal by 1950 for women to work until the arrival of children and to return to the labour market after the age of 35. In Britain this pattern was not so obvious until the late 1950s.[12] By 1975, a new feature was clear in the United States. This was a sharp rise in the participation rates of mothers aged 20 to 24 years old with children under school age.[13] A similar change in Britain is, as yet, hardly noticeable and is likely to be impeded by the recession.

Increased rates and longer periods of participation by women might have been expected to affect the distribution of men and women across occupations and, hence, their rates of pay.[14] Such an expectation is based on the view that the early relatively weaker attachment of women to the labour market made it irrational for employers to train and promote them. But there were few signs of desegregation in either country in the periods preceding equal rights legislation.

Segregation is labelled 'horizontal' when women and men work in different occupations and 'vertical' when both sexes work in the same broad occupational category but where each sex predominates in different levels. According to Hakim, the former has declined slightly in Britain while the latter has increased. Horizontal segregation decreased at a slightly faster rate in the United States than in Britain but both countries are more notable for the continuity, despite shifts, in the broad patterns of different occupational destinations for women and men. Hakim's figures, Table 1.5, for the decline of horizontal segregation are undramatic.

TABLE 1.5 *Occupational concentration, 1951–71; US*

Total number of occupations identified at each census	Per cent of all occupations which have:			
	No women workers	*70% women workers*	*A higher per cent of women workers than the labour force*	*A higher per cent of men workers than the labour force*
1951 : 587	6	11	28	72
1961 : 201	9	10	26	74
1971 : 223	2	12	26	74

SOURCE Hakim, *Occupational Segregation*, p. 23.

Although a few occupations exclusive to one sex have disappeared, men are more likely to find themselves working in an occupation in which they predominate. In the United States, she argues, horizontal desegregation despite its faster decline than in Britain, is also the result of men entering 'female' occupations and not of the branching out of women.

She quotes Gross's observation that 'sexual segregation in occupations is considerably more severe than racial segregation'.

So far as vertical segregation is concerned, broadly similar patterns appear in both countries. Using a variety of sources,[15] which are not strictly comparable but which can give a general picture, the figures given in Table 1.6 for the main British occupational categories can be derived.

Within the professional categories, women are poorly represented at the higher level compared to the lower, they are clerks but not administrators and more often are semi-skilled than skilled manual workers.[16] Occupations within these categories that are notable for their degrees of horizontal segregation include medicine, where women are more likely to be nurses and para-medical staff than doctors; teaching, where they are less likely to be university lecturers than school-teachers; and management, where they are probably in personnel instead of sales and contracting. In the manual sector, women are concentrated in the low to moderately paid industries of electrical engineering, food, drink and tobacco, textiles, clothing and footwear and miscellaneous services. Men are more likely than women to be employed in the moderately to highly paid occupations of construction work, mechanical engineering and mining. So, in manual and non-manual work, women are well represented in those occupations that are an extension of their domestic roles. Electrical engineering might be thought of as an exception but the stereotype of female manual dexterity operates strongly here. In both sectors promotion and on-the-job training are less likely for women, contributing to vertical segregation. At most, 10 per cent of nurses are male; yet one-third of senior posts are held by men. In teaching, headships of co-educational schools usually go to men. In manual occupations even where women are numerically dominant, such as textiles and food, drink and tobacco, women are more likely to be located at the semi-skilled level than the skilled.

In the United States similar inequalities exist within and between occupational categories. This is shown in Table 1.7.

The professional category looks better than its British counterpart but this is because it includes all occupations that

TABLE 1.6 *Women as per cent of each occupational category, 1951–66; Britain*

	Year	Higher professional	Lower professional	Employers, proprietors, managers, administrators	Clerks	Skilled manual	Semi-skilled manual	Unskilled
A	1951	8.0	53.2	18.5	58.2	15.8	40.5	20.9
	1959	9.5	57.8	20.1	62.4	15.2	42.2	22.7
	1961	8.1*	61.9‡	26.0 6.2	—	—	—	—
B	1966	8.9*	60.5†	30.0	63.0‡	18.4§	42.2§	22.9§¶

* If anything, these over-represent women since Seear, unlike Routh, does not include authors, the clergy and senior members of the armed services.

† Similarly, this is based on total figures which exclude air-crew, artists, librarians, musicians, navigators and sportsmen.

‡ 1968 figure.

§ Manufacturing industries only.

¶ Seear's figures refer to 'other' but, since she specifies all other categories, this figure probably refers to the unskilled.

SOURCES See Note 15: A, Routh, p. 49; B, derived from Census data for 1961, 1966 and from Seear, pp. 3–4.

TABLE 1.7 *Women as per cent of each occupational category, 1950 and 1960; US*

Year	Profes- sional technical	Managers adminis- trators	Sales	Clerical	Craft	Opera- tives	Services
1950	40	14	34	62	3	27	45
1960	38	14	36	68	3	27	52

SOURCE Hakim, *Occupational Segregation*, p. 35.

are divided in the British case into two categories. The breakdown of occupations within it reveals similar differences. Few American women in this pre-reform period were account- ants or engineers. An even smaller proportion of doctors were women. But, as in Britain, almost 100 per cent of nurses were women and in teaching, while a higher proportion of university and college lecturers were female, American women were also badly represented in the university sector and more heavily concentrated than British women outside it. In management, women were better represented in the food industries than any other. Secretaries and other non-administrative office staff were overwhelmingly female. And in manual occupations, women were even more poorly represented at the skilled level than in Britain. Among unskilled manual occupations women were heavily concentrated in quasi domestic jobs like dress- making, laundry, food and health and personal services.[17]

Economic explanations for employment patterns

Explanations for pay and occupational differences between women and men fall into three broad categories. First, many sociological approaches concentrate on the supply side by dealing with characteristics of women and employers' percep- tions of them.[18] In this kind of analysis, the structure of the labour market is seen as a product of the attitudes of individuals that constitute it. Secondly, some economists look for relation- ships between pay differentials and the occupational distribu- tion of women and men. This approach distinguishes between discrimination before and after entry into the labour market. As a result, factors like education and family arrangements that are primary in the first approach are exogenous to the second. However, developments on early models of post-entry discrimination now include more systematically the effects of social arrangements on pay and occupational distribution.[19] Finally, other economists and sociologists claim that a division by gender of the labour market into primary and secondary sectors explains the pre- and post-entry behaviour of women and employers.[20] Each approach has overlapping components and hence, despite different starting points, some similar implications for a government wishing to modify the pattern of employment.

Supply side analyses: education and training

British and American employers in their evidence during enquiries leading up to legislative reform adopted the first approach in an effort to distinguish between 'sheer prejudice' and 'reasonable discrimination' on grounds of cost.[21] They cited poor education in inappropriate subjects. This was, they thought, possibly the result of poor careers advice but they also believed that certain innate female attributes hindered the development of certain skills and made it difficult for women to deal with crises or to fit into work relationships. Family commitments and lack of ambition were, in their view, the cause of poor motivation, high turnover and absenteeism. In additional physical, as well as emotional, differences and male reluctance to accept female supervision all meant that investment in training women for higher paid jobs was a poor risk. Leaving side emotional dispositions for later discussion, it is clear from education statistics that women in neither country before equal pay and opportunity laws were being educated in scientific or industry oriented subjects. In both countries, specialisation began early in the school curricula and continued into higher education. In Britain, about five times as many men as women studied science and social science. And, of those women, about three-quarters qualified in education and ancillary health subjects, usually from colleges of education and specialist institutions instead of universities. Quotas operated in British medical schools which required higher passes at 'A' level from women candidates. For industrial subjects, the British figures are shown in Table 1.8.

Even in 1974 more American men than women enrolled in college. But the number of female students grew steadily after the Second World War until they represented almost half the graduands in 1971. Beyond that, the higher the degree the less likely it was to be won by a woman. At the diploma and first degree level, American women, like their British sisters, studied a narrow range of subjects. Non-degree awards for women were mainly in nursing, dental hygiene, secretarial and commercial subjects and data processing. First degrees conferred on women were mostly in education, sociology, history, foreign languages and ancillary health subjects. In the physical sciences, business studies and engineering, women received between virtually none and a quarter of degrees awarded.[22]

Thurow argues that employers do not offer jobs but opportunities for on-the-job training.[23] Broad differences in the educational backgrounds of different groups, he argues, affect employers' perceptions of their suitability for training. Those with approved backgrounds are therefore higher up in the queue for recruitment. Furthermore, investment in training will need to yield not merely profit but the highest possible profit. Evidence of broad differences between groups in their attachments to the labour market will be used to justify more investment in the training of one group than of the other. Employers' beliefs about women, referred to earlier, will make them treat women (as a class) as a poor investment and this will be reflected in recruitment. Again, leaving aside emotional and intellectual dispositions and family obligations for discussion later, it is possible to show that employers behave as predicted. This behaviour, involving apprenticeships, also implicates trade unions. The evidence presented to the Royal Commission on Industrial Relations and Employers Associations[24] showed that 98 per cent of technical and craft apprenticeships in Britain were held by men. Even in clerical and office work, only 31 per cent of apprentices were women. Of all female apprenticeships 72 per cent are in hairdressing.[25] In the United States women constitute about 1 per cent of craft apprentices while, in at least one state, women formed about 82 per cent of cosmetology apprentices.[26] Male employees also benefit more

TABLE 1.8 *Men and women on advanced industrially oriented courses, 1967; Britain*

Advanced	Men	Women	Non-Advanced	Men	Women
University First Degrees			*OND*		
Engineering/technology	1 450	4	Engineering/Technology	4 767	30
Science	2 923	893	Science	338	82
CNAA First Degrees			*ONC*		
Engineering/technology	5 177	5	Engineering/technology	36 118	218
Science	2 031	299	Science	6 779	2 573
			Business/commerce	12 091	1 871
HND			*CGLI*		
Engineering/technology	7 893	24	Engineering/technology	418 107	5 207
Science	1 484	242	Science	4 525	1 970
HNC					
Engineering/technology	32 943	80	Social admin., business	6 244	4 643
Science	6 343	1 267	Wholesale and retail	3 035	2 808

SOURCE Association of Teachers in Technical Institutions (now NATFHE), *Education, Training and the Employment of Women and Girls*, 1970.

than women from day and block release schemes. So-called protective laws restricting the hours, times and locations of work are in Britain, and were in the United States, often used as a justification for inhibiting on-the-job training for women.

Interaction of supply and demand factors

As it will be shown, many sociological explanations can be criticised for concentrating too heavily on supply side factors. But 'demand side' explanations can also be attacked for being too simplistic. This approach describes a situation where profits may be sacrificed to enjoy the commodity of discrimination (the opposite of the previous approach in which discrimination occurs to maximise profits). Such theories predict lower pay for women when an employer has a 'taste' for discrimination and segregation when the 'taste' comes from employees. Where there is competition from non-discriminating employers, both forms are expected to diminish. Although employers cite prejudice among male employees, this model cannot be regarded as adequate because both pay differences and segregation have persisted despite, albeit imperfect, competition. Chiplin and Sloane[27] develop a more complex model that analyses the interaction of supply and demand. In addition, they analyse more thoroughly than Thurow the workings of factors outside the labour market in combination with relationships between pay differentials and occupational distribution. In other words, they try to assess how much differences in pay are caused by differences in occupation and to what extent differences in both are connected with what they regard as economically rational estimations of women's market values or with the free choice of women themselves.

Writing in 1974, the fourth year of voluntary compliance with the British Equal Pay Act, they conclude that inequality is seldom present between women and men doing the same job and argue that the major depressing effect on aggregate female earnings is vertical segregation within occupational categories. In a case study, they found that 40 per cent of differentiation between the gradings of women and men could not be explained in terms of supply side factors. Although further effects of the Equal Pay Act are, in their view, limited, they accept that the Act was necessary because of persistence of employers' 'taste' for discrimination. In addition, however, their own findings indicate the necessity of an anti-discrimination law to weaken vertical segregation. But, in their view, the most productive use of labour in Britain may need to be based on some, if less, continued differentiation because of supply side factors.

They do suggest, however, that social and economic behaviour in families may be changing and they acknowledge that the existing operation of the labour market may discourage the acquisition of sought after skills by women and changes in their labour market attachments. This is central to segmented or labour market theories.

Dual or segmented labour markets

Dual labour markets exist when there is a more or less pronounced division into higher and lower paying employment sectors and where mobility across the boundary is limited.[28] In the higher paid primary sector, recruitment is internal and stability and more definite career structures are evident. In the secondary sector, pay is poor, training rare, voluntary and involuntary dispensibility is high. The division may be expressed between manual and non-manual work but also in vertical segregation within occupational categories. Readily identifiable characteristics like educational qualifications, race or gender form a cheap screening device with the object of maintaining stability in the primary sector. A 'vicious circle' results in workers taking on the characteristics that go with jobs in the secondary sector which, it is argued, are not innate but used to rationalise confinement to that sector. Examples of these characteristics are absenteeism, high turnover and an apparent lack of interest in acquiring skills before or after entering the labour market.

Components of other explanations are relevant to the mechanism of division. Hakim points out that, in the dual labour market model, women's collective exhibition of discontinuous work profiles leads employers to treat all women as equally likely to move in and out of the labour market, debarring them from many primary sector occupations. This is central to Thurow's ideas about the returns on investment in training and important to Chiplin and Sloane. But the causal relationship is different. In the dual labour market model, family arrangements are not objective supply side factors. Instead, the present constitution of the family is a rationalisation for dividing the British (and American) labour market by sex instead of (or as well as) some other factor. Hakim points out that where there is a dual labour market, an equal pay law on its own would depress women's earnings still more because, to evade the law, employers might reorganise and reclassify jobs. This would increase the degree of vertical segregation identified by Chiplin and Sloane, as well as Barron and Norris, as the most significant source of differences in earnings.

Circumstantial confirmation for the segmented labour market model which would modify the claims of the other types of explanation is found in psychological and sociological debates in both countries about the nature of women and men. These controversies are whether different aptitudes are innate or learned, whether training patterns, absenteeism and turnover rates reflect inherent weaker motivations or other factors, whether differences are, in any case, statistically significant and to what extent allegations of unreasonable prejudice among male workers are well founded.

Aptitudes and dispositions[29]

The evidence about mental aptitudes and emotional dispositions is not as overwhelming as employers seem to think. Psychologists point out that while more of one sex than the other show up at the extremes of surveys of aptitudes and dispositions there is a large overlap and differences within one sex are larger than those between them. Paradoxically, flexibility and imagination which are 'female' at one end of a range of characteristics are also those which employers claim are most relevant in senior management. And yet, British managers reported in 1973 that, even where women and men were equally well qualified, they would give preference to male applicants in all occupations except catering, domestic and office work.[30]

With respect to the 'nature' or 'nurture' debate about the acquisition of particular skills, the evidence suggests that the expectations of parents, teachers and careers advisers all affect willingness among girls to study untraditional subjects at school or in higher education. In wartime, when explicit public efforts were made to alter conventional attitudes about female skills and employment, women learned to do jobs that employers believed to be beyond their capabilities. In subsequent surveys, women's responses confound the beliefs of employers by revealing a widespread interest in training and retraining.[31] The need for 'brawn' if not 'brain' in manual occupations and, possibly, some professions like engineering may once have justified the use of gender as a cheap screening device. But it always denied opportunities to women with appropriate physical characteristics but not to men without them. Modern technology is reducing the numbers of jobs whose main requirement is sheer strength. Obviously many heavy jobs remain and there are others which require the periodic shifting of a load. From the passing of protective legislation in both countries, the release of women from heavy labour was seen as a sign of civilisation. But, particularly in the United States, suspicion has arisen that protection is an excuse for denying capable women both the freedom of rational choice and access to higher paid jobs. In Britain, the emphasis in the argument is that there are inadequate safeguards against hazards for men and that both groups should be covered by protective legislation.

There are almost no statutory restrictions now in the United States. In Britain, they are less constraining than might be supposed. Few industries are covered by laws about the weights which women may lift. Where there are such regulations, this is often because of union agreements (which are sometimes anomalous).[32] Exemptions from laws regulating the shifts women may work can be secured by application to the Secretary of State for Employment. These are rarely refused.

Turnover and absenteeism rates as measures of commitment to work also seem to be ambiguous. In Britain, figures show that until 1963 the most common reasons for women leaving an employer after less than a year were connected with the family. But in both countries, turnover rates vary considerably among occupations, age groups and levels of responsibility. Since 1963 in Britain, a majority of women seem to stay with the same employer for more than three years and the proportion of those with more than ten years service increases rapidly with age. In the same decade, continuous employment with the same employer was less likely in America for older women than men, but 'quitting' rates for women and men in manual work were the same.[33] As with turnover rates, absenteeism in both countries is associated with monotonous, low status and poorly paid employment. For those women not in this type of employment, their absence rates are similar to those of men. Ironically, employers sometimes justify confining women to monotonous jobs because they are more 'reliable' than men.

The idea that women's earnings are not essential has lost much of any validity it once had. Apart from single women, married women increasingly need their earnings if their families are to remain above what is publicly defined as the poverty line. This is true of women in both countries and especially of ethnic minority women in the United States. As a result, working women appear to make every effort to be at work even when children are ill or on holiday. But it is evident that good, not merely any, child care facilities are an important factor in decisions about employment.

Women and trade unions

Reluctance among male workers to accept female supervision in Britain is discussed by Creighton.[34] He points out that male fears of female competition in the labour market have a real base in so far as women competing for the same jobs at lower rates could lead to under-cutting and reduction in male employment. This is said to have been at the root of male support for a TUC resolution in 1888 calling for equal pay. No such evidence can be found for espousal by the American Knights of Labor of the cause of equal pay. But Samuel Gompers was renowned for his opposition to women's equality in the craft unions that made up the American Federation of Labor.[35] Another possible objection is that women are believed to be poor trade unionists. Women workers in Britain and the

United States did show themselves capable of militancy in the late nineteenth and early twentieth centuries but they have been less organised than men. Structural factors, however, may have more explanatory power than gender. Women tend to work in smaller plants, in service industries with shifting and seasonal work forces and in the junior levels of non-manual occupations. All of these are notoriously difficult to organise even where employees are male. Nevertheless, a large part of the absolute increase in union membership is accounted for by women. In Britain, they do attend branch meetings less often than men and fall into arrears of subscription more often. But it should be noted that only a minority of men are active in running their unions and they may not always encourage women to participate. Union meetings may be held at inconvenient times for women. In neither country are there many female 'role-models' to encourage activism among others. Even unions with large female memberships have suspiciously few female full-time representatives or delegates. For example, in 1971 59.4 per cent of the National Union of Public Employees were women but only one of its 90 full-time officials was female and two of its 25 delegates to the TUC Conference. The trade union movement in general in the United States is less well established than in Britain but women's experience of it is similar. Women rarely serve on the governing bodies of even those unions with high female membership. Only one woman before 1940 served on the board of the International Ladies Garment Workers Union and even by 1972 women were still only 7 per cent of all board members in general. The 'vicious circle' affecting behaviour like that posited in the dual labour market theory may operate here too.

Another more deep-seated, difficulty has been suggested by Sennett and Cobb.[36] This is that if a man's job is one which lacks status, is brutalising or does not add dignity to his life, he will try to make it worthwhile by thinking that he works for a dignified purpose; that is to support and sustain his family, an institution that society values. If women appear to him to devalue this by saying that they no longer want to be dependent or if governments appear to devalue his purpose by encouraging equality for women, his *raison d'être* is under threat. This argument particularly applies to working-class men. But it may not be universal. Studies reveal that some British working class husbands and men who work in the public sector think it natural that their wives should seek paid employment and not merely to supplement the family income.[37]

The psychological analyses and the surveys referred to here at least cast strong doubt on employers' beliefs about female attributes and, in so far as they do, they support the possibility that the beliefs serve to maintain stability in the primary sector. In conclusion, it is necessary to summarise the policy implications that arise both from these studies and more general labour market theories.

Policy implications of the preceding analyses

What emerges first and foremost is that an equal pay policy must be accompanied by one on equal opportunities. This is clear in both the explanation of Chiplin and Sloane and dual labour market theories. Beyond that the implications of economic theory are contradictory. For Chiplin and Sloane, policies must acknowledge the possibility of some continued differentiation. They argue that the British policy does not. If that is so, neither do the American Equal Pay Act or Civil Rights Act. In contrast, the implication of Barron and Norris is that a pattern undifferentiated by gender is possible. Chiplin and Sloane believe this can only be done with much greater intervention into the structure of family life. Thurow's arguments imply that another form of intervention could modify patterns of employment. This is that, on the one hand, governments could influence the patterns of female education before entry to the labour market and, on the other, could alleviate employers' costs of post-entry training. Despite their interpretation of the limitations of British policy, Chiplin and Sloane also suggest that the very presence of norms specified by law could reinforce self-generating changes that may, in any case, be taking place in women's education and family life. It is possible to dispute their interpretation of the British legislation by arguing that all it does is to insist on equality of treatment for comparable workers. The Sex Discrimination Act does not insist on the training or employment of women in traditionally male occupations, although it facilitates this by advocating an end to discrimination in schools and enabling but not compelling positive discrimination in training for either sex in occupations predominately the field of the other. Indeed, so limited were the effects of the American Civil Rights Act that it became necessary for Presidential Orders to be promulgated requiring (not merely permitting) positive action programmes to be undertaken by government contractors to accelerate changes in womens' expectations, education and eventual employment destinations. This is discussed more fully in Chapters 3 and 4. It will also be shown that, although family or marital status is a consideration in the laws, the legislation of neither country directly affects family responsibilities. Consequently outcomes might be expected to be closer to the expectations of Chiplin and Sloane than to Barron and Norris. At present public and work-place provision for the care of pre-school children is poor. In Britain its availability is still often a consequence of the location of essential wartime production. To some extent in the United States and especially in Britain, child care provision is subject to ideological debate about whether it is a matter for the public or private sectors.

The limits of existing laws, or their application, with respect to eliminating sex-based differentiation in the labour market, are discussed more fully in the final chapter. At the same time, suggestions are also made for using what laws and institutions are available with greater effect. It is also argued that use can be made of what could be construed as the biggest drawback to the laws as they stand. This is that the policies of both countries were based on optimistic views about the future of their economies which were expected to provide an expanding pool of opportunities. High unemployment now makes such hopes seem misplaced. Nevertheless, it is suggested that recession can be used to accelerate the necessary social changes identified by Chiplin and Sloane and, if used carefully, could improve the quality of domestic life and employment for women and men.

PART TWO
Policy Initiation

2

The Politics of Pressure for Reform

The close timing of the American Equal Pay Act (1963) and Civil Rights Act (1964) on the one hand and the British Equal Pay Act (1970) and Sex Discrimination Act (1975) on the other and the economic analyses discussed in the last chapter suggest that equal pay and opportunity laws may be seen as complementary. To some extent this is true. The latter laws, in principle, prevent evasions of the former. But the history both of pressure for change and of willingness by governments to respond suggest that the issues are distinct, especially in Britain. Demands for public enquiries into equal pay had appeared since the nineteenth century. But widespread pressure for an anti-discrimination law did not 'take off' until after the Equal Pay Act. And in any case, although this book is about employment only, employment is but one of several aspects of economic and social life covered by The Sex Discrimination Act. In the United States, although public responses clearly distinguish between equal pay and equal opportunities, early feminism showed a much greater integration of political, social and economic demands than in Britain. In both countries, something of a hiatus occurred in the inter-war period. After 1945 pressure for an equal rights amendment gained some momentum in the United States. But there is more evidence of public pressure for specific policy changes in Britain than America in the periods preceding government action in the 1960s and 1970s. It was, indeed, the failure of the Civil Rights Act for women and not its initial absence that was a precipatory

factor in the growth of modern American feminism. Consequently, the first section of this chapter on nineteenth-century
feminism discusses both countries but the second, on the period
leading up to the reforms of the 1960s and 1970s, necessarily
concentrates on Britain. The activities of modern American
feminist groups are discussed in Chapter 4 on implementation.

The nineteenth and early twentieth centuries[1]

Although some feminist thought existed in pre-industrial
Britain and America, systematic analyses of the position of
women in both countries were spurred on by the French
Revolution and the spirit of the Enlightenment. But, despite
the creation of a Constitution that was an enlightened one for
most white American men, the lives of women in both countries
continued to be regulated by codes based on *Blackstone's
Commentaries on the Laws of England*. However, the persistence of
slavery had important consequences for American feminists
that did not exist in Britain.

America[2]

The many histories of feminism and accounts of the lives of its
participants reveal several basic themes. These include the
relationship between feminism and anti-slavery movements,
interest in improving the economic and social position of
women and, of course, the suffrage campaign from which a
demand for an equal rights amendment grew.

The similarity of domestic laws governing the conduct of
slaves and females was thrust upon American women by their
day-to-day proximity. By the 1830s, the obvious analogies were
being drawn by a hundred or more female anti-slavery
societies. A convention on women's rights was held in 1848 at
Seneca Falls attended by three hundred women and men many
of whom, like Elizabeth Cady Stanton, her husband and Susan
B. Anthony were feminists and abolitionists. The Declaration
of Sentiments drawn up at this convention called for an end to
all legal disabilities placed on women including the denial of
suffrage and barriers to equality in employment. Until the Civil

War feminists and abolitionists worked closely. But, despite their war contributions, particularly in nursing, the 14th Amendment of 1868 extended the 'equal protection of the laws' to former slaves but not women and, for the first time, specified in the Constitution political rights for *male* citizens.[3] The women's movement became fragmented.

Some feminists argued that there was a special role for women in social and economic matters which could be fulfilled with or without the vote. This line of thinking had radical and conservative aspects. The radical strand followed the tradition of the Lowell Reform League which, for years before the war, had been petitioning Congress about women's rights at work, as well as slavery. Delegates attended the first Convention of the National Labor Union in 1868 which called for improvements for working women. Susan B. Anthony was unseated as a delegate to it in 1869 because she was thought to be against organised labour but, in the same year, the Knights of Labor was formed and adopted the aim of equal pay for blacks and women. In 1886 it created a women's department to investigate 'the abuses to which the other sex is subjected by unscrupulous employers' and to 'agitate' for equal pay.[4] The American Federation of Labor, founded in that year by Samuel Gompers, was in favour of protective legislation but against equal treatment for women workers. Ironically, in the bitter labour disputes of 1890s, the unions of the AFL which were closed to women depended on them as picketters during the violent upheavals of the period. At the Boston convention of the AFL in 1903, the National Women's Trade Union League was founded. A coalition of middle and working-class women, it aimed to do what the AFL would not – to support strikes predominantly by women about better conditions for women. One of its first actions was to support the New York Shirt Waisters in 1909 who then formed the International Ladies Garment Workers Union – which disaffiliated from the AFL – CIO (Congress of Industrial Organisations) in the 1960s because of its lack of commitment to women's rights.

This was also a creative period in education. Efforts were made to use the courts to enable women to qualify as doctors and lawyers. Educational settlements were founded for working-class women and courses put on for them at prestigious female colleges like Bryn Mawr. By the end of the century 'social feminists', if they were not involved in the labour movement, had, like Jane Addams, joined the Progressives in their campaigns for general political and social reform. Educational and social issues were also pursued in the numerous women's clubs that were a feature of American society. It was here that the conservative strand of 'social' feminism was evident. Many of their policy demands stemmed from a fear that the 'American way of life' would be diluted by immigration from southern Europe and at least one row at a Convention of the General Federation of Women's Clubs happened because of antipathy among Southern women to the idea that black men had more rights than white women. The Federation even deliberately left female suffrage out of its aims until the twentieth century to avoid alienating conservative women.

Two societies after 1868 concentrated on the vote. Later on, although Americans disapproved of the British resort to direct action, an English Quaker, Alice Paul, introduced some militancy into the campaign. She also founded the National Women's Party which adopted a variety of objectives that were not necessarily feminist and, from 1923, presented an annual equal rights petition to Congress. Working-class women and men suspected that her motive was to attack the tenuous establishment of protective legislation recently won by the Progressives.

The general climate, however, in the post-suffrage, inter-war years confirmed Charlotte Perkins Gillman's nineteenth-century pessimism about the relaxation of sexual mores. The dominant ideology of the 1930s was in the words of O'Neill one 'where women's place was at home and in the bed'.[5] As before, war was accompanied by efforts to dispel such orthodoxies. These succeeded, most women claiming in 1943 that they would remain in the labour market after the war. But renewed idealisation of family life came quickly. Few women in the early 1950s questioned the allocation of women to the private sphere and men to the public. Women graduating at Smith College in 1955 were told by Mr Adlai Stevenson that their task was 'to influence man and boy' through the 'humble role of housewife'.[6] Betty Friedan was one of the audience of graduands who, soon afterwards, set herself a rather different task.

Britain

In Britain, the main basic themes were 'social' feminism and suffrage. Philanthropic women like Elizabeth Fry were opposed to slavery and in favour of public duties for women. But belief in Britain that slavery was immoral did not generally precipitate campaigns for the emancipation of women. The British version of the view that there was a special role for women, enfranchised or not, lay behind campaigns in 1860s – earlier than in the United States – to protect women and children from the vicissitudes of factories. Such measures were bitterly opposed by 'another small group of middle-class women'[7] who argued, long before Alice Paul, that protection would be used to deny women equal rights. Another example of British 'social feminism' was Josephine Butler's campaign against the Contagious Diseases Acts. In Britain too, there were several examples during the late nineteenth century of women who tried to use the courts to secure access to higher education and improve the health of women by providing women doctors for them to consult. Working-class women were becoming organised by the late nineteenth century. The British Women's Trade Union League was founded by Emma Paterson in 1873 and it was a woman, Clementina Black, who proposed the 1888 resolution on equal pay at the Conference of the Trades Union Congress. But the unanimous support it got from male trade unionists was largely the result of their fear that lower pay for women threatened their own employment.

Without the close links with anti-slavery to force women into a more comprehensive critique of economic and social arrangements, the best known element of British feminism concentrated on the vote.

What is described by Randall as 'the first recognisable female suffrage pamphlet'[8] was published by Annie Knight in 1847. The original Fawcett Society was founded in 1866 as the London Association for Women's Suffrage but, as Randall points out, it was John Stuart Mill's failure to amend the 1867 Reform Act to cover women that sparked off a national campaign. More closely allied at first with a political party – the Liberals – than its American counterpart, it later split when the emergent Labour party failed to support it in 1904. The

Women's Social and Political Union, led by Mrs Pankhurst
and Christabel Pankhurst, initiated the campaign of direct
action so disliked in the United States. Sylvia Pankhurst did
what she could to ensure that political inequality continued to
be linked with the economic deprivations suffered by working-
class women.

The First World War, which was followed by votes for
women in both countries, was also the occasion of a public
enquiry into the question of equal pay for women workers in
Britain.[9] Between then and the Second World War the subject
was brought up a number of times in the House of Commons.
Several suffrage societies – such as the Fawcett Society and the
Women's Freedom League – transformed themselves; and
others, like the Six Point Group, were started in order to secure
the full emancipation of women. During the 1920s and 1930s
they petitioned Members of Parliament about equal pay,
public appointments and remaining legal barriers which,
despite the Sex Disqualification (Removal) Act, continued to
discriminate against women at home, in public life and in
employment. But, as in the United States, it was not until after
the Second World War, that new forms of organised feminism
became widespread and well-known.

The rise and fall of the first wave of feminism are explained
by Randall.[10] She argues that industrial capitalism was the
precondition for feminism because it at once released middle-
class women from many domestic responsibilities and confined
them to inactivity to demonstrate the new found wealth of their
husbands. At the same time, diminished domestic production
increasingly pushed single women into the labour market
either into a narrow range of socially acceptable occupations or
into factories, depending on their class. But contemporary
politics developed along Lockean ideas of natural equality and
individual responsibility. The inconsistency of not applying to
all individuals a doctrine which allowed men to be physically or
intellectually different yet morally equal was not lost on
middle-class women.

The question of suffrage which, in its day, divided women,
also had a longer-term frustrating effect. Despite the enforced
return of women to the home after the war, the winning of the
vote made it appear that equality had been achieved. Compla-

cency set in; dissenters were regarded as freaks.[11] It was not until after 1945 that conditions became such that resentment could be expressed effectively at the strains imposed by rhetorical lip-service to equality, the idealisation of domesticity and continued material inequality.

Post-war renewal of feminism

The conditions for the renewal of feminism in both countries were provided by the Second World War. The 1918 exodus from the labour market was not replicated. And it has also been argued that the new, widespread availability of contraception for married women was significant in facilitating this.[12] Middle-class women had made moderate gains in employment but had reached a plateau, unsurpassable without intervention to eliminate all remaining barriers and to ensure that there was equal pay in all professional occupations.[13] Nevertheless, the general picture of the period in Britain is one of anomalies. The welfare state was regarded at first as providing equality universally. Demands for equal pay in the non-manual public sector succeeded in 1955. In the early 1950s, Lady Pakenham observed that there was no longer any need for anyone to call herself a feminist and Justice (now Lord) Denning also believed that female equality was a fact, although he feared it marked the end of civilisation.[14] At the same time, however, ideas about child care and family life went into reverse. Wartime propaganda about the benefits of independence arising from the absence of constant maternal attention was replaced by psychological theories that urged mothers to stay at home.[15] In the United States such ideas were put even more forcefully by professional psychologists and politicians. Suburban family life was almost reified and feelings among women that the reality of home life did not live up to its idealised portrayal were diagnosed as individual difficulties requiring individual psychological readjustment.[16]

Inconsistencies in the position of women were not contained for long in either country. Despite, or perhaps because of, the greater emphasis in the United States on women's confinement to the private sphere, widespread anger appeared there first. In 1963, Betty Friedan published the first edition of *The Feminine*

Mystique where discontent at the discrepancies in women's lives was described in a phrase that became famous: 'the problem with no name'.[17] Her publishers did not expect the book to sell widely. But it touched a fuse and within weeks was a best seller. After that, the coming together of a number of phenomena gave birth to the new women's movement in America. President Kennedy had set up a Commission on the Status of Women in 1962. Together with similar state commissions, it provided a network of women who were aware of the role strains placed on educated middle-class wives and of inequalities imposed upon a growing number of unattached working women. The almost accidental way in which gender was included in the Civil Rights Act, followed by unwillingness in the Equal Employment Opportunities Commission to take women seriously, was a catalyst in the formation of the National Organisation for Women. Civil rights groups gave rise to the younger branch of the women's movement. Analogies were drawn again between the position of women and blacks. And it was discovered that radical men could be as chauvinist as others. Experience in civil rights and anti-Vietnam war groups at once spurred women to form their own and provided them with political skills. But although feminist issues were widely discussed in the early to mid-1960s, organised feminism did not get under way until the first legislative steps had been taken. Since its objectives were enforcement and improvement of existing laws, it is dealt with in Chapters 4, 5 and 6. The rest of this chapter concentrates on the growth of pressure in Britain for new laws.

Pressure for reform in Britain

The literature on pressure group politics classifies groups broadly into two types: sectional economic groups and 'cause' or promotional groups.[18] In this policy area, as in many others, the sectional economic groups are business and labour. In principle, the TUC could have acted more like a promotional group than it actually did until quite late in the day. Over the years, its attitudes to the principle of equal pay were ambiguous. By negotiating the content of equal pay and opportunity legislation with governments, it followed the classic pattern of a sectional economic group. And it will be argued in Chapter 5, its behaviour since 1975 lends some support to corporatist theories about British government. Nevertheless, while obviously not a feminist group, militancy among some trade unionists helped feminists to bring the issue of equality to public attention and this will be discussed before moving on to the myriad of shifting and overlapping groups that make up the real promotional lobby.

Trade unions and reform in Britain

It has been noted already that support among trade unionists for equal pay was, in effect, a demand for protection of male employment. During the late nineteenth and early twentieth centuries, employers were explicit to them and to governments that they would not employ women at the same rate. When trade unionists opposed equal pay, they did so on the basis that men needed to earn a wage large enough to support a family. But the entry of women into wartime labour markets led to active campaigns among male trade unionists for equal pay. These satisfied two interests. Male workers whose jobs were taken over by women wanted to protect their own rates and positions for the end of hostilities. And women preferred not to be exploited. The president of the engineering union told the 1943 Women's Conference that 'the system which allows women to be brought into industry as "cheap labour" and uses them with the double effect of exploiting them and undermining men's rates has left its scars on all of us.'[19] The engineers went on to press for nurseries and special leave arrangements for childbirth. When a campaign for equal pay in the public sector began in the 1940s, the Amalgamated Engineers were involved, together with the engineering technicians, mineworkers, transport workers, the distributive and allied workers, post office engineers, and scientific workers, in lobbying for a phased introduction of equal pay. Other groups were perhaps professional organisations rather than trade unions and included organisations of insurance workers, civil servants, teachers and women public health officers. They were demanding its immediate introduction.

Both the TUC and some affiliated unions made overtures in

the next few years. The TUC put its weight behind the Whitley Council recommendations for equal pay in the public sector. After that it was relatively silent until 1961 when it asked the government to take steps to ratify ILO Convention 110 and in 1963 specifically asked for legislation to create the necessary conditions. In the same year the TUC Women's Conference drew up a Charter for Working Women calling for progress on equal pay and opportunities in jobs, apprenticeships and training. The Conference was particularly concerned with the problems of occupational segregation. Direct action was not recommended until it appeared clear that the government would continue to subordinate the issue to other economic aims.

Nevertheless, its stance did not satisfy some unions. In 1956 at the conference of Transport Salaried Staffs a representative of the National Union of Railwaymen stated that women had heard too many words and seen too little action on the issue. In 1963 the Shipbuilders and Engineering Workers Unions set up a committee under John Boyd to press for higher gradings for skilled women, and the Transport and General Workers Union inaugurated an 'intensive female recruitment drive'.[20] In 1964 the Amalgamated Union of Engineering Workers committed itself to the idea of equal pay in three years.[21]

The beginnings of a more noticeably militant phase from 1968 were evident in 1965 when Ray Gunter postponed government action and the TUC general secretary made it clear that industrial action would be supported. Such a course had already been advocated in a series of articles in *The Sun* on 'The Wasted Sex' and was supported by David Ennals in *Tribune*. In 1966, the TUC Women's Conference reiterated sharp criticisms of government tardiness on equal pay. In 1967 a national union of women workers was formed to work for better treatment,[22] possibly because of a feeling that official TUC policy had not been firm enough. Certainly by 1968 feelings were running high. A successful strike by women at Fords which held up £50m worth of exports took place, the women marching on the House of Commons, and was reported to have stirred the government into renewed action.[23] Strikes also took place at Vauxhall and Rolls-Royce. In November Mrs Castle promised that equal pay would be a reality in seven years.[24] Later in that month there were angry scenes at the TUC conference on equal pay when TUC leaders were accused of having been hoodwinked for too long by the government. More strikes were threatened unless women were not immediately paid at the male minimum. A National Joint Action Committee was founded by the Vehicle Builders Union and held a rally in the spring of 1969 in Trafalgar Square, attended by an estimated 30 000 people. This venture is reported by Randall as having attracted the interest of left-wing groups looking for ways to mobilise the working class.[25]

Despite renewed tripartite discussions, there were more equal pay strikes in 1969 in Skelmersdale, Manchester, Coventry, and Dundee. TUC leaders were reluctantly coming to terms with the government's views on definition and implementation.[26] After the Act was passed, slowness at voluntary compliance was the occasion of TUC demands for an Order-in-Council to accelerate progress and then grassroots militancy when the demands failed. A particularly successful strike occurred at Hawker Siddeley and this was followed by several others, which made 1973–4 a year of an unprecedented number of strikes by women, many of which were explicitly about equal pay.

Although the Working Women's Charter of 1963 had covered more than equal pay, the main focus of demands until 1973 was this question. But in 1973, the Union of Shop Distributive and Allied Workers reactivated calls for government intervention on the non-contractual aspects of employment. The TUC supported intervention when it prepared evidence for a House of Lords Select Committee considering an anti-discrimination bill introduced by Lady Seear. But there were problems. General anti-discrimination proposals reopened the question of protective legislation in a more far-reaching way. A simple rate for the job or equal pay for work of equal value begged questions about whether or not women were allowed to do certain kinds of jobs. Some women's groups believed protective legislation was being used as an unjustifiable reason to pay women in general less than men. But the TUC could not agree to the repeal of such legislation because of their view that this would lead to exploitation. Ideally, the TUC hoped for general legislation covering men and women restricting the hours they worked and controlling the environment in which they did.

The other problem was that enforcement was proposed by both the Select Committee and then the Labour Government through industrial tribunals. Since they had been set up, the National Industrial Relations Court had been created. This had so soured government/TUC relations that in 1973 it was official union policy to boycott government institutions that sought to regulate what the TUC saw as part of collective bargaining.

However, maintaining a separate position on these points, the TUC did present evidence favourable to the general tenor of the Anti-Discrimination Bills and co-operated with other groups, particularly the National Council for Civil Liberties (NCCL), which shared its views on protective legislation, to encourage government action. They were consulted by the Home Secretary, Roy Jenkins, in the preliminary stages of the Sex Discrimination Bill and were particularly interested in ensuring trade union involvement in proposed conciliation processes. By this time, tribunals were, on the whole, back in favour as the previous government's industrial relations innovations were repealed. The TUC was much concerned that the burden of proof should be the same in a sex discrimination case as it was under Labour's Trades Unions and Labour Relations legislation; that is, removed from the complainant on to the employer. Successful at first, this in the end was modified as the result of counter suggestions from the Scottish Law Office.

In general, the indicators of trade union attitudes are contradictory. In some cases the impetus came from grassroots rather than leaders. It can also be argued that once the leaders got the rhetoric right, much opposition came from the rank and file. Allen explains the beginnings of interest with anti-discrimination legislation in terms of the realisation that new technology would increase the number of jobs requiring the 'female characteristic' of manual dexterity at the expense of traditionally male occupations.[27] But one of the early proponents of a better deal for skilled women, the Amalgamated Union of Engineering Workers, has not been in the forefront of insisting on proper enforcement. In 1973–4, while some TUC leaders were working for a Sex Discrimination Act, an engineering union official told the Select Committee on Expenditure that he did not approve of women working. It was reported that he believed part of the explanation of football violence to be 'greedy mothers working'.[28] And, in general, where neither lack of conviction nor principled objections to legal interference in collective bargaining appear, there are substantial pockets of complete ignorance of the law.[29]

Feminist groups in Britain

So far as promotional groups are concerned, women are sometimes argued to be ineffective political actors. Even as late as 1970, when he might have been confounded by the evidence, an eminent American historian was still purveying the view that women were not 'natural joiners' because the 'privateness' of their biological characteristics and emotional dispositions meant they could not function in groups concerned with public issues.[30] This kind of theory is often used to explain the low rate of female participation in trade unions referred to in Chapter 1. So far as politics are concerned, Richards notes without the theoretical implications of necessity, that women's lobby groups fail because women are inexperienced in dealing with politicians.[31] That the impact of women's groups is low is to some extent borne out by the British evidence on employment between 1918 and 1970. But it must be remembered that there v as a substantial overlap between active Members of Parliament and outside groups which was important in focusing attention on equal pay in the 1940s and 1950s. Further discussion of this appears at the end of this section. Pressure groups were being effective in this respect when one of their members wore a pressure group hat in Parliament. Evidence in the United States suggests that inefficiency does not follow from innate characteristics but is diminished as the practice of participation among women increases.[32] The proposition that women are not natural joiners, even if they are not always efficient, is difficult to sustain in the face of the numbers of women's groups that there are in twentieth-century Britain. That some of them deliberately chose not to be 'efficient' in what are conventionally regarded as politics is sometimes overlooked by writers on pressure groups.

In 1972, the Central Office of Information published a booklet on 'Women in Britain' which listed over two hundred organisations wholly for women or with women's branches. This represented a large increase in preceding decades. But, even in 1964, it was reported that three million women were active in 120 national groups, although it was also argued that only 15 of them could be described as 'feminist'.[33] Between 1966 and 1967 women's societies proliferated rapidly.[34] Feminist groups of the mid-1960s shared the aim of emancipating women in all spheres of life; occupational, economic, social, moral and legal. These were generally the remains of the suffrage movement. But a younger women's movement also came into being in the eight years between 1964 and 1972. This arm of feminism is concerned with equality but does not necessarily follow the rules described in conventional pressure group literature. In 1970 the first Women's Liberation Conference was held in Oxford where a resolution to support legislative reform was only narrowly accepted. Appendix I at the end of this book lists about fifty organisations involved in one way or another in the campaigns for equal pay and sex discrimination legislation.

Attention was drawn by one commentator to the proliferation of bodies with similar aims determined to maintain their own structures and activities.[35] It was pointed out that methods were amateur, petitions being presented too late and complaints formulated too vaguely. Such a view is supported by Mrs Joyce Butler's claim that she would find few people to turn to who had any concrete ideas when considering how to introduce an anti-discrimination bill.[36] The realisation that proliferation and vagueness were dissipating efforts finally led Virginia Novarra of the Fawcett Society to try to develop a coherent strategy and coordination with other groups to get an Act in the 1970s. The Fawcett Society became something of an umbrella organisation in the latter stages of the campaign, with Parliamentary links through the all-party group on equal rights and with Women's Liberation through the Women's Lobby. The National Council for Civil Liberties (NCCL), having been prodded by members in the mid-1960s, also acted as a direct lobby and an umbrella group.

The difficulties of tracing the impact, let alone the activities, of such an amorphous collection of groups are enormous. In one account of the stances of major interest groups, promotional groups are specifically excluded for this reason.[37] The information that follows here comes very largely from the files of the two umbrella organisations. This has revealed much of the activities of the other groups linked to them and has been supplemented by interviews and unpublished papers.

Campaigns in Britain

The first round of equal pay.[38] Post-1945 efforts for equal pay began during a Second World War campaign for equal compensation for men and women who were civilian casualties. This led to two equal pay campaigns, one led mainly, but not exclusively, by Conservative women MPs and the other by the Labour member, Charles Pannell. With the affiliation of various extra-parliamentary associations, about four million women were represented. Pressure from inside and outside Parliament is thought to have led to the setting up of a Royal Commission in 1944.[39] Dissatisfaction with both its slow start and its final report were the causes of a series of mass meetings between 1944 and 1946. Resolutions were passed and sent to the government, the Opposition, London County Council, the Association of County Councils, the Trades Union Congress and the British Confederation of Employers. All resolutions recommended a single rate for the job. Parliamentary candidates were lobbied in the 1950, 1951 and 1955 elections and delegations called on the Minister of Labour and the Chancellor of the Exchequer between 1951 and 1954. In 1955 the government agreed to introduce equal pay into the civil service in stages and, soon afterwards, to do the same for local government officers and teachers in the state sector. For the next few years, there was little further action. When an equal pay campaign began again in the 1960s, it was mainly among trade unionists. Campaigns for the elimination of other forms of employment discrimination did not take on a mass character until the 1970s. But there were a handful of attempts to keep the broader issues alive in the 1950s.

Broader issues of women's rights. Groups, including the NCCL,

protested when marriage bars began to be reintroduced in the
tobacco industry, banks and the post office. The Six Point
Group held meetings in 1952, 1954 and 1956 about the United
Nations Commission on the Status of Women and the government's failure to take steps to ratify the United Nations
Convention on the Rights of Women. They were also concerned with the general attitude of United Kingdom
Representatives at the United Nations on questions about
women. At one of these meetings in 1956 with Dame Lucille
Sayers, United Kingdom Representative to the United
Nations, it was revealed that the government believed any
further application of equal pay ought to arise from industrial
bargaining. When publicising this, the Six Point Group also
called for mechanisms to ensure that companies in contract
with the government treated men and women equally. In 1962
Thelma Cazalet-Keir tried to activate interest in the wider
aspects of women's equality at work by writing to the
newspapers about the lack of equal opportunities for women in
the civil service and public bodies like the BBC.[40] But a year
later Dee Wells was expressing disappointment at the lack of
action by women's groups on equal opportunities.[41] Also in
1963, Dr Margherita Rendel and two other members of the
National Council for Civil Liberties tried to prod the Council
into taking up women's rights. They were warned that this
would be unlikely to happen. In the event they succeeded,
although it was not until the 1970s that a permanent women's
rights section was established in the NCCL.

In 1963, the Status of Women Committee coordinated a
lobby to defeat a bill proposed by Lord Balneil that would have
removed from women the right to choose for themselves when
to return to work after childbirth.[42] The Six Point Group was
working on a bill that would mean that absence from work due
to pregnancy would be treated as absences for health reasons;
that would rectify the shortage of nurseries; and introduce a
more imaginative approach to part time work. They were also
working on the elimination of barriers against women in the
Stock Exchange, engineering, the Church, the foreign service,
senior management and education posts and apprenticeships.[43] Lady Summerskill had been a member of that group
but had resigned in the 1950s because of its criticisms of

Western policies towards Formosa and Korea. However, she introduced a bill to the House of Lords covering similar objectives through an industrial charter for working women.[44] None of these had much immediate impact. In 1964 women's groups, with the Trades Union Congress, concentrated on persuading the government to implement its election pledge on equal pay. Responses were non-committal, admitting the pledge but arguing that much detailed analysis would need to be done before specific proposals could be announced.

Signs of cohesion on equal pay and equal opportunities. However, 1964 to 1965 was a year of increased publicity for the position of women. Although the Society for the Protection of Utter Femininity had been formed in 1962 because 'equality had gone too far', it was argued in 1964 that 'everyone was talking about women' because it had not gone far enough.[45] Reports were drafted and published in 1964 and 1965 by the Liberal Party, the Over 40 Association, the Women's Employment Federation and the NCCL, all of which basically said the same thing. These were widely commented upon in the press. In April 1965, *The Sun* carried a series of articles on the position of women and reported a response of thousands of letters from women who wanted to get involved. In March 1965, the Six Point Group held a conference to conquer differences among groups and 'to blast off a new campaign to accomplish things that feminists have worked for unsuccessfully for years – especially equal opportunities and rewards, the treatment of unmarried mothers and equality of taxation'.[46] Women's groups were heartened by the Trades Union Congress's renewed interest in equal pay and in 1966 many of them formed an alliance, including the Six Point Group, the Status of Women Committee, the Suffrage Fellowship, the Association of Headmistresses, the British Federation of Business and Professional Women and the National Council of Married Women, in order to produce a set of election demands on equality at work, in social security and in taxation. But despite all the reported activities, the Women's Information and Study Centre took the view that, while there were signs of a more organised drive to eliminate inequality, there was still a good deal of confusion and even apathy.

In 1967, the Fawcett Society tried to bring order to the confusion. A conference was held on Women in a Changing Society. It was attended by eleven unions, twenty other groups, and various foreign experts. Perhaps because told by one of its speakers, Dr O. MacGregor of London University, that the women's movement had to broaden its class base, the society soon afterwards advised women to join trade unions and to strike, if necessary, for equal pay. Other groups, spearheaded by the NCCL, tried to thwart one trade union leader, Tom Jackson, in his opposition to allowing equal opportunities in the Post Office. The publication of Hunt's report on women workers, sponsored by the Department of Employment, lent weight, according to one commentator, to the demands for equal pay, if not equal opportunities.[47]

In the following year Mrs Butler made her first attempt to get at these non-contractual elements of employment. Her experience, referred to earlier, confirms the pessimism of the Women's Information and Study Group. But, in the same year, the British Federation of Business and Professional Women published a booklet entitled *Justice or Prejudice* in which specific proposals for an anti-discrimination board were suggested. The year was both Human Rights Year and the fiftieth anniversary of female suffrage. To celebrate, the Fawcett Society organised a conference on 11 November which brought together a variety of groups and individuals with an interest in women's employment. They included Barbara Castle, Robert Carr, Lady Summerskill, David Basnett (ironically, representing the Trades Union Congress Women's Advisory Committee), Ann Mackie (CBI Committee on the Employment of Women and its Working Party on Equal Pay), Lady Seear, Margaret Allen (economics correspondent of *The Times*) and Pauline Pinder (PEP research project on women's employment).

Members of the Fawcett Society and other women's groups attended the rally organised by the National Joint Action Campaign in Trafalgar Square in the spring of 1969. Its purpose was to demonstrate the need for action on all fronts but emphasis was on equal pay with messages of support for the equal pay strikes that were taking place in various northern cities. The wider issues were taken up by an actress, Diane

Hart, when she set about founding a national women's party. But, although Una Kroll stood as candidate for the Women's Rights Party in Sutton and East Cheam, this was not a tactic that could work as easily in Britain as it has on occasion in America.[48] The NCCL was taking a more conventional approach by expressing alarm that the government's equal pay proposals would contain nothing about the non-contractual elements of employment.

Support for private members' bills in Parliament. All the same, there appears to have been something of a hiatus on the wider issues between 1968 and 1971. Renewed activity in the older women's movement seems to have been spurred by the formation by Mr Bishop and Mrs Butler of the Parliamentary ginger group on equal rights which met the Fawcett Society, other groups and unions in March 1971 to discuss Mrs Butler's bill. Several amendments covering educational endowments, the powers of the proposed anti-discrimination board and advertising were suggested by the Fawcett Society. When Mr Hamilton agreed to take on Mrs Butler's Bill in the next session, Mr Bishop again wrote to the Fawcett Society urging women's groups to support him.

The new radical women's movement had in the meantime been attracting national attention. During the late 1960s Women's Liberation Workshops were started. They drew attention to problems such as the lives of women in high rise housing, the poverty of crèche facilities and low pay among unorganised women workers. Consciousness raising groups were formed, although as Randall points out, this was less common in Britain than in America. Randall also argues that Women's Liberation and the increasingly militant unionised women workers fuelled one another's efforts at direct action.[49] Attitudes to political reform were, however, mixed. It was only by a slim majority that it was agreed in 1970 to support campaigns for legislative changes. In the winter of 1971–2, the Women's Lobby, part of Women's Liberation, began to cooperate with the Fawcett Society to provide a bridge between the two broad wings of feminism.

The Women's Lobby circulated a note about Mr Hamilton's Bill explaining why it should be supported and organised a public meeting to discuss it. On the day of debate (28 January 1972) angry hisses from the public galleries greeted the Home Office Minister's rejection of the idea of change. His attitude and Ronald Bell's filibustering were attacked on the women's pages of the national newspapers.[50] The Fawcett Society set about an assessment of what to do next. One result was the formation in conjunction with the Women's Lobby, of a national newsletter, *Women's Report*, which made its first appearance in January 1973. This two-monthly periodical with a high circulation kept many women informed about the activities of a wide variety of groups, the unions, the parties and government.

In the meantime, Lady Seear had introduced her bill which had been sent to a Select Committee and groups got together to coordinate their evidence. Callender estimates that over 50 per cent of the Committee's evidence came from women's groups.[51] To coordinate it, five conferences were held in 1972 including one on 28 January organised jointly by the Fawcett Society and Women in the Media. Eighty organisations attended and were addressed by Lady Seear, Shirley Williams, Joan Bakewell, Margaret Corbett-Ashby and Joyce Butler. Delegations visited 10 Downing Street to support Mr Hamilton's bill. The Fawcett Society and Women in the Media each presented evidence to the House of Lords Select Committee and the Fawcett Society followed up that of Dr Rendel by writing to the Committee to express strong support of her views. Betty Lockwood (Women's Secretary of the Labour Party and Chairperson of the National Joint Council of Working Women's Organisations) was worried by evasions of the Equal Pay Act because of the absence of an anti-discrimination clause. In November 1972 she wrote to the Fawcett Society requesting joint action. At the end of the month, a workshop was held with the Fawcett Society, the Parliamentary group and others including Ms (now Baroness) Lockwood. On the agenda were the powers of an anti-discrimination board, the protection of complainants, damages and rewards, promotional activities of the board, compliance by government contractors and strict control of exceptions to the law.

In the first month of 1973, the main interest of women's groups was not the next round of an anti-discrimination bill.

Instead they, as well as trade unions, were concerned with the question of an Order-in-Council to ensure more rapid progress towards equal pay. The Fawcett Society, the National Joint Council for Working Women's Organisations and the Status of Women Committee were among those who wrote to the Secretary of Employment. Replying, Mr Chichester-Clark reminded the Fawcett Society that the government was in any case committed to equal pay by 1975. Lady Seear, for the Fawcett Society, persisted over the next few months but was disappointed; no Order was promulgated.

In the meantime, a lobby was organised around Mr Hamilton's second attempt at a Private Members Bill. Women in the Media, with easy access to communication channels, organised a mass meeting at Caxton Hall, the old suffrage venue, to coincide with the second reading on 2 February. When information was relayed from the House of Commons that the bill was about to fail again, 300 women marched to Downing Street to protest. When debate resumed on 14 February, Sally Oppenheim MP was jeered from the gallery when she announced that, although she had supported the Bill, she wished to dissociate herself from women's liberation. Cheers, however, rang out when the Bill got a second reading.

Because it was felt in some quarters that the issue had been well aired already in the House of Lords and that the Commons Select Committee was being used to delay legislation, extra-parliamentary activity was stepped up. On 10 March 1973 on International Women's Day, 2000 people marched from Hyde Park to Trafalgar Square. Six women and one man were arrested. On 31 March the Status of Women Committee held a well-attended conference on equal pay and opportunities. Women's Liberation began to collect signatures on a petition demanding immediate action. This was delivered by Mr Raphael Tuck (Labour) to the House of Commons in November. In the summer of 1973 the Fawcett Society set up a working party to publicise the need for speedy implementation. The Conservative government then tried to regain the initiative and pressure groups had to consider how to react.

Responses to preliminary governmental proposals. Three hundred groups and individuals responded to the Conservative

Government's consultative document, *Equal Opportunities for Men and Women*. From November 1973 to January 1974 detailed criticisms were published by both the NCCL, which by then had a full-time women's rights section, and the Fawcett Society. Most of the NCCL objections to the government's proposals were shared by other groups. For example, it was felt that the scope was too narrow; the exclusion of small firms was too generous; enforcement procedures were inadequate, relying too heavily on discredited tribunals and granting too few powers to the EOC; and there were, in general, too many loopholes. These were the views, too, of the Runnymede Trust, the Six Point Group, the National Union of Teachers, Women in the Media, the National Joint Council of Working Women's Organisations, Women in Parliament and Una Kroll. Views diverged, however, over protective legislation, the NCCL being opposed to its repeal and the Fawcett Society suggesting that such laws should be gradually removed.

The last point was included in a report – *What Next?* – prepared by Virginia Novarra throughout 1973 and circulated in the spring of 1974, setting out aims and tactics for the Society and other groups. In February 1974, there was a new Labour government and the Fawcett Society Anti-Discrimination Committee argued that the Fawcett Society was well placed to coordinate pressure on it to maintain its interest in early legislation. As a result the Society initiated an inter-organisational Committee which met in July to prepare for the forthcoming government statement. About thirty organisations attended,[52] although some of them were not wholehearted about working together because of divergences on protective legislation.[53] But there was a large amount of agreement on the proper scope of anti-discrimination legislation, the powers of any enforcement board, the need for legal aid for individual complainants, and for affirmative action to positively promote equality. A committee was set up to coordinate the group's activities which Mrs Millie Miller MP subsequently chaired. A resolution was passed and sent to the Home Secretary: 'that this meeting urges Her Majesty's government to bring forward without delay legislation to make discrimination illegal in education, training, employment, membership of trades unions and professional bodies, pensions, goods, facilities and services, mortgages, hire purchase, housing, advertising, tax and social security.' The resolution also called for a strong enforcement body that could initiate legal action with or without complaints and the encouragement of affirmative action to promote equality.

In the meantime, the NCCL had also been preparing for the advent of concrete proposals. From the beginning of the year conferences had been held in London, Nottingham and Cardiff. The one in London was attended by 500 people and included the participation of thirty trade unions, twelve trades councils, women's liberation workshops, women's groups and students. In May 1974, a model bill was published and widely circulated.

When the government's outline of proposals was published in late July, newspaper comments ranged from seeing the proposals as a vote winner in the next election to the view that they were a waste of time. *The Sun* described them as a Bill of Rights for Women, while the *Express* thought the Home Secretary would be better employed trying to discover the perpetrators of the bombing of the Tower of London. The *Daily Telegraph* believed there to be little demand for statutorily enforced equality and that most people would regard legislation as an unacceptable reduction in freedom. *The Times'* 'cautious welcome' was shared, although for different reasons, by pressure groups.[54] The Women's Liberal Federation issued a statement saying that proposals were all right as far as they went. The NCCL was worried about the exclusion of small firms, pensions and about reliance on industrial tribunals. Both the Fawcett Society and the Trades Union Congress were bothered about the exclusions of pensions and social security. The CBI refused to comment.[55] The All Party Equal Rights Group told the Fawcett Society that it would be necessary to 'keep the Home Secretary on his toes'. The NCCL met Shirley Summerskill (Home Office), John Fraser (Department of Employment) and departmental officials almost immediately to discuss the contents of the proposals using their own Model Bill to make recommendations about enforcement mechanisms, private clubs, and affirmative action.

A White Paper was published in September and the Inter-Organisational Committee met again to respond to the Home Office invitation to comment. Both the NCCL and the

Inter-Organisational Committee believed that the drafters of
the White Paper had taken some notice of earlier criticisms. But
the latter initially listed 22 points of interest and later sent a 14
page document with over forty points of criticism to the Home
Secretary. These included suggestions for tightening wordings
to avoid loopholes, criticisms of permitted exemptions, disappointment that tax and social security were excluded,
disquiet that there was nothing on positive discrimination, and
unease about many details of enforcement. The Committee
members were particularly uneasy about the proposal to
enforce the education provisions through the Secretary of State
for Education. They were also 'dismayed' that a complainant
would have to prove an intention to discriminate. Their
comments on protective legislation brought all groups into line
since they stated that it should not be repealed but extended to
men. The views of the Inter-Organisational Committee were
generally shared by other groups, including the NCCL,
Women in the Media, and the newly formed Equal Pay and
Opportunities Campaign. The last seems to have been the only
other group to ask for the discriminatory effect of an action
rather than a proven intention to discriminate to be a crucial
factor in whether an unlawful act had been committed.

As drafting got well under way after the October election –
the second in 1974 – the Inter-Organisational Committee
urged affiliated members to lobby the Home Office to produce
a bill as quickly as possible and made standby arrangements
with Parliamentary contacts in case of delay. The Fawcett
Society wrote to Roy Jenkins to emphasise points previously
made about marital status, intention to discriminate, exceptions and exemptions. At his invitation the group met Shirley
Summerskill on 6 December to expand upon written comments. In February 1975, Roy Jenkins was guest of honour at a
Fawcett Society dinner for International Women's Year where
he again assured the audience that the criticisms of various
groups had been studied with care. But he warned that full
equality could not be brought about in the forthcoming Sex
Discrimination Bill. On the one hand, family arrangements
would still militate against full equality and, on the other, he
disliked the idea of positive discrimination because it would be

difficult to formulate without eroding the very principles on which the legislation would be based.

But a month later the bill was published and did provide an enabling clause facilitating, but not compelling, a limited amount of positive discrimination in training for either sex under certain conditions. In April the NCCL and the Inter-Organisational Committee prepared their comments. The latter produced a long document in which it was stated that many of their original points had been met. They particularly welcomed the inclusion of the idea of indirect discrimination stemming from acts not necessarily intended to be discriminatory. According to a participant, however, this was not included as a result of British women's groups but on American advice.[56] Women's groups were still disappointed about exemptions and felt that the exceptions allowed on the grounds of occupational qualification were too broad. Moreover, many details of enforcement still worried them, particularly in connection with the absence of legal aid at tribunals and the lack of opportunity for women's groups to assist individual complainants to present cases. Of special concern was the reversal of the original placing of the burden of proof on employers. This point also caused the NCCL considerable anxiety. It was noted that the precedent set by the Trades Unions and Labour Relations Act was reversed. The NCCL shared concern about the denial of legal aid as a result of the intention to enforce employment cases through tribunals and not courts. They were, however, pleased about a strengthening of a procedure whereby the EOC would issue non-discrimination notices and about the small shift in the idea of positive discrimination. The NCCL went on to prepare a memorandum on points of concern for consideration by the Bill's Standing Committee. The groups affiliated to the Inter-Organisational Committee also continued to try to get amendments passed during various stages of the Bill. These efforts will be referred to in the next chapter and set in the context of other pressures on the government.

Linkages among groups and between them and MPs

Before summarising and turning to the politics of public

responses in Britain and the United States, it is important to deal briefly with the point made earlier about linkages between groups and overlapping memberships within and outside parliament.

In the period leading up to the first round of equal pay, two Members of Parliament stand out. Irene Ward, also a member of the Fawcett Society and the British Federation of Business and Professional Women, was prominent in the Equal Pay Campaign Committee. Charles Pannell led the Equal Pay Coordinating Committee which was the focus of many sections of the labour movement. The campaign committee was chaired by another MP, Thelma Cazalet-Keir, and through its affiliated groups and overlapping memberships linked at least thirty women's societies and professional associations to the parliamentary campaign. Irene Ward has the reputation of being 'an unusually outspoken and persistent prodder of front benchers even when her party is in office'.[57] Her doughtiness was particularly evident in her fights for women's rights – even to the extent of entering the Chamber waving the library steps that were supposedly too heavy to allow the employment of female librarians in the House of Commons.

Barbara Castle was the heroine of the second round of equal pay. Where her predecessor had signally failed, she devised solutions that secured the acquiescence of the Trades Union Congress and the CBI. Although she disappointed Mrs Butler and appears to have no close links to women's groups, she had to badger her colleagues. Obviously irritated references in Richard Crossman's diaries describe her 'shoving this through without consideration to others', because she thought it would be 'immensely popular' in the country at the forthcoming election.[58] Another commentator noted that 'equal pay would give her a place in history as secure as Nye Bevan; . . . that . . . legislation was long overdue since the government was behind public opinion of which seventy per cent was in favour; and that her bill would be one of the most popular for a long time'.[59] According to Edith Summerskill, it was only because there was a woman at the Department of Employment that there was an Equal Pay Act at all.[60]

The National Executive Committee of the Labour Party seemed more open-minded than the Parliamentary party. In

1967, Edward Leadbitter, who had come to believe that women were treated as second class citizens in all matters, succeeded in getting the NEC to initiate an enquiry and was applauded by Margaret Drabble and Brigid Brophy.[61] Joyce Butler and Edward Bishop were tireless in their parliamentary efforts and in fostering links outside with groups like the Fawcett Society. But it was not until 1974 that they found a critical mass of kindred spirits among MPs. That their bill was pursued by William Hamilton was almost accidental. He was lucky twice in the private members ballot and agreed to take it on.

The Liberal peer, Baroness Seear, came to be interested in women's employment through her academic research in personnel management which convinced her that discrimination existed and was both economically irrational and unjust. It was consideration of her bill that brought promotional groups close to the centre of the policy process and which convinced the government of the need for some intervention. Strongly supported by Baroness Summerskill (Labour), both women, like many other interested politicians, had personal connections with lobby groups. Lady Seear and Lady Summerskill, whose daughter Shirley was known to share some of her views, belonged to the Fawcett Society. So did Lena Jager (Labour). Lady Summerskill also belonged to the Six Point Group. By the 1970s, Joan Vickers (Conservative) and Irene Ward were also peers. The former was a member of the Fawcett Society and of the Status of Women Committee; the many memberships of the latter have already been mentioned.

Such a pattern was obvious outside Parliament too. Margherita Rendel, for example, gave evidence of the House of Lords Select Committee on behalf of the British Federation of University Women. She had also written a Fabian booklet on the subject, was part of the Labour Party NEC Study Group, encouraged the NCCL to take up women's rights and was an active member of the Fawcett Society and the Equal Pay and Opportunity Campaign. Also active in the extra-parliamentary Labour Party was Anthony Lester (now QC and SDP), who, with other labour lawyers, had pressed for race relations legislation. By 1974 he was political adviser to the Home Secretary when the Home Secretary, originally cautious about equal pay, became convinced for the need for 'race-relations-type' laws for women. It was these three who, in different ways, explicitly introduced American legal influences into British thinking. This important feature of British policy is discussed more fully in Chapter 3.

Although trade unions and women's groups were, in comparison to Britain, conspicuous by their absence in campaigns in the United States for the Equal Pay Act and the inclusion of women in the Civil Rights Act, there were some notable individuals involved in the shaping of American policy who were also active in the cause of working women's rights. Their contributions will be discussed in the next chapter on public responses. For the moment, it is necessary to summarise the contrasts and cross-fertilisations between the two countries that have been referred to in this one.

Summary of contrasts and mutual influences between British and American feminism

Broadly speaking, both societies experienced similar industrialisation processes and the development of political liberalism in the nineteenth century. But because of slavery, the discrepancy between Enlightenment thought and the reality of women's lives was much more dramatic for American women than for British women. But Americans were more reluctant than the British to resort to action that might lead to violence. It is possible that this is a product of different political cultures. In the United States, its written Constitution was the creation of men who believed that the best constitutions were the product of reason. In the absence of a 'clean state', British constitutional changes were an accretion of reforms which, as the militant suffragettes pointed out, were seldom solely the result of rational discussion. Instead, they argued, almost all democratic reforms had necessitated recourse to direct action. Despite earlier advances in the United States than in Britain in analyses of and expressions of discontent about women's oppression in general, American suffragists were obliged to accept, although selectively, some British ideas about tactics. In the twentieth century, rebellion against the prevailing attitudes of the 1950s apparently came to the surface at about the same time. But specific campaigns occurred in Britain to secure reforms, while in the United States they arose to ensure the implementation of laws largely passed for other reasons. At this time the trade union movement and working class women were more important in Britain than in America. Despite trade union ambivalence towards women's rights, the combination of newly adopted Trades Union Congress attitudes and rank-and-file female militancy affected governments to an extent that would be difficult in the United States. Although, on the face of it, similar labour movement institutions exist in both countries, fewer American workers are unionised and trade unions have a more tenuous role in policy-making. Formed after the creation of the Democratic Party, the AFL-CIO has no constitutional link to it like that between the Trades Union Congress and the Labour Party which grew out of the labour movement.

However, British feminism was influenced in the late 1960s by the women's movement that was emerging in the United States from underground political activity into the forefront of national politics. As in the nineteenth century, analogies were noted between the positions of women and racial minorities and, through radical political activity and consciousness-raising groups, American women became adept at articulating injustices and their needs and at developing political strategies for dealing with them. Randall points out that British feminists, whose roots were also in radical and peace group politics, found a coherence in the thinking and writing of American and West German women for their own inchoate resentments.[62] Rowbotham reports that it was an American who suggested the holding of the first British Women's Liberation Conference.[63]

One problem for radical British women that took a different form in the United States was the question of what kind of equality had priority and for whom. In the Labour Party and in groups further to the left, there was a strong current of opinion that the pursuit of democracy entailed the primacy of ending class inequalities and that women's equality would be a natural by-product. For such thinkers, feminism is a conservative diversion. In the next chapter it will be shown that this was a hindrance to espousal by the Labour Party of the cause of women's rights. In the United States, parties are less explicitly class-based and this kind of argument appeared in other circles. Although the links between civil rights groups and feminists were a source of strength, and sometimes an incentive to feminism, they also caused divisions on the ground that the women's movement diverted attention from the more important goal of racial equality. It was also felt that drawing analogies belittled the cruelty of racial oppression. This was an acute problem for black women but, by 1970, having been too often the victims of the views on women of Stokely Carmichael and degrading treatment like that received by Shulamith Firestone, they were sure that both movements were necessary.[64]

An important difference between the two societies is that democracy, posed by the British left in material terms, is defined procedurally in the United States. The consequences of this will be discussed more fully in Chapter 5 but the relevant point is that, in America, democracy is thought to be present when groups, which like women may cut across classes, are able to participate in the political process. So, while in Britain class based parties and classes have acquired legitimacy as political actors, individuals and groups of individuals count for more in American ideas about the rectitude of political arrangements.

3

The Politics of Public Responses

The history of changing public attitudes

In nineteenth-century Britain and the United States, the justifications for keeping women out of public life, for denying them access to professional qualifications and for protecting them in manual occupations were similar. In Britain, women were not persons in the full legal sense and, while American women were deemed to be citizens, it was asserted that citizenship did not necessarily confer the same rights on all persons. Women in both countries were treated differently from men sometimes as a punishment for fecklessness, sometimes in compensation for delicacy or vulnerability and sometimes in reward for moral superiority.[1] Despite votes for women and greater consistency in definitions of person and citizen, such ideas persisted between the world wars in welfare, family and employment policies.[2]

Early moves on equal pay and opportunities in the United States

Ideas about differences between women and men coexisted, however, with indications of improvement in ideas about women's pay. In America, these appeared most frequently in state legislatures – perhaps because of female involvement in Progressivism which was strongest at this rather than the Federal level of politics.[3] Between 1912 and 1923, several states passed laws guaranteeing minimum rates for women but these were controversial, often being linked with restrictions on the number of hours that could be worked by women. Nevertheless, the policy was eventually adopted by the Federal government in 1938 under the Fair Labor Standards Act. Straightforward equality of rates was the stated policy of the National War Labor Board during the First World War. At the end of hostilities, Michigan and Montana passed their own equal pay laws. The Second World War was the occasion of renewed state interest and ten others passed similar reforms. By the time of the Federal Equal Pay Act of 1963, twenty-two states already had their own equal pay laws and two others banned discrimination in pay under fair employment legislation.[4]

Discrimination in the non-contractual elements of women's employment was banned in Hawaii and Wisconsin before the Federal Civil Rights Act of 1964. For religious and racial minorities, anti-discrimination laws existed in twenty-five states and there had been a number of Federal initiatives; notably the Pendleton Act of 1883 which outlawed religious discrimination in the civil service and New Deal efforts to ban religious and racial discrimination in defence contracts and federally funded public works projects. Presidents Truman and Eisenhower made some attempts to extend and improve existing laws but did not devise adequate enforcement procedures. Alice Paul's proposed Equal Rights Amendment, which would probably have ensured that such laws also applied to women,[5] rarely reached the floor of the House of Representatives. In the 1940s, the Republican Party endorsed the ERA. But Democrats, worried that it would supersede minimum wage and maximum hour laws, looked for alternative ways of improving the position of working women. A number of bills were introduced to the House in the 1950s by Congressmen Cellar, McDonell and Clayton-Powell, supported by groups of Jewish and Catholic women and trade unionists who were unhappy about the loss of protective legislation.

President Kennedy's Commission on the Status of Women

Soon after President Kennedy's inauguration a Commission on the Status of Women was set up. The suggestion for it came from two women. Katherine Ellickson, who had helped Congressman Cellar in the 1950s, and Esther Petersen, appointed by the President as Director of the Women's Bureau, raised the matter in February 1961. They were both active trade unionists who had tried and failed to persuade the AFL-CIO to promote greater equality but who were opposed to the ERA. Their idea was taken up by the Secretary of Labor who justified it to the President as a constructive alternative to 'the futile agitation about the ERA'.[6] The wish to overcome the ERA controversy was accompanied by a desire to transcend party politics. Labour women had identified themselves with President Kennedy's victory but the Commission was to be bipartisan. Eleanor Roosevelt was chosen to lead it because she was 'an outstanding symbol of humanitarian accomplishment'[7] for Republicans as well as Democrats.

President Kennedy later became a supporter of the ERA mainly, it is claimed, because of an unauthorised alteration to a speech drafted by a pro-ERA member of his staff.[8] In the meantime, he gave his full support to the Commission, instructing Federal departments to cooperate fully and to review their own practices affecting female employment. The Commission's recommendations, made in 1963, were modest. The rapid introduction of a Federal equal pay law and a Presidential Committee on appointments in public and private employment were proposed. But, with one exception, its members felt that the latter should be advisory and compliance with its recommendations voluntary. More research and promotional activity, especially by the Employment Services Agency, were suggested and the creation of inter-departmental and citizens' advisory committees recommended.[9]

The Equal Pay Act of 1963 was accelerated accordingly and the advisory committees were set-up. Various states also created their own Commissions which, after the Civil Rights Act, provided a network through which dissatisfaction with poor policy implementation was expressed. But, in the meantime, no action was taken on the recommendation for a Presidential Committee. Women were not included in the President's civil rights proposals and female employment was not considered during the 1963 hearings on his Civil Rights bill. That women were dealt with in Title VII (employment) of the

Civil Rights Act was the result of a curious combination of circumstances.

The inclusion of women in the Civil Rights Act

In 1963 the first concern of most liberal women as well as men was to end racial discrimination. This objective was given special priority by President Johnson in 1964. Southerners were of course opposed to it. In order to split the bipartisan liberal civil rights coalition, the Virginian Congressman Judge Howard Smith introduced an amendment to the employment section to ban sex discrimination. He believed that some liberals would support it while others would reject it because the added controversy would make it even more difficult for the bill to be passed. He also believed that, if he failed to destroy the bill, at least implementation would be impeded by an unwanted extra burden of enforcement.[10] The northern Democrat, Martha Griffiths, supported the amendment because of her genuine concern about sex discrimination and her hope for an opportunity to bring in a sex discrimination clause. She was opposed by her colleague, Emanuel Cellar, who cited Esther Petersen's assertion that the amendment was not in the best interests of women. Congressman Smith succeeded at first in dividing the civil rights alliance but, in the end, liberal women carried their colleagues and there was a majority for the amendment and the whole bill. When it went to Senate, the longest filibuster in the whole of American history began and went on for 83 days. For 57 of them, normal business came to a halt. The only feminist pressure from outside Congress on its proceedings came from the tireless Betty Friedan, the Women's International League for Peace and Freedom and a Presidential aide, Liz Carpenter, who is believed to have secured administrative acceptance of the amendment on sex discrimination. Eventually, after a vast number of amendments and the tabling of a new bill, just four votes more than the necessary 67 were cast in favour of ending discussion and the bill itself was passed by a similar majority. At no time was there any serious discussion of how the Act would work for women and, at the signing ceremony of 2 July 1964, President Johnson's remarks were couched entirely in male terms. Ironically, many of the strengthening amendments, which the conservative coalition had succeeded in deleting from the original bill, were to be re-installed largely as a consequence of the organised women's movement that grew out of anger at the refusal of the new Equal Employment Opportunity Commissioners to take sex discrimination seriously.

Affirmative action

While the idea of compliance with anti-discrimination laws by government contractors had existed since the New Deal, the notion of affirmative action was coined by President Kennedy in 1961. In that year he called upon employers to take positive steps to improve career prospects for racial minorities and gave some enforcement powers to the Fair Employment Practices Commission over government contractors. The extension of the idea of remedial action for individuals to the removal of deeply embedded patterns and practices of discrimination through affirmative action plans was developed by his successor, President Johnson – at first for racial minorities and then for women. What is entailed by these plans is discussed later in this chapter.

Early attitudes to equal pay in Britain

Britain, of course, has no counterpart to state legislature. Of local governments, the Borough of Poplar was the only one to be concerned at an early stage – the 1930s – with the question of equal pay. But the issue was raised a number of times in Parliament around the turn of the century. It was the subject of official investigation in 1912 (in the public sector) and during the First World War. The Atkins Committee[11] recommended equal pay for the same work and pay proportional to productivity. Between 1918 and 1931, various efforts were made to secure implementation, especially in the public sector. But members of Parliament were told, at first, that men had greater family responsibilities and, later, that, while the government approved of the principle, the country could not afford it.[12] In 1935, however, the government denied belief in the principle. Duff Cooper, Parliamentary Secretary to the Minister of

Labour, stated that the government would not incur expenditure or pledge itself to a principle that was represented in the House and country by 'a slogan which (it) did not believe to represent the facts'.[13]

The next year, Ellen Wilkinson (Labour) supported by Mr Pethwick Laurence (Labour), Eleanor Rathbone (Independent) and Conservatives Colonel Clifton Brown, Florence Horsburgh and Lady Astor reminded the House that although the principle of equal pay in the civil service had been accepted in 1920, nothing had been done except to grant it at the point of recruitment.[14] In 1944, Thelma Cazalet-Keir succeeded in amending the Education Bill to give equal pay to teachers in state schools.[15] On both occasions, Parliamentary feelings were suppressed by Prime Ministers who turned the issues into votes of confidence. Mr Churchill, however, made a concession by appointing a Royal Commission,[16] although he gave it very limited terms of reference. The modesty of these and inaction on the Commission's report led to a period of further debate during which the Labour governments of 1945 and 1951 announced that nothing could be done because of costs, practical difficulties, the national incomes policy and the likelihood of repercussions in the private sector.[17] But, as the equal pay campaigns discussed in Chapter 2 reached their zenith in 1954, the Conservative Chancellor undertook to discuss a phased introduction of equal pay in the public services with the Whitley Councils.[18] A seven-year period for non-industrial civil servants was agreed upon in 1955 and similar arrangements followed for teachers and local government officers.

Governmental attitudes to the extension of equal pay in Britain

The predicted effects in the private sector began to be felt in 1961 when the TUC requested the government to comply with the International Labour Organisation's Convention 110 on equal pay for work of equal value and pointed out that, should Britain join the European Economic Community, equal pay for the same work would be required under Article 119 of the Treaty of Rome. The Minister of Labour replied that equal pay in industry was not a matter for government intervention but for industrial negotiation.[19] The TUC and others persisted and, in 1964, the new Labour government, having made equal pay an election pledge, set up a committee to consider the matter, chaired by the Minister of Labour, Ray Gunter. But in May 1965, he told George Woodcock, General Secretary of the TUC, that equal pay raised such complex issues that industry could not be expected to introduce it during a period when there was a pay norm of $3\frac{1}{2}$ per cent. A month later, Mr Gunter's Parliamentary Secretary, Roy Hattersley, confirmed that all election pledges would be fulfilled but that Parliament still had four years to run.[20] A tripartite study group was set up in 1966 but, by the middle of 1967, talks were deadlocked over definitions and estimates of costs.[21] At the end of the year, substantive action was postponed pending improvements in the economy, but a study was commissioned to consider costs in specific industries and departments were instructed to review the implications of the Treaty of Rome.[22] In 1968, there was a bipartisan flurry of back-bench pressure but the most immediately important event was the replacement of Mr Gunter by Mrs Castle. Tripartite talks were resumed. The Confederation of British Industry remained unhappy about costs and persisted in its preference for the Treaty of Rome definition which was narrower in scope than that of the ILO.[23] Nevertheless, both sides agreed, albeit reluctantly, to the compromise devised by Mrs Castle and the general principle of equal pay became law in 1970.

Governmental views on other forms of discrimination

The government was unwilling, however, to intervene in the non-contractual elements of employment. Mrs Castle told Mrs Butler that she was not interested in including an anti-discrimination clause, although she had irritated Cabinet colleagues by trying to badger them into including pensions and social security.[24] During the passage of the bill, the Conservative Robert Carr warned that her bill would be ineffective without an anti-discrimination clause[25] but, although both parties were agreed about the justness of equal pay, Mr Heath's government did little at first to rectify this omission. Indeed, in January 1972, the Home Office Minister,

Richard Sharples, incurred wrath from the public galleries when he rejected Mr Hamilton's private members' bill by saying that women were best suited to occupations that were extensions of their domestic roles.[26] Effective filibustering in an earlier debate by Ronald Bell compelled the Speaker to withhold a second reading. Angry MPs demanded a revision of rules that allowed a single member to thwart the wishes of a majority that was '95% of a House unusually crowded for a Friday night'.[27] Mr Sharples was removed from his ministerial post for political ineptitude; he should have been aware that concern had grown since 1971 when Mrs Butler's similar bill was deferred because of lack of interest.[28] Although embarrassed, the government took no further action. The peers, however, had agreed to send an almost identical bill, introduced by Baroness Seear, to a Select Committee. Not unanimous at first about the need for intervention, its members were all convinced by the evidence received. That of Dr Margherita Rendel and two distinguished American women, Sonia Fuentes of the Equal Employment Opportunities Commission and Catherine East of the National Women's Party, for the first time referred systematically to possible lessons from the United States.[29] By the end of the Committee's hearings, the scope of the bill had been widened and enforcement proposals strengthened.

In 1973 Mr Hamilton tried again in the House of Commons. Once more the bill was about to fall because of filibustering. Following uproar on the Floor and in the galleries, the question arose of whether the government would grant extra time. In the end, the opposition guaranteed half a Supply Day and, on 14 February 1973, the bill got a second reading and was sent to a Select Committee.[30] Mr Hamilton regarded the referral as a delaying tactic because so much evidence had been collected already in the House of Lords. The Committee published a brief report to coincide with the final report from the House of Lords.

In the meantime, the government was preparing a *volte face*. Instead of relying on the normal progression of the two existing bills, it allowed rumours to appear in the press that it would bring in its own measures – a discourtesy for which it was reprimanded by the peers.[31] In November 1973, a consultative document was published called *Equal Opportunities for Men and Women*. The eventual Equal Opportunities Commission was christened in it but its recommendations bore few other resemblances to either private members' bills or later Labour proposals. Conservative leaders were obviously hoping for an enforcement body with narrow jurisdiction which would rely mainly on persuasion, especially in education,[32] instead of sanctions. Baroness Summerskill believed that the 'proposals were an election ploy to obtain women's votes with the minimum of sacrifice to male prestige'.[33]

Criticised by many women's groups, the document probably would have failed as an election ploy. But, in any case, the Prime Minister rested the election of February 1974 on the single issue of: 'Who governs – the miners or the government?'. The electorate did not give a clear answer but the Labour Party took over and, on 23 July, announced an intention to legislate on women's rights.[34] After consolidating its position in a second election, it published a White Paper.[35] During the winter of 1974–5, the Home Secretary, Roy Jenkins, and his adviser, Anthony Lester, visited the United States where they discussed their hopes to eliminate race and sex discrimination. In March 1975, their bill was published. The White Paper had taken account of 'the Select Committee findings, the experience of earlier race relations laws and the views of many individual groups'. The bill was stronger in some respects than the White Paper, partly as a result of discussions in America; of particular importance was the introduction of the new idea of indirect discrimination.[36] It was weakened in that, as a result of advice from the Scottish Law Office, the burden of proof was partly shifted back on to the complainant.[37]

American equal pay and opportunity laws

Equal pay[38]

Originally covering the same categories of workers as minimum wage laws, the Equal Pay Act of 1963 was extended in 1972 and 1974 to protect most workers in private and public employment. Employers must pay the same wages to women and men in the same occupation, under similar conditions, or if

they do work requiring equal or substantially similar skill,
effort, or responsibility. Differences are allowed if they are
based on merit, seniority or extra productivity under a
piece-work system. Case law has confirmed that work does not
have to be identical.[39] Differences in duties can be discounted if
employees of the better paid sex rarely have to do them; if they
are minor; or if employees of the other sex also have extra,
though different, tasks to do. The obligation to do shift-work
has been discounted in the courts as a justification for extra
differences in pay over and above the shift premium. Some
American courts have grafted the notion of indirect discrimination on to the law about equal pay. Differences must be resolved
by putting the lower rate up and not by reducing the higher
rate. Between 1963 and 1974, compliance was the responsibility of the Wage and Hour Division of the Department of
Labor. Individuals could file complaints with the Department
for themselves or on behalf of groups. This could be done
anonymously to avoid retaliation. If the Department could not
negotiate a solution, the complainant could go to court. The
Department itself could initiate investigations without complaints and often did so automatically when reviewing companies for breaches of other laws. President Carter transferred
responsibility to the Equal Employment Opportunities Commission during a rationalisation exercise. Sanctions are strong.
Employers may have to pay up to two years back pay and, if
discrimination is 'wilful', this may be extended to three to
compensate for damages to feelings. 'Wilful' discrimination
may also bring a large fine and two similar convictions could
lead to six months imprisonment.

Discrimination[40]

Taken together, Title VII of the Civil Rights Act of 1964,
Executive Order 11478 of 1969 and the Equal Employment
Opportunities Act of 1972 cover most employees in private
employment, in Federal, State and local government. Exemptions are allowed for firms employing fewer than 15 people
(before amendments, 100 and then 25). Title VII of the Civil
Rights Act makes it unlawful for an employer: to refuse, on
grounds of race, colour, religion, natural origin or sex, to hire,

discharge, discriminate in compensation, terms, conditions and privileges of employment; or to segregate or classify employees in such a way as to deprive them of opportunities. Employment agencies must not refuse to refer potential employees on the same grounds. Nor may labour unions discriminate in excluding, restricting, segregating or expelling members. Neither employers nor unions are allowed to discriminate in offering on-the-job training or apprenticeships. Exceptions are allowed where sex can be shown to be a bona fide occupational qualification (BFOQ) for reasons of authenticity, in religious institutions, in cases of national security and if the individual is a member of the Communist Party. Different treatment is also lawful if based on merit or productivity. In the original Act, it was stated that, except in the case of Indians in enterprises near Indian Reservations, nothing could be construed as justifying preferential treatment on account of an imbalance. Remedial treatment has, however, become lawful in the courts and under Executive Orders requiring affirmative action. Other unlawful practices include retaliation by an employer, union, or employment agency against an individual known to be bringing charges. The Act also bans advertisements for jobs which state preferences for sex or nationality except where there is a BFOQ. The courts have since largely ruled out the listing of jobs under the separate headings of 'women' and 'men'.

The Equal Employment Opportunities Commission (EEOC) is a bipartisan body whose commissioners are appointed by the President. At first it could only investigate individual complaints and conciliate. Its powers were circumscribed where State institutions already existed and it was not allowed to file suits itself. Legal proceedings were the responsibility of the plaintiff or, in the case of alleged 'patterns and practices' of discrimination where there might not be a specific plaintiff, the Department of Justice. The EEOC could assist by submitting *amicus curiae* briefs but did not, and still does not, have the 'cease and desist' authority of the National Labor Relations Board. This was always controversial since there was no compulsion on the Justice Department to follow EEOC recommendations to litigate. A concession, however, was made which allowed the EEOC to file its own suits in private sector employment cases. This has given it considerable scope because individual suits can become class actions which may affect very large numbers of employees. The EEOC may also issue guidelines which are not mandatory but which are treated seriously by the courts. Its guidelines include the idea of indirect discrimination. It was not until 1971, however, that the Supreme Court embodied this in case law. The wording of the Civil Rights Act suggests that action is discriminatory only when it is intended to be so. But in *Griggs* v. *Duke Power Company*, the Supreme Court decided that the aim of legislators had been to end the detrimental impact on racial minorities of arbitrary conditions imposed by employers whether or not they had intended to discriminate.[41] This was the legal origin of the idea that it was not always necessary to look for improper motives, and that neutral rules were discriminatory if they were unrelated to job performance and had a disproportionately detrimental (or disparate) impact on a particular group.[42] In public sector employment, Executive Order 11478 and the 1972 Equal Opportunities Act mean that Federal agencies have to draw up affirmative action plans and provide remedies (reinstatement and back pay) in the Civil Service similar to those in the private sector.

Affirmative action by Government contractors and bodies in receipt of federal funds

Executive Orders 11246 and 11375 of 1965 and 1968 outlaw discrimination by government contractors and require positive steps to remedy the effects of past discrimination. Many employers are affected; Contractors with fifty or more employees whose contracts are worth more than $50 000, subcontractors and bodies involved in projects receiving Federal funds, including universities.[43] Trade unions are not directly covered, but employers are not allowed to cite union policies as a reason for avoiding legal obligations. The first Order was amended by the second to deal with sex discrimination in the provision of services and supplies. After a number of lawsuits in the 1970s, construction industry plans also have to include targets for female employment. Enforcement responsibility was placed originally on the contracting departments under the guidance of the Office of Contract Compliance Programs (OFCCP) in the Department of Labor. Later, more responsibility was centralised in the Department of Labor, although the application of sanctions remained in the hands of the line agencies. Sanctions could include the temporary suspension of a contract, its cancellation, the debarring of the company from *any* government contracts, or court action.

The affirmative action plans in which contractors are expected to show how they will promote opportunities are not intended to be simple quota systems.[44] In 1970, the OFCCP defined such a plan as:

> a set of specific and result oriented procedures to which a contractor commits himself to apply every good faith effort. The objective of these procedures plus such efforts is equal employment opportunity. Procedures without effort to make them work are meaningless; and effort, undirected by specific and meaningful procedures, is inadequate. An acceptable affirmative action program must include an analysis of areas in which the contractor is deficient in the utilisation of minority groups and women, and further goals and time tables to which the contractor's good faith effects must be directed to correct the deficiencies, thus to achieve prompt and full utilisation of minorities and women at all levels and in all segments of his work force where deficiencies exist.[45]

In determining where there is under-utilisation, the contractor should consider: the local population; how it compares with the company's work-force; the availability of skilled members of the affected group; the promotability of members of the group already in the company; and, in order to improve the pool of qualified applicants, what the company can do to improve training opportunities. Plans should include targets, measures of progress, comprehensive data about company practices as well as demographic factors, detailed procedures for internal review and descriptions of how employees, unions, local schools and community action groups will be encouraged to make use of its equal opportunity policies.

The British legislation[46]

The contractual elements of employment; equal pay

The Equal Pay Act of 1970 provides for equality in the terms of a contract of employment. It requires that a woman (or a man) be treated no less favourably than a man (or a woman) in all contractual matters if both employees are engaged in the same or broadly similar work in the same or an associated establishment, or where their jobs have been given an equal value under a job evaluation scheme. The Act covers all constituent parts of pay, including bonuses, holiday pay, working time and overtime rates. It deals with individuals, collective agreements and wage regulation orders in all establishments in Great Britain including the Crown, the Police and Armed Services, although enforcement procedures are different for the last.[47] Individuals may make claims through regional industrial tribunals and may appeal on questions of law to the Employment Appeals Tribunal. It is for the plaintiff to show that work is the same or broadly similar. If there are differences in work, it is for the employer to show that they are legitimate because they are of practical importance. Differences in pay can be allowed, too, if the employer can show that there are material differences between employees which are not based on sex discrimination; for example, qualifications or length of service. Tribunals may award back pay for up to two years. The Central Arbitration Committee, to which employers, trade unions and the Secretary of State for Employment may refer collective agreements, can award arrears of pay from the time of referral. Legal enforcement of the Act was made voluntary for the first five years. But the Act contained a clause allowing the Secretary of State for Employment to introduce an Order, should voluntary compliance be too slow, requiring that women's pay be 90 per cent of men's by a specified date. This was never used. When the Act was amended by the Sex Discrimination Act, responsibility for enforcement was placed in the Equal Opportunities Commission.

The non-contractual elements of employment[48]

The employment provisions of the Sex Discrimination Act of 1975 complement the Equal Pay Act by dealing with the non-contractual elements of employment. The Act does not directly deal with pensions, taxation or social security. Maternity leave for working women, which in the United States is treated controversially in the courts as an aspect of the Civil Rights Act, is dealt with in the British Employment Protection Act.[49]

The Act defines what is unlawful behaviour as direct discrimination where a person is less favourably treated on grounds of sex and, in employment, on grounds of marital status; indirect discrimination, where a substantial number of one sex is unable, to their detriment, to comply with an apparently neutral rule, applicable to both sexes, which cannot be shown to be related to job performance;[50] and victimisation where a person thought to be seeking redress under the Act is unfairly treated.

The sections dealing with employment cover areas excluded by the Equal Pay Act; for example, recruitment, promotion, training and transfers. Certain exceptions are allowed: for example, where sex is a genuine occupational qualification for reasons of authenticity; or where personnel or welfare services are concerned; or where an employer cannot reasonably be expected to provide separate accommodation; or when the job involves work to be done in other countries where law and custom would make it difficult for persons of a particular sex to be effective. The armed services, ministers of religion and midwives are treated separately and less stringently.

Pressure or instructions to discriminate by an employer on, for example, a personnel officer are unlawful. Nor may trade unions, professional associations, employment and training agencies deprive one sex of membership or services. Advertisements must make it clear that jobs covered by the Act are open to both sexes. A limited amount of positive discrimination is allowed but not compelled. Unions previously restricted to one sex may temporarily reserve places in their organisations for members of the excluded sex. Employers and public bodies may treat one sex favourably in the provision of training opportunities if that sex has been badly represented in occupations to which the training leads.[51]

Remedies can be sought by individuals and by the Equal Opportunities Commission. As in equal pay law, employment cases go first to industrial tribunals, then the Employment Appeals Tribunal and, thereafter, the normal Court of Appeal.[52] Individuals may be assisted by the EOC if complex issues or important principles are involved. Only the EOC may start proceedings in 'victimless' cases: for example, where a discriminatory practice means that no person could ever put herself or himself in a position to be a complainant[53] or in cases of discriminatory advertising. The Commission was given the unprecedented power to carry out formal investigations into particular industries, companies or services. A non-discrimination notice, backed up by a court injunction, can be served and the EOC may monitor to ensure that non-compliance does not persist. The Commission may issue Codes of Practice which would be admissible evidence in a court of law. Its other functions are conciliatory, persuasive and educative. These involve informal investigations, research and the allocation of grants to others for the analysis of problems and the promotion of equality. The EOC is expected to review the workings of the Acts, of protective legislation and of tax and social security regulations.

A comparison of the two sets of legislation

In many ways, the two equal pay acts are alike. Both stemmed in part from worries about irrationalities in the labour markets and, in neither country, were proposals controversial at their legislative stages. The British Conservative MP, Sir Douglas Glover, an opponent of Mrs Castle in 1964, was moved to peroration:

> It is one of the glories of Britain that when . . . the mood is right, the fundamental agreement within society manifests itself . . . there is far more fundamental agreement . . . than there is division between the parties.[54]

The contents of both acts make it clear that work is not expected to be identical. Although the American act contains nothing about job evaluation, judges have been bolder than their British counterparts about the effects of indirect discrimination on pay and about what is comparable when jobs are not the same. In effect, therefore, American law takes into account some job evaluation considerations such as levels of responsibility required in different jobs.[55] Both laws allow similar exemptions and, in both countries the courts have disallowed formal obligations to work on 'unsociable' shifts as a reason for different basic payments. The American law, however, makes disobedience more expensive.

On broader questions of discrimination, British law is both stronger and weaker than the American. Marital status is included in the policy of the former but not the latter. Nor does Britain exempt members of the Communist Party from legal protection. Formal investigations give the EOC a 'cease and desist' authority that the EEOC does not have, although to some extent this is counterbalanced by the potential impact of class action cases which can involve large numbers of employees in the United States. By statute in Britain and by case law in the United States, both countries ban indirect discrimination. Both protect victims from retaliation and potentially provide for damages to feelings. Guidelines in the United States are, and British Codes of Practice could be, taken seriously in the courts. Both countries allow exceptions to the law where sex is a genuine occupational qualification, in particular for reasons of authenticity. The Civil Rights Act in the United States has been deemed to supersede differences between the sexes in protective legislation while, in Britain, most protective laws remain and are, for the time being, subject to review. The British law contains nothing about contract compliance and has no compulsory equivalent of affirmative action.

Because of the different patterns of origin of the Civil Rights Act and Sex Discrimination Act, particular provisions were the subject of more detailed discussion in Britain than in the United States. The Home Secretary claims to have been persuaded to introduce indirect discrimination and his limited proposals for positive discrimination by 'the validity of criticisms of many women's and other organisations'.[56] He also met the objections of groups discussed in Chapter 2 when he included marital status, victimisation and damages. But it is also the case that he was advised by American policy-makers that his proposals would be ineffective without the notion of indirect discrimination, victimisation and damages.[57] He rejected the urging of women's groups for provision for positive action on the ground that his observation of the practical application of affirmative action in the United States reinforced his belief that it undermined the philosophy on which his proposals were based.[58] In effect, he rejected American judicial views that affirmative action did not constitute the preferential treatment that was specifically outlawed in the Civil Rights Act but could be upheld because it was remedial. The government's rejection of contract compliance and full scale positive action gave rise to unsuccessful protests initiated by Jo Richardson (Labour) in the House of Commons and Baroness Vickers (Conservative) in the House of Lords.

In addition, there was Parliamentary discussion of other points of detail that has no parallel in the United States because of the history of the Civil Rights Act. For example, women in both Houses, sharing the concern of feminist groups, tried but failed to reintroduce the idea that the onus of proof should rest on employers – as in the case of the Equal Pay Act and Trades Union and Labour Relations Act. The Government maintained that other alterations had been made to assist victims in eliciting information and securing damages. Because of these controversies and various other objections, Maureen Colquhoun (Labour) indicted the Act as a piece of 'shabby window-dressing for this hideous International Women's Year'.[59]

Nevertheless, there were few explicitly anti-feminist alterations that succeeded.[60] The innovatory idea of indirect discrimination and novel powers granted to the EOC were less controversial than expected. The main changes arising from wishes to limit women's rights at work were the exceptions involving work in other countries and living-in posts. A Government amendment was inserted and an Opposition amendment accepted as a result of representations from the CBI and the General Council of British Shipping. More or less satisfactory compromises were reached on the clergy and male midwives. On protective legislation Conservatives tried to push the CBI line that it could not coexist with equal rights policies. But the government argued that enough had been done by making the EOC responsible for a review required by the European Economic Community and by placing a time limit on it of 1978. It agreed, however, to an incomplete removal of restrictions on the cleaning of machinery by women who themselves operated it and to a further review by the Health and Safety Commission. However, all that is involved in protective legislation is still controversial to an extent that is no longer evident in the United States.

In general, though, the principles of the Sex Discrimination Act were accepted in all sides of both Houses. Behind the relative harmony over the Act itself was acceptance of the idea that it was right to use the law to shift attitudes by specifying what was unacceptable practice. This relatively new view of the proper role of the law had been expressed by Robert Carr (Conservative) during the Equal Pay Bill and was continued by Sir Ian Gilmour in 1975:

> It is a huge relief to find a piece of legislation which is not designed to undermine what the last Conservative Government did but is designed to build on what we achieved. . . . A country which considers itself just and democratic cannot afford to institutionalise prejudice against half the population, particularly when it is almost broke. Legislation is necessary because it affects the climate of opinion . . .[61]

In the House of Commons, only Ronald Bell (Conservative) and Enoch Powell (Ulster Unionist) disagreed, arguing that, since there were no legal impediments to women doing whatever they wanted, there were no extra rights which governments could confer upon them. It was inconceivable to both that the market would not, by itself, reflect changing attitudes or that it would give different rewards for identical services. Ivor Stanbrook (Conservative), without the theoretical justifications, argued that the Government's own amendments had made 'this Draconian measure' even worse than it had been at Second Reading.[62] The cross-bench peer, Lord Monson alone opposed the principle of the bill in the Upper

House, describing it as 'profoundly anti-libertarian . . . with all the hall-marks of American earnestness . . . and . . . Puritanism'.[63] Like Mr Bell, he believed that legal reforms should only occur when changes in social thought had already taken place. He did not believe they had.

Most peers deliberately disassociated themselves from him. According to Lord Gardiner (Labour), 'there could be no rational argument against the claim that there should be equality for women', and Viscount Colville (Conservative) in a House usually noted for its politeness, referred to Lord Monson as a 'caveman'.[64]

The reasons for capitulation

Liberal democracy and public opinion

A number of factors make it seem as though the governments of Britain and the United States were responding to public opinion in a fashion expected by the conventional understanding of liberal democratic politics. Ellickson observed that the Republican and Democratic parties were realising that they had to appeal to women voters.[65] Friedan, because of her university and radical connections, thought that she was 'in touch with something much larger than herself' and was vindicated when her book, despite her publisher's pessimism, became an instant best-seller.[66] Mrs Castle thought she was on to an election winner.[67] Mr Hamilton spoke of mass lobbies.[68] Mrs Williams believed that legal recognition of women's equality at work had the 'power of an idea that had found its time',[69] and Mr Jenkins credited many women's groups with his innovations in the Sex Discrimination Bill.[70] Because, by the nature of things, one set of events follows another, it is tempting to see a chronological description as a causal explanation. But to argue that the growth of public opinion made representative and responsible governments legislate is to leave unexplained a number of anomalies. It does not explain why governments choose to hear public demands when they do or why they act slowly or not at all on some issues and quickly on others. For more than a century and a half there were intermittent, and at times strong pressures for equal pay and opportunities in the United States. Yet a Federal Equal Pay Act owed as much to opposition to the Equal Rights Amendment as it did to acceptance of public pressure for equal pay. Equal opportunities for women came in at the last moment on the 'coat-tails' of a race relations reform, with no obvious widespread organised pressure. In Britain there was public pressure for equal pay for about one hundred years and yet the government responded comparatively rapidly to relatively brief pressure for an anti-discrimination law. Goodin argues that timing of governmental action depends on particular configurations of powerful interest groups with which they are confronted.[71] Often, as in the case of women's rights, inaction is justified on the ground that the time is not right – a device which, he argues, is a technique for manipulating public opinion in order to placate potentially disruptive forces. British members of Parliament and trade unionists were sometimes driven to argue that, since the time never seemed right for women's equality, women would have to become disruptive,[72] and in the United States, poor enforcement at the start of equality policies for women was explained on the ground that the Department of Justice was 'in the business of social turmoil and that women were not out in the streets demanding their rights.'[73] Conversely, governments could be seen as the protecting stronger interests of employers and labour when the perceived needs of the economy were given as reasons at first for inaction and then for reform. On the other hand, it is also possible that governments said that the labour forces needed to be rationalised in order to persuade reluctant employers to accept anti-discrimination laws that were thought necessary for other reasons. And it is more than likely that there was a complex interplay of a number of factors in the timing of equality laws.

Connections among women's rights, race relations, class and welfare issues in both countries

In the United States, apart from the Equal Rights Amendment and ideas about business rationality, there was considerable concern in the then dominant liberal coalition about the extent of poverty and failures in welfare policy, especially in the cities to which poor whites and racial minorities had migrated. Racial discrimination was seen as a significant cause of poverty and civil rights reforms were part and parcel of President Johnson's great society programme.[74] Riots in the inner cities were followed by the Kerner Commission report which recommended that positive steps had to be taken to remove legitimate grievances.[75] Although it was a combination of a political stratagem and genuine concern that had resulted in the banning of sex discrimination at work and not governmental anxiety about female poverty and disruption, women became part of a political constituency that liberal Presidents could not afford to alienate.[76] This, together with the growth of cohesion in the women's component of the civil rights alliance, gave women a certain political leverage. In the background was the fact that an individualistic political philosophy had to be adapted to the needs of a complex industrial society. This facilitated the idea that individualistic rights could be defined in social and economic terms[77] and that they could be conferred legitimately on groups of individuals. Even the Democratic Party which, since the 1930s, had acquired something of a class connotation, was losing its tenuous (in comparison to Britain) 'labour' approach to politics,[78] and reverting to liberalism, albeit in its new form.

In Britain, the progression was different although some of the immediate causes were similar. Older political beliefs that were less strongly individualistic and more 'organic' than in the United States, gave way in the twentieth century to a collectivist approach in general and class-based views of democracy in the Labour Party. For the latter, especially, the classical liberal formulation of democracy defined in the procedural terms of political rights for individuals was inadequate. To be democratic was to pursue substantive material equality between the classes. While the idea that economic and social needs might be in the same category of human rights as liberal political liberties remains disputed among philosophers, the welfare state has been widely accepted in Britain.[79] In its ideal form welfare legislation does not differentiate between groups of citizens. Its provisions should be universally available as of right on an anonymous basis. The provision of education and health services are like this. At best, in order to preserve anonymity, the only admissible information about claimants of selective benefits (rather than rights) is, according to Sen,[80] their levels of welfare. The Equal Pay and Anti-Discrimination Laws are different in that they appear to offer economic and social rights to specific groups whose membership is not universal and whose composition does not alter with changes in levels of welfare. They are not anonymous but are identifiable by immutable, innate characteristics.

Equal rights laws – especially those dealing with women – present particular difficulties for the Labour Party. For some time, a strong strand of opinion existed on the political left that feminism was a conservative diversion from the pursuit of class equality and that women's rights would be a natural by-product of general social transformation.[81] There is a class element in the Equal Pay Act in so far as Mrs Castle wanted working-class women to have the same rights as middle-class women in the public sector. But, since very few women of any class were paid completely equally, its effects cross classes. And, unless it is claimed that women and the working-class are coterminous, it cannot be argued that a sex discrimination law reduces class inequality.[82]

This theoretical problem prevented the Labour Party from wholeheartedly adopting equal rights policies at an early stage. It may have been compounded by the surprisingly radical stance adopted by the Conservative Women's Reform Report of 1947, by the active involvement of Conservative and Liberal women in equal pay and opportunity campaigns and by Mr Heath's investigations in the late 1960s into how to modernise laws about women, their work and families. Fears of feminism in the Labour Party dismayed Douglas Houghton in 1963[83] and it was obvious that they were still there by the end of the decade, despite the inclusion of equal pay in the 1964 manifesto. The Crossman diaries reveal that Cabinet opinion over equal pay was split.[84] Some ministers thought that equal pay was an essential part of socialism; others believed that, although desirable, it should not be pressed to the extent of upsetting the trade unions; and others still believed it to be entirely of secondary importance. On anti-discrimination measures, Joyce Gould, who succeeded Betty Lockwood as Women's Officer of the Party, and MPs Joyce Butler, Edward

Bishop and Ted Leadbitter, had to work at convincing leaders
of the rightness of intervention. It was not until 1972 that the
party produced a discussion document and it was only in 1974
that equal rights for working women appeared in the manifesto.[85]

The difficulty does not appear in the United States, where
parties do not have close class connections, in exactly the same
form. There, the disagreement was paralleled in disputes about
the priorities to be given to race or sex discrimination.
Historically American conservatism and liberalism have cros-
sed party lines, mainly on a geographical basis and the parties,
as opposed to cross party alliances, have not been consistently
distinguishable over questions of state intervention. British
conservatism has always been more agnostic than American
about the idea of state intervention. The past history of the
Conservative Party, combined with its reforming dispositions
of the 1960s, enabled it to arrive fairly readily at the view,
adopted by liberal Republicans and Democrats in the United
States, that intervention on women's rights was possible. But,
of course, given that the Conservative Party also contains
old-fashioned *laissez-faire* elements, its action on equal opportunities would have been characteristically moderate. It was,
however, the Labour Party that introduced reform; and its
measures, in keeping with its philosophy of the State, had a
much greater interventionist thrust. Its new way of increasing
material equality, however, was not an accretion of eclectic
past traditions but a product of difficulties it confronted in
solving class inequalities by collective means.

*Political and economic factors encouraging the British Labour Party to
adopt group rather than class-based solutions for inequality*

While the Labour Party was compelled to change by economic
considerations, it was helped by changing attitudes in Parliament about law-making. Equality laws occurred during a
decade of moral reforms, such as the abolition of theatre
censorship and abortion, homosexual and divorce law reforms.
One writer has credited these to the advent of a Labour
administration in 1964.[86] But all were preceded by a flurry of
private members' bills and are notable for the extent of

bipartisan back-bench cooperation. Other writers argue that changes in the sociological composition of the House of Commons were significant.[87] Members elected after 1960, with university (but not Oxbridge) educations, it is argued, share dispositions towards reform and towards the idea that policies should not be based on blind partisan attitudes but on research, probably carried out by select committees.[88] These backgrounds and attitudes are generally to be found in the Labour Party but the correlation holds for Conservatives too. Between 1960 and 1975 the House came to be dominated numerically by new members, many of whom were reformers. Mrs Butler's experience of the more favourable attitudes towards anti-discrimination policies of new members in the 1970s provides some circumstantial support. So, too, does the influence of the evidence taken by select committees on race relations and sex discrimination. But a sociological explanation is not a complete one. Individual members discriminated between the reforms they favoured or opposed. One example of many is Mrs Knight (Conservative) who opposed abortion reform but supported equal pay and Mr Hamilton's bill. Furthermore, many important initiatives came from the House of Lords whose members had often spent much of their lives in politics; for example Baronesses Seear, Summerskill, Ward and Vickers and Lords Gardiner, Houghton and Amulree.

Moral reforms and anti-discrimination laws share a structural dimension that contributes to bipartisan activity and House of Lords activism. In a system such as the British that is, or has been, characterised by rotating majorities for parties that are largely based on class, governments have built in majorities on class issues.[89] But they do not on issues that involve the interests of minority social groups or of groups that cut across classes. Because of dissidence in the ranks and because as many voters may be lost as gained, such governments cannot afford to respond to appeals from minority pressure groups. This revitalises the role of the back-benchers, making the reformers among them, whatever their party, worthwhile targets for lobbyists. And, since they are well disposed to select committees, another useful forum is provided for the expression of opinion by affected groups. The House of Lords was able to take on its 'progressive' air in the period

precisely because its members do not have appeal to class based
constituencies. While sociological and structural factors provided a favourable legislature, Labour governments were
forced to take advantage of them for other reasons. Sen argues
that the pursuit of equality is almost bound to become
prohibitively expensive if based on universalism and anonymity and this necessarily leads to the need to clarify specific
characteristics as signposts for distribution.[90] Politicians of the
late 1970s and 1980s have made the *costs* of welfare salient. But
in the 1960s optimism about the *effects* of the welfare state was
exploded by the public discovery of continuing poverty and the
realisation that minority groups gained little from the public
provision of health services, housing and higher education.[91]
From the middle of the 1960s, there was a convergence of
resource problems, worries about ineffectiveness and a mood in
Parliament which at once compelled and facilitated a logic
leading the welfare state from the universal to the particular
and towards laws for the economic and social well being of the
inhabitants of specified areas or citizens of specific types.

The latter was seen first in the field of race relations.[92] In the
early stages of immigration, the idea that the law be used to
guarantee economic and social rights was not contemplated. It
was assumed, almost universally, that legal equality sufficed
and that, since immigrants were legally equal, they had no
relevant special characteristics for which government should
take responsibility. Indeed, to pick out a group for specific
treatment was considered dangerous. One dissenter in the
1950s recommended a law to ban racial discrimination in
economic and social affairs. But it was not until local
authorities had to grope towards *ad hoc* solutions to economic
and social problems that pressure was put on central government to take a different approach. The first major review of
policy, carried out in 1965, incorporated the idea that special
measures for special groups were necessary and justifiable. In
the Street Report of 1967 on the use of the law for this purpose,
it was recommended that the law be used primarily to create a
climate of distaste for discrimination and, as a last resort, to
seek out and punish discriminatory behaviour.

If anything was 'an idea that had found its time' by 1973, it
was the view that it was proper to protect particular and readily

identifiable groups in this way. The trend was continued, not initiated by the Equal Pay Act, and it culminated in the Sex Discrimination Act. It was believed that, while racial and sex discrimination were not identical problems, certain consequences had common features which the law could help to eliminate by banning anti-social practices, by providing remedies and, through changing behaviour, by indirectly reducing prejudice. The events leading to the Sex Discrimination Act were occasions for assessing race relations laws and institutions. Lessons about their shortcomings were drawn and contributed to the content of the new law – in particular to the provisions for remedy and the powers of the EOC. The Act and the Commission were used the next year as models for a new race relations act.

The effects of Britain's membership of the EEC

The precise timing of British governmental action in equal pay and opportunities is, at least in part, a consequence of expected and actual membership of the European Economic Community – a factor absent in the United States. In 1961 the then six member states agreed upon a three stage programme of implementation of Article 119 (on equal pay) of the Treaty of Rome. It was reported that the French were insisting on legislation in order to avoid competition from other member countries with lower labour costs.[93] At that time, the Conservative government in Britain was trying to negotiate entry. It was thought that its negotiator, Mr Heath, would state Britain's willingness to accept the principle but its preference for leaving the matter to collective bargaining. This was expected to be enough to avoid holding up negotiations but not satisfactory for a full member. The EEC programme of implementation was strict. By June 1962, disparities in pay were to be no greater than 15 per cent, by 1963 this was to be 10 per cent and, by the end of 1964, pay was to be exactly the same.

The force of EEC requirements was much greater than the ideals expressed in United Nations declarations on women's rights and in the International Labour Organisation Conventions on equal pay and opportunities. Despite many appeals to the government to ratify these international agreements, it remained possible to respond by saying that Britain was not ready to do so.

But the EEC provisions included the intention to send questionnaires to governments, employers and trade unions to ascertain progress. In addition, member state governments refusing to implement EEC Directives could be arraigned before the European Court of Justice. Expulsions could follow, although violations would probably have to be widespread. Although there were no intermediate enforcement steps that could back-up an unfavourable ruling from the Court, it was noted at the time that members had never defied it.[94]

The probing on equal pay experienced by Mr Heath and Mr Butler in 1961 and 1962 continued during Mr Wilson's government. And it was reported that the government was worried that the rules of the Treaty of Rome would be applied strictly.[95] As noted already, a special study of the implications of Article 119 was carried out. In the end the British Act was more generous than would have been required by the EEC at that time. In 1975, however, an EEC Directive extended the definition of equal pay to 'cover work to which equal value is attributed' and proceedings have been brought against the British Government for incomplete compliance with European law.[96]

By the beginning of the 1970s, it was clear that the EEC was likely to ban discrimination in the non-contractual elements of employment too. By January 1974 a Social Action Programme had been drawn up encouraging member states to promote equal opportunities for working women. Soon afterwards, Britain's continued membership was in the balance. By that time, the possibility of a Directive, with all the usual compliance steps, was being discussed. The British government passed the Sex Discrimination Act three months before the Directive was published in February 1976. (It was this Directive that also required member states to review their protective legislation.) The Debate on the Directive, however, had taken place in April 1975, at about the same time as the first Parliamentary stages of the Sex Discrimination Bill. A British conservative, Lady Elles, was the rapporteur in the European Parliament. Other European conservatives, unlike Mr Bell in Britain, argued that it was shameful for the West that Eastern Europe had taken the lead on women's economic equality.[97]

The Directive contains no suggestions about specific ways in which such a lead might be matched. It was pointed out in the debate that there were no tried and tested methods in Western Europe. It is hardly surprising that a British government should not look to Eastern Europe for detailed guidance about how to enshrine women's rights in legislation or to enforce the law. Both the Home Secretary and his adviser knew about and admired the Kennedy–Johnson civil rights reforms and were persuaded by the views put to them strongly during their visit that anti-discrimination policies would not work unless they were aimed at the effects of employment practices instead of the motives behind them. It was realised, too, that the idea of aiming at effects is a common European legal concept. Consequently, there is a European contribution not only to the timing of government responses but also to the inclusion in the British Act of the indirect discrimination as well as an EEC influence on its sections on victimisation and a limited version of positive action.

PART THREE

Policy Implementation

4

Implementation and Enforcement

To leave the story of new laws about the point of introduction would be to exclude important components of the policy process. This is because a policy is not only a discrete decision or a new law but an accumulation of strategic and operational decisions made in a variety of bodies and the effects of decisions and actions taken before and after legislative reform. The administering of new laws is not the neutral process implied by the disciplinary separation of politics and public administration. The continuation of political processes during implementation influences the extent to which states of affairs change as intended by legislators. Consequently, while this chapter provides some information about post-legislative developments in pay and occupational distribution, it concentrates on the political aspects of implementation. That is, it discusses the efforts of institutions and groups engaged in changing the labour market patterns described in Chapter 1.

Post-legislative patterns of women's pay and employment

Pay

A startling contrast exists between the United States and Britain. The ratio between men's and women's pay is much worse in the former than in the latter and, in all major occupational groups except service workers, the gap has widened since 1963. In 1963, variations in average annual

earnings ranged between 39.0 per cent for female sales workers
and 64.8 per cent for professional women. In 1973, the same
groups were still at the extremes at 37.8 per cent and 63.6 per
cent respectively.[1] Between 1973 and 1983, the aggregate
difference continued to hover at around 60 per cent. Despite
widening differences between men and women, the incomes of
white and minority group women narrowed from 25 per cent in
1967 to less than 7 per cent in 1974. In Britain, however,
women's pay improved quite rapidly after 1970. Between that
year and 1977 women's average hourly earnings moved from
63.1 per cent of men's to 75.5 per cent. Thereafter, a decline
began which has continued slowly ever since.[2]

So far as the United States is concerned, the Department of
Labor is thought to have discharged its equal pay obligations
properly and so analysts have tried to find other explanations
for the disappointing effects of the Equal Pay Act.[3] In some
accounts, part of the difference is attributed to the success of
equal opportunity legislation.[4] This means that as women
increasingly enter new occupations or re-enter the labour
market, more women earn entry-level salaries and this depres-
ses average pay figures. In other research, it is argued that
poor education and restricted opportunities continue to explain
75 per cent of the differentials.[5] Part of the remaining 25 per
cent is thought to include some unequal pay for the same work
but the main conclusion of the research is that continued
pressure is needed, not for equal pay, but for equal work
opportunities. Early improvements in Britain reflect the granting of equal pay for the same or broadly similar work. Chiplin
and Sloane argue that, by 1975, few women, engaged in work
where there were comparable men, received lower rates.[6]
Some, though not many, gains were made through the section
of the Act dealing with jobs rated as equivalent under a job
evaluation scheme. And between 1975 and 1977, general pay
restrictions made allowances for progress towards equal pay.[7]
The absence of full equality and the decline from 1978 result
from inadequacies in the equal pay law and from practices that
contravene the Sex Discrimination Act. For example, the job
evaluation section does not outlaw schemes with discriminatory factors unless a particular case is proved. And under the
'like work' section a woman has to be able to compare herself

with a man. According to some reports, the extent of job segregation and manipulation of job evaluation schemes mean that very few women are now in a position to claim equal pay.[8] The Equal Pay Act actually encouraged increased segregation as employers and unions reached agreements on grading structures that moved women into jobs where there were no men or that, as a result of modifications to job descriptions, ensured that lower-paid grades were occupied by women and higher paid grades by men.[9]

Occupational distribution

Both optimists and pessimists about women's pay in the United States can find some vindication of their views in developments in occupational patterns. At the beginning of the twentieth century, occupational segregation was greater in the United States than in Britain. By 1960, it was similar in the two countries and, by 1970, America had overtaken Britain in its rate of decline.[10] At first, this was mainly because of permeation by men into 'female' occupations. But by the mid-1970s, women *had* increased their share of some occupations in which men predominate; for example in the professional, craft and operator categories. Within the professional category, the rates of increase of female accountants, architects, engineers, physicists, lawyers and judges increased by two to four times between 1960 and 1970. Sharp rises also took place in female enrollments on degree courses in subjects leading to these occupations. In engineering, degree courses and part-time training schemes are more flexible in the United States than in Britain and attract more women students. In the manual sector, similar rates of improvement occurred during the same decade in the skilled trades; in particular, among carpenters, electricians, plumbers, car mechanics, painters, toolmakers, machinists, compositors and typesetters. In general, the rate of increase of skilled women workers was eight times that of skilled men. Nevertheless, while rates rose rapidly, absolute numbers remained very small. And, even in 1973, the staff of Federally funded training programmes were found to be profoundly ignorant of the possibilities of breaking down traditional patterns in apprenticeships and skilled trades.[11]

Since 1975, improvements in manual work have been slowing down, whereas 1980 Census statistics show that women now form 30.5 per cent of executive, managerial and administrative employees compared with 18.5 per cent in 1970.

In contrast, the British Sex Discrimination Act appears to have made very little impact so far on the degree of occupational segregation. In 1978, *The Sunday Times* reported that

> the next time you ask for a plumber . . . or a roofer . . . it is quite possible that when you open the door, the figure in overalls will be a woman.[12]

The report went on to say that a growing number of women were joining the construction industry as a result of the Sex Discrimination Act. But the change – even if considered in terms of its rate – is very small. Between 1975 and 1980, women as a percentage of men in construction rose by less than 1 per cent from 6.8 per cent to 7.6 per cent.[13] Among middle-class women, the largest gain has been made in medicine. By 1979, 30 per cent of doctors were female. British women have always been better off than American in this field. In both countries, their share of engineering has never been impressive in absolute terms but, as in America, the rate of increase for British women has been quite high. A small gain in the general management category for British women can be accounted for, as might have been expected, by an increase in female personnel managers. The overall position is, however, depressing. In its Annual Report for 1980, the Equal Opportunities Commission states that:

> All available information about women's position in the labour force points to their being concentrated in industries and occupations which are largely female; this has remained so since 1975.[14]

Publicly sponsored enquiries[15] between 1978 and 1980 revealed that the occupational distribution of women and men still correlated closely with the division between low and well paid work; that more than three-quarters of employers hired men exclusively as sales managers, scientists, and supervisors; and that 84 per cent of managers in a small sample of firms admitted to specifying sex to local job centres, turning down applicants for jobs and training on grounds of sex and applying apparently neutral rules that were discriminatory in effect. In a later, larger sample, most firms claimed to offer equal opportunities but only 3 per cent of them could offer documentary evidence that they did so.[16]

Attitudes of employers, trade unionists and women workers

Credit for the comparatively more rapid improvements in the United States, especially in manual work, has been given by the Department of Labour to the affirmative action plans required by its own Office of Contract Compliance.[17] American employers claim to feel bound to object in public to the burdens placed upon them by affirmative action plans. Procedures are complex and failure to comply can be expensive. The first major and expensive settlement was completed in 1972 with the American Telephone and Telegraph Corporation. More recently, the General Electric Company had to spend $32 million dollars on back pay and to develop affirmative action policies in order to resolve charges initiated by the EEOC. On the other hand, some large corporations admit discreetly that legislation has forced them to modernise outdated labour utilisation policies and grievance procedures.[18] As a result of improved labour use and industrial relations, they sometimes find it difficult to be precise about the real costs of reform or the advantages of dragging their heels. In smaller firms, where bureaucratised procedures and public intervention are comparatively more burdensome, there seems to be more reluctance to use and train women in new ways until forced to do so.[19] Trade unions, as in Britain, have varied in their attitudes. The main source of dissent, where it was not inherent conservatism, was the question of protective legislation. But in 1974, women in 58 trade unions formed the Coalition of Labor Union Women to encourage female union membership and to persuade cautious unions into unequivocal opposition to discrimination. By the 1970s, special laws about the hours of women's work had been declared void by the courts which also instructed that regulations about exposure to hazards should apply to both sexes. The AFL-CIO then ended its opposition to the Equal Rights Amendment and joined a campaign against states that had not ratified it. Sheer economic necessity that faces rising numbers of poor families, especially single parent families headed by women, has contributed to the expansion of the female labour force and has fostered the belief that it is normal for women to work. But during the 1970s, there was a widespread belief that the normality of working women was reinforced by political acknowledgement of it through the creation of new laws and institutions. These and improvements to them, instigated often by women's rights groups, helped to promote the idea that it is also normal for working women to expect to be treated equally. Many professional women believed that, without Federal intervention, the advances of the period would have taken decades.[20] Ironically, this view became public as major setbacks were beginning to appear.

British employers, despite admitting discrimination in training, were less likely to believe in 1979 than in 1973 that women were unfairly treated in this respect.[21] What is indisputable, however, is employers' unwillingness to use the nearest equivalent in Britain to affirmative action; that is very few of them have used the enabling clause of the Sex Discrimination Act to train women for occupations that have been predominantly male. Recently the EOC and TUC have taken up this question, which from the start was on the agenda of women's groups. Few unions did much about the Act at first, some positively limiting its impact deliberately or out of ignorance. Female membership, however, has risen rapidly since 1974 and several unions have cooperated in experimental, voluntary positive action programmes.

During the lifetime of the Equal Pay Act and the Sex Discrimination Act, the attitudes of women workers became more informed and more demanding. While the argument that in periods of unemployment men should have priority remained powerful, the number of women giving high priority to their own paid employment increased significantly. In 1971, two out of three working wives considered themselves housewives first and employees second. In 1977, half of them saw themselves as working women who also ran homes. In 1979, four out of five said they would work even if millionaires. By 1981, ignorance of the laws was giving way to dissatisfaction about their ineffectiveness, by the knowledge that Britain was lagging behind Europe and by 'widespread and popular support' for amendments like those proposed by the Equal Opportunities Commission.[22]

Paradoxically, given such developments and changes, albeit slow and often rhetorical in trade union thinking, British employers increasingly claimed that social attitudes and traditions were the main barriers to equal treatment.[23] These prevented women from being 'career conscious'. They may have had to resort to such arguments because they no longer felt able to refer – and fewer of them did in 1979 than 1973 – to innate inabilities and deliberate prejudice. All the same, it is odd to make such claims when it was becoming a more common social attitude to favour the idea of women's equality and when this was acknowledged by the creation of institutions to persuade the unconverted and punish the disobedient.

Institutions responsible for enforcement in the United States

With its more complex system of government, the United States has many more units of responsibility for equal opportunities than Britain. At the Federal level, the Civil Service Commission, the Equal Employment Opportunities Commission, the Departments of Justice and Labor are all involved in enforcement, while the Civil Rights Commission and Women's Bureau of the Department of Labor carry out research and offer advice to political leaders. In addition, each government department has its own equal opportunities office. Central bodies like the EEOC and Department of Labor have regional and field offices. And most states and some cities also have their own offices of fair employment, equal opportunities and contract compliance. In the judicial system, suits may be filed in State and Federal courts. To review them all would involve a book in itself and, because of this, this section concentrates on Federal institutions responsible for private sector employment. In this and the next section on Britain, the structures and functions of enforcement bodies are outlined. In addition important contributions to substantive policy development are discussed. A comparison of the broad roles of the institutions within their respective political systems is made in Chapter 5.

Wage and Hour Division, Department of Labor[24]

This Division was responsible until 1978 for investigating violations of the Equal Pay Act by private employers or State and local governments; negotiating settlements; and, when necessary, securing compliance through the courts. Employees did not have to file suits through the Division and, conversely, it could, without specific complaints, pursue violations which were revealed by other investigations. Employees were protected from victimisation by the Division's right to maintain anonymity. In 1979, responsibility for equal pay was transferred to the EEOC.

Until 1977, the Division had a good reputation but in that year the Civil Rights Commission reported that regional staff had become lax in following up violations revealed during other investigations. The national office was criticised for its guidelines for employers on equal pay, which were inconsistent with those of the EEOC on pensions and fringe benefits and uninformative about the effects of amendments to the law in 1972 and 1974. Since the courts generally give great weight to agency guidelines, this was a serious criticism. It was felt by some that credit for advances in the enforcement of equal pay should be given to the courts rather than the Division. At the same time many women's groups were relatively content with the Division, believing that, if the courts were important, it was because the former, using a broad definition of equal pay, was more willing than other agencies to litigate. They also noted that the Division was quicker than others at reaching settlements and, as a result, had a minimal backlog of unresolved cases. Consequently, they opposed President Carter's proposal to transfer responsibility to the EEOC and only agreed to it after several commitments and guarantees had been made.

Equal Employment Opportunities Commission[25]

The EEOC is responsible for resolving individual charges and eliminating 'patterns and practices' of discrimination. In scope the latter responsibility resembles formal investigations in Britain but the EEOC has no 'cease and desist' power to issue the equivalent of the British non-discrimination notice. Until 1974 the Department of Justice and, since then, the EEOC would need to seek such action through the courts.

The EEOC is headed by a chairperson and four other commissioners appointed by the President with the advice and consent of the Senate. The most senior staff positions are the Executive Director and General Counsel, the latter also a Presidential appointee. The national office is the apex of several regional litigation centres and many district offices. It is responsible for all groups protected by the Civil Rights Act; about one-third of its cases are about sex discrimination.

Its reputation is mixed. On the one hand, disappointment with its performance is widespread. On the other, it has adopted advanced positions on the rights of working women. One problem involves leadership. To begin with, the first chairperson, F. D. Roosevelt, Jr, was adamant that sex discrimination had been included in the Act to bring it into disrepute and was not a genuine part of his brief. Difficulties were compounded by conflicts between different ethnic groups represented on the Commission. President Nixon's appointees were believed to be uncommitted to rigorous enforcement and, although under President Carter, new appointments and reforms appeared very promising, President Reagan's administration does not attach high priority to civil rights and, in particular, to equality for women. New commissioners are less willing than their predecessors to involve women's groups in the business of implementation.

In addition to leadership problems, the Commission experienced management difficulties. Until 1977, it was beset by a high turnover of personnel and by organisational problems which caused disputes about policy-making responsibility; poor coordination among legal, investigation and conciliation staffs; delays and duplication of effort; acceptance of standards of evidence later rejected by the Justice Department; inadequate monitoring procedures; and huge backlog of cases and little action on 'patterns and practices' of discrimination. In 1977 President Carter appointed the respected and experienced Eleanor Holmes Norton to the chair of the EEOC[26] and she overhauled its structures and procedures, using her experience of the New York City Commission on Human Rights. The EEOC's organisation was rationalised, functions changed, and intake procedures reformed and accelerated. Special plans were introduced to deal with the backlog and a vigorous programme to eliminate patterns and practices of discrimination was initiated.

The Commission's favourable reputation stems from the fact that, despite organisational chaos, it has advanced the rights of women in substantive legal developments. Even when it had no power to litigate itself, its many *amicus curiae* briefs had a significant influence on the law. These can be used to present wide ranging economic, sociological and statistical information about general issues and need not be confined to the specific details of particular cases. They are especially useful in demonstrating patterns and practices of discrimination. Use was made of them in the EEOC's enquiry into the American Telephone and Telegraph Corporation (ATT). When ATT applied to the Federal Commerce Commission (FCC) for a price increase, a legal officer on the EEOC, which had received over 2000 complaints from ATT employees, suggested petitioning against it because the Corporation was violating the Civil Rights Act. In 1972, after two years of discussions among the corporation, government agencies, pressure groups, and social scientists and the submission of evidence and briefs by the EEOC arising from its own investigations and from outside research commissioned by it, the Supreme Court handed down consent decrees. These ordered the payment of $38 million and the restructuring of personnel procedures to end discrimination against all protected groups. The case was particularly important for women because it finally laid to rest the belief among commissioners that sex discrimination was not a serious problem.

From the start, EEOC guidelines on sex discrimination were quite strict. Judges argue that administrative guidelines are entitled to 'great deference'[27] and this gives them a legal status that is comparable to what is envisaged for British Codes of Practice. The first version, published in 1965, stated that stereotypical assumptions about the nature of women could not count as a defence under the bona fide occupational qualification clause. It also articulated for the first time the idea of indirect discrimination by stating that discrimination meant more than evil intent or differential treatment of two similarly situated people and could be established by proof of an adverse impact on a class of people. This definition was accepted by the Supreme Court in 1971 in *Griggs* v. *Duke Power Company*.

Many were disappointed, however, that the first guidelines did not deal with the separate advertising of jobs for women and men, protective legislation, fringe benefits and pregnancy or seniority rules. On protective legislation and seniority, the EEOC awaited judicial guidance and incorporated court rulings into revised versions of the guidelines. Job advertisements were the occasion of disputes among the EEOC, pressure groups and the courts. On fringe benefits, the EEOC decided between 1969 and 1972 that higher costs revealed in actuarial analyses could not justify different treatment in medical, accident or retirement insurance schemes. In the 1972 guidelines, it also recommended that pregnancy should be treated in the same way as sickness and disability in leave and insurance arrangements. In these respects the EEOC was more rigorous than the Department of Labor which has responsibilities under the Equal Pay Act, not the Civil Rights Act. The Equal Pay Act allows different payments based on actuarial factors. Until 1976, the courts fully upheld EEOC policy but in *Gilbert* v. *General Electric Company* the Supreme Court ruled in favour of the Department of Labor guidelines about benefits.[28]

With its *amicus curiae* briefs, strict guidelines and its power to litigate after 1974 the EEOC is thought to have become, in the 1970s, a strong and successful proponent of women's rights.[29] As part of a complex system of government, its policies were reinforced by the Supreme Court. By the same token, its boldness has been curtailed as much of the substance given to the law has been whittled, and sometimes stripped, away as a result of the permeation into all corners of government of the right wing coalition that put President Reagan into office.

Office of Federal Contract Compliance Programs (OFCCP), Department of Labor[30]

Although affirmative action may result from charges filed

successfully by the EEOC or Department of Justice, the OFCCP, responsible for Executive Orders 11246 and 11375, has developed the typical plan expected of employers as described in Chapter 3. These orders cover at least 30 million workers and over 325 000 contractors.

Administrative arrangements have changed several times, mainly because of poor compliance. Part of the problem was internal to the OFCCP and its regional offices but the main original difficulty was its lack of control over line agencies; that is, other departments and bodies simultaneously responsible for specific plans and parties to contracts. Different agencies such as the Treasury and Department of Health, Education and Welfare set different standards, which was especially confusing when one contractor was engaged by more than one department. Often line agency requirements departed from the regulations and guidelines of the OFCCP. Line agencies rarely applied sanctions against offending contractors. The Department of Health, Education and Welfare, the Treasury and the General Services Agency were particular culprits and many charges, sparked off by the Women's Equity Action League, were brought against the first of these. Thus, the degree of centralisation introduced by President Carter in 1978 was welcomed by the business community as well as women and minorities.[31] His reforms, however, left some doubt about which department would be responsible for the ultimate sanction against a recalcitrant company. Most administrators believed that the application of sanctions would depend on the strength of Presidential willingness to intervene in disputes between official bodies about the enforcement of civil rights legislation.[32] Since 1980, affirmative action has incurred disapproval in highest political circles and, among those favourably disposed, it is thought that remedies need to be more carefully formulated to meet the different circumstances of different protected groups.

Affirmative action policies, now vulnerable and in need of improvement, were in any case articulated slowly. the OFCCP did not produce regulations until 1971 to 1972 for industries other than construction. Rules about women in the construction industry did not emerge until the late 1970s. In 1974, a plan for the Alaska pipeline was submitted which included goals and timetables for female employment and was rejected because the office had no policy on opportunities for women. After two law suits, filed by feminist groups, in 1976 and 1977, the Department announced that female construction workers would be covered by its Orders and funded two appropriate apprenticeship schemes for women. But the goals and timetables set have been criticised for being based on existing participation rates and not being broken down geographically by trade. Participation varies in both these respects. In 1974, for example, 11 per cent of electrical trade unionists and 13 per cent of painters unionists in California were women and yet the OFCCP produced a national goal of 5 per cent in both crafts. The conservatism of the OFCCP on sex discrimination affected other institutions. In 1977, the deputy director of the New York City Contract Compliance Office found that contractors responded to representations by stating that the United States Employment Service Agency (ESA) did not refer women to them. The ESA defended itself by saying that, since there was no OFCCP policy on the matter, it had no need to take special steps.

Conservatism in the OFCCP was evident not only in its affirmative action plans for women but also in its guidelines on sex discrimination in general, which were the same as those of the Wage and Hour Division and not the EEOC. When criticised, the OFCCP invoked the *Gilbert* case but, as the Civil Rights Commission pointed out, that judgment did not over-rule the entire guidelines but only the one section dealing with pregnancy.

Nevertheless, the OFCCP has some supporters, mainly because of its broad interpretation of equal pay and because most people concerned about civil rights agree that past inequalities and present discrimination cannot be eliminated on a piecemeal, individual basis.

Employment section of the Civil Rights Division of the Department of Justice[33]

This civil rights unit has not suffered the same organisational and managerial problems of the EEOC and OFCCP. Turnover is low, staff are well trained and internal monitoring is close.

But it is small having, in 1977, only 37 legal specialists and eleven clerical officers. While this probably explains its good characteristics, it may also be the cause of the cautious approach adopted by it. One of the reasons for transferring its litigation responsibilities in private employment to the EEOC in 1972 to 1974 was because it had filed too few 'pattern and practice' cases and none with more than a limited impact. Nevertheless, it was also praised for its skill when it did act. Because of this, when State and local governments became covered by the Civil Rights Act in 1972, litigation in public sector 'pattern and practice' cases was made a Justice Department responsibility.[34] Relations with the Department of Labor have been uneventful. Some co-operation with the EEOC, such as in the ATT case, has had excellent results. But there has been friction between the two over litigation authority and differences of opinion about class actions between the employment and civil sections of the Department itself.

Most civil rights leaders and feminists concede that the Department has played a useful role on indirect discrimination, affirmative action and the like, but no more so than the EEOC. Many feminists were alarmed at the relatively higher priority it gave to racial minorities over women, particularly in terms of relief for past discrimination. In 1969, the Department justified their priorities to the Civil Rights Commission by saying that they were in 'the business of social turmoil' and that 'women were not out in the streets demanding their rights'.[35] After 1972 a little higher priority was given to cases which involve either women alone or women and racial minorities and anxieties were reduced by the transferring of private sector litigation authority to the EEOC.

Coordination[36]

The first ten years of enforcement were seriously hindered by the multiplicity of agencies and a lack of coordination among them. Employers and employees were confused by the plethora of institutions and their inconsistent demands for information and interpretations of specific issues. In 1972 an Equal Employment Opportunities Coordinating Council was set up but, according to most participants and observers, it was completely ineffective in resolving differences of opinion over selection procedures in affirmative action plans, the legality of voluntary plans, seniority systems and redundancies, pensions and fringe benefits. For example, despite the Council, two different sets of regulations about job selection criteria existed until 1978. The Council's only success was in data collection.

The Council was abolished in 1978 by President Carter, who had made an election pledge to improve the enforcement of civil rights. His reforms transferred functions from the Wage and Hour Division and the Federal Civil Service Commission to the EEOC. The relationship between the EEOC and the Justice Department was clarified and contract compliance was more centralised within the Department of Labor with the idea that it might one day be taken over by an efficient and effective EEOC. These changes, which include modifications asked for by the civil rights lobby, were supported and even recommended by minority and women's rights groups.[37] Improvements and standardisation did occur but some institutional confusion continued into the 1980s.

The Courts[38]

Recourse to the courts for policy enforcement is much more extensive in America than in Britain. Until the second half of the 1970s, the courts tended both to interpret statutes broadly in advance of other institutions and to give clear confirmation of the views of these bodies when they were in the lead. There followed a more ambiguous period as the demise of the liberal coalition began to be felt in all political quarters. In the 1980s the courts, with some exceptions, reflect the dominance of a non-interventionist political philosophy.

Comparable work. In equal pay cases, the courts were swift to treat the wording of the statute, which refers to work requiring equal levels of skill, effort and responsibility, as meaning comparability not identity.[39] Extra tasks for men had to be shown to be regular, recurring and time consuming. Even if substantial, they could not count if they were also infrequent. Extra pay for secondary duties, if allowed, had to be commensurate with the obligation. In the 1970s, courts were confused

about whether unequal pay, arising from indirectly discriminatory employment practices, was unlawful. But legal
clarification appeared in 1981 which recognises that some
equal pay claims may in such instances be heard under Title
VII instead of the Equal Pay Act.[40]

Equal value. The Equal Pay Act appears to be limited where
segregation exists and this was confirmed in one case where it
was argued that similar monetary benefits for employers
arising from different jobs could not justify equal pay.[41] But
other judges, in deciding what constituted equal effort, skill and
responsibility awarded equal pay for janitors and maids and for
jobs requiring manual dexterity on the one hand and heavy
lifting on the other. Similarly, it has been ruled that equal pay
may be merited in decision-making jobs that carry similar
responsibilities even if their contents differ.[42] Since 1981, the
possibility of claiming equal pay for 'comparable work' under
Title VII – if other discriminating employment practices are
found – may further limit the depressing effects on pay of
segregation.

Justifiable exceptions and equal pay law. Legitimate exceptions have
been construed narrowly.[43] Although different rates are
allowed for shift work, the differential must be uniform and
must not arise from discriminatory employment practices.
'Red-circling' – the protection of pay rates when an employee is
moved from a higher to a lower paid job – is allowed only under
the strictest circumstances for very temporary periods. Employers cannot defend themselves by arguing that an incentive
of higher pay is necessary to attract male employees. To allow
this market consideration as a material difference between
employees 'would completely undercut the remedial purposes
of the Act'.[44]

'Disparate impact' (indirect discrimination) under Title VII. A
'landmark' anti-discrimination case was *Griggs* v. *Duke Power
Company* of 1971, which deals with race but is applicable
elsewhere and has even been cited in British and European
courts. It was here that the idea that neutral rules which had a
disparate impact on a particular protected group could be

unlawful was confirmed. Preconditions for employment in the Duke Power Company were a high school diploma and success in two admission tests. Overruling judgments in the lower courts against Griggs, the Supreme Court stated that the Act proscribes

> not only overt discrimination but also practices that are fair in form but discriminatory in operation . . . Congress directed the thrust of the Act to the consequences of employment practices not simply motivation. What Congress has forbidden is giving these devices (tests) and mechanisms controlling force unless they are demonstrably a reasonable measure of job performance.[45]

Rules, tests and stereotypical assumptions. The 'disparate-impact' concept may well have been restricted by a case heard in 1982 to be discussed later but to start with, rules and tests, later the subject of EEOC guidelines, were scrutinised strictly in the courts. This was so whether they appeared neutral, as in the *Griggs* case, or applied to one group only. Height and weight tests effectively debarring women from employment were struck down. So too were promotion criteria that depended on experience such as military service but not, for example, teaching.[46] Explicitly different treatment can only be justified if there is an overriding objective like safety and if there is no less discriminatory way of meeting it. Consequently no blanket rules are allowed that force pregnant teachers to take leave when no such rules exist for other forms of disability.[47] Marriage and school-aged children cannot be used to deny women employment unless the same rule applies to men, or unless it can be shown that most married mothers perform badly at a specific job.[48] It is not enough to appeal to embarrassment, unpleasantness or 'woman's nature' to justify discrimination against would-be women bar-tenders, underground workers, telegraph repairers or car mechanics.[49] The elimination of stereotyping has benefited both sexes employed by airline companies which discriminated against men in recruitment and required women to retire early or on marriage. The courts confirmed EEOC views that customer preference for young female attendants was not a bona fide occupational qualification; sex and age being 'tangential to the essence of the business of transportation'. Narrow interpretations of bona fide occupational qualification have continued to be upheld in the 1980s.[50]

The courts and the EEOC – protective laws and job advertisements. Issues on which the EEOC and the courts were out of step to begin with were protective legislation and job advertisements. On the first the EEOC, confronted by conflicting views among pressure groups, awaited judicial guidance. The courts took the view that state protective laws based on stereotypes and 'romantic notions' conflicted with Federal law and, because of Article VI of the Constitution, had to fall. Consequently, protective laws can only be upheld if they also apply to men.[51] Clashes occurred between the EEOC and the Washington DC Court on job advertisements. Separate listings in newspapers of male and female jobs are not banned by the Civil Rights Act but, after intense pressure from womens' groups, the EEOC incorporated such a prohibition into its guidelines. The guidelines were suspended during an appeal by a newspaper proprietor in the Washington Court but some states reformed their equality laws in line with the EEOC and the Supreme Court eventually confirmed that separate listings were unlawful in such states.[52]

Affirmative action and seniority systems. Notwithstanding a cautionary note in the Civil Rights Act about preferential treatment, the courts at first accepted the constitutionality of affirmative action in private employment under Title VII as well as under Executive Orders. This is because such an action can be described as remedial not preferential. Two factors have recently attenuated the impact of such schemes. One involves constitutional principles and will be dealt with later. The other has arisen because of the growing problem of redundancy. Until 1976, it was the view that awarding retrospective seniority was necessary to accomplish affirmative action goals and to provide fair remedies for individuals. One effect of this was to limit the effects of the 'last-in, first-out' redundancy principle on newly recruited or promoted members of protected groups. In 1976, it began to be ruled that wholesale retrospective seniority negates the rights of other workers; that retrospective seniority could not be given to whole groups but only to individuals who could demonstrate that they, personally, had been victims of discrimination. In a 1982 judgment about seniority systems, strictness has been extended beyond redundancy. In that year, the Supreme Court decided that bona fide seniority schemes were those adopted after the Civil Rights Act which, at the time of adoption, were not in violation of Title VII. Such systems could not be challenged on the basis that they had a 'disparate impact' of the type discussed in *Griggs*. Plaintiffs would have to establish discriminatory motives in the design or application of such systems. At the same time, it was argued that, since the adoption of a seniority system was an employment practice subject to Title VII, the same general standards might apply to hiring, promotion, discharge and compensation practices.[53] Consequently, this ruling could affect the outcomes of equal pay claims made, as permitted only the year before, under Title VII.

Procedural and evidential matters. Until the seniority cases, the courts appeared to be trying to lighten procedural and evidential burdens faced by plaintiffs, although this was not always clear. On the relationship between the two Acts, the courts vacillated between allowing Title VII concepts in equal pay cases and arguing that violations of Title VII could not be remedied indirectly through the Equal Pay Act. In the *Gilbert* case about pregnancy benefits, the Supreme Court ruled clearly, but for women negatively, that if no violation could be found under one, none could be found under the other.[54] The matter has been reopened by the question discussed earlier of work that is of 'comparable worth'.

One easing of the burden for equal pay plaintiffs that has persisted is that they may compare themselves with predecessors.[55] The burden of proof in equal pay cases has been mitigated by insistence that improper motive does not have to be demonstrated and that there is a very strong evidential onus on employers to show that different pay rests on legitimate factors other than sex.[56] The *Griggs* case also seemed to indicate that a Title VII plaintiff need not establish improper motive but simply had to show a *prima-facie* case of denial of opportunities to a protected group; and that a strong evidential burden of proof relating to performance and business necessity then passed to employers. Since then, the circumstances in which improper motive need not be established have been restricted. At first, it was thought that *Griggs* would stand as a principle in class action cases but that single plaintiffs would need to show discriminatory intent. The seniority system case described above seems to indicate that individuals forming part of class actions also have to do more than show disparate impact. In general, plaintiffs now seem to be expected to show that any justifications presented by respondents as lawful are not true reasons for decisions.[57]

In both equal pay and Title VII cases, the courts confirmed the acceptability of a whole range of evidence that makes it easier for Americans than the British to present *prima-facie* cases of discrimination, particularly indirect discrimination. This includes census statistics, official research reports and guidelines; Congressional records; *amicus curiae* briefs from parties, including pressure groups, not directly involved in the case; and the work of experts in law, history, and the social sciences. Until 1982, this tended to help plaintiffs. But in 1982, Supreme Court judges depended heavily on the view that lawful 'liberal interpretations' of Congressional deliberations were those that did not go further than the objectives that Congress expressly wished to serve, and judges refer more frequently now to denials in congressional debates of preferential treatment. And it is also clear that courts are now looking for even more refined statistical data.[58]

Women also benefited at first from the use that judges allowed of class actions. Theoretically, American rules are similar to those in Britain which limit such action to five or six plaintiffs because they also require typicality and common questions of law. In practice, they have been used to cover numbers of employees comparable to those of a British formal investigation. In the 1970s American judges resisted efforts to limit them and, on the contrary, once allowed a black woman to represent all other female and black employees in her company. Since 1979, however, this device for securing rulings with large impacts has become less useful as judges have begun to be stricter about common characteristics and, hence, to insist on more narrowly drawn classes of employees.[59]

The constitutional framework. Finally, it is necessary to discuss the relationship between women's rights and the Constitution.[60] Any laws or regulations are set in its guiding framework. Its 5th Amendment protects individuals from Federal action without 'due process of law' and its 14th Amendment orders states to guarantee the 'equal protection' of the laws to all persons. Since the nineteenth century, public and private and state and Federal relations have become infinitely complex and 'equal protection' has become an inherent part of 'due process'. The position of women, however, is somewhat ambiguous under the 14th Amendment, which is why there has been so persistent a demand for the Equal Rights Amendment. Nineteenth-century women were dismayed when the 14th Amendment referred to male persons and former slaves. Although that amendment in many ways now covers women, the Supreme Court has developed a different standard of review for women in allegations that laws and regulations are unconstitutional. A standard of 'strict scrutiny' has been adopted where the 'suspect' classifications of race, religion or national origin are involved. It must be shown, not merely that there is a rational relationship between the differentiation and its intended outcome, but that there is a compelling governmental interest at stake and that no other non-discriminatory rule could accomplish the same purpose. The only racial classification to have been upheld was the internment of Americans with Japanese surnames during the Second World War. Once, the Supreme Court came close to making sex a 'suspect' classification,[61] but, since then, has adopted an intermediate standard of review. Without declaring sex to be a 'suspect' classification, the Supreme Court has insisted on the presence of a rational relation between the classification and its purported intent. This was revealed by the Supreme Court's treatment of the pregnancy cases and cases about stereotypical generalisations. Proponents of the ERA believe that the Supreme Court would have to make sex a suspect classification if the Amendment succeeded.

However, the 'suspect' classification analysis may be used to limit as well as promote the advancement of racial minorities and might do so for women too. This is because of the question of whether it is *ever* legitimate to take race into account. This was the central issue in challenges to the constitutionality of affirmative action plans. Two white men, Defunis and then Bakke alleged that they had been denied entry, because of their race, to law and medical schools, while members of other races had been accepted with lower grades. By the time of the Bakke case, the civil rights lobby was divided. Most felt, as they had before, that the cause of civil rights would receive a severe symbolic blow if Bakke were to win. Others believed that the University of California Medical School had not produced a proper affirmative action plan that expanded the pool of qualified applicants but that it was little more than a quota system based on racial labels. Consequently, they believed that a defeat for Bakke would legitimise the use of the single factor of race as a classification device; the very outcome that liberals had fought against for a century. In the end, the Supreme Court ordered Bakke to be admitted but upheld the constitutionality of affirmative action to eliminate the effects of past discrimination, provided plans were more than quota systems. Since then affirmative action has come under fire from other quarters and controversy still rages about what makes a good constitutional plan. In none of the challenges to affirmative action considered so far by the Supreme Court, has any systematic guidance been given as to what kind of plan would be a good one.

Institutions responsible for enforcement in Britain

Equal Opportunities Commission (EOC)[62]

When he created the Equal Opportunities Commission, Mr Jenkins thought he had established a powerful body 'to enforce the law in the public interest' which was superior to the Race Relations Board with its unworkable remedial procedures and to the conciliatory body proposed by the Conservatives.[63] The Commission was given conciliatory and legal powers to help individuals. It was also given enforcement powers to eliminate what Americans call patterns and practices of discrimination and promotional powers to encourage widespread equality. It was also given responsibility for monitoring the two Acts and for reviewing the future and the operation of protective legislation, taxation and social security regulations. Consequently, it may take on important individual cases, carry out formal investigations and issue Codes of Practice which could be, subject to Parliamentary approval, admissible evidence in the courts; it may also undertake informal enquiries, its own research, and fund outside research by academics and pressure group projects which educate and inform people about equality and the law.

The headquarters of the Commission are in Manchester, a location that was controversial in 1975,[64] and it has two regional offices and a London press department. It has a full-time chairperson and deputy and between eight and fifteen commissioners. In between monthly full meetings, subcommittees oversee specific aspects of its work. Financial allocations reflect its early emphasis on the educational and persuasive components of its powers. Between 1978 and 1984, more resources were allocated to enforcement but research and publicity have always been given a high proportion of the small budget granted to it through the Home Office. This kind of expenditure has produced a large amount of information. Surveys have been conducted of employers and trade unions to determine precise forms of discrimination, awareness of legal rights and obligations and appropriate changes in practices and procedures. In the light of discussions with other bodies and extra-governmental groups, these findings have been used as the basis of a draft Code of Practice on employment. Evidence has been presented to public enquiries into income distribution, the health service, legal services and public appointments. Research has been carried out into the employment of women in small firms, childcare, pensions, taxation, new technology, job evaluation, segregation, protective legislation, education and training to name but some. Often this has been done in conjunction with the Department of Employment and academic bodies like the London School of Economics and the Social Science Research Council. Most findings are published both to seek out opinion and inform, and most publications elicit large responses. Thousands of pamphlets and publications are distributed without charge to individuals, trade unions, job centres and the like. One important booklet is a guide to preparing cases for tribunal. Grants have been given by the EOC to pressure groups to train people in making use of the laws. The EOC has assisted and co-operated with the National Council for Civil Liberties (NCCL) and trade unions in developing voluntary positive action policies. It has also tried to persuade reluctant governments that such action needs to be facilitated by changes in the law. In 1984, the EOC, in co-operation with the Engineering Council, launched a large promotional project to encourage women to become engineers and scientists (WISE).

On law enforcement, the Commission has been much more cautious. A deliberate decision was made at the start not to issue Codes of Practice because Commissioners were 'very conscious that busy managers and trade union officials have had to come to terms with a great deal of complicated legislation over recent years'.[65] Despite controversy, which will be discussed in Chapter 5, drafts of a code were produced in 1981. But on job evaluation, only a guide, with no legal status, has appeared so far, even though the Commission has stated that segregation, is now, after unemployment, the main barrier to equality.

The Commission has initiated far fewer formal investigations than the architects of the Act expected. They hoped for at least one and possibly five in the first year but difficulties in the Commission's first investigation into Tameside Education Authority led to reluctance to initiate others immediately. Consequently commissioners did not willingly take on the second, into Electrolux Ltd, but were urged to do so early in 1977 by a judicial decision of Mr Justice Phillips, then Chairperson of the Employment Appeals Tribunal.

To comply with the Equal Pay Act, Electrolux had introduced a grading scheme without male and female labels. But it turned out that all the jobs in one grade were occupied by men and those in the lower-paid grade by women. Although it became a *cause célèbre*,[66] as ATT had in the United States, the local branch of the Amalgamated Union of Engineering Workers accepted the arrangement and justified its action because it carried a pay rise for most women workers. It was disputed by one female shop-steward, Ms Anne Hutchinson, because she believed the difference between her work and that of men in her department was insubstantial and that the company was disobeying the Equal Pay Act. The Bedfordshire tribunal agreed with her and the four other women who were considered in the same case. When a second complaint failed, the company decided to appeal against the first. By the time of the hearing, over two hundred applications were in the pipeline. Mr Justice Phillips upheld the first decision but, with no British equivalent of a large class action resulting in company-wide reforms, he had to point out that the impending avalanche of claims could not produce a coherent wage structure and he suggested that the EOC should intervene. Part of the dispute about the grading system involved criteria for selection into the higher paid grade which also carried extra payments for a contractual obligation to do shift duties. Such issues raise the question of indirect indiscrimination and therefore need to be considered in the light of the Sex Discrimination Act. Because both Acts were relevant, the investigating commissioners led by Lord McCarthy, who was brought in from outside as an expert in industrial relations, were given wide terms of reference. The breadth of their duties and slender staff resources meant that the investigation took much longer than expected.[67] In August 1978, a non-discrimination notice was issued requiring changes that the company had already seen fit to initiate itself. These changes involved relatively straightforward equal pay issues. It is not clear whether the Commission believes the company to be contravening the Sex Discrimination Act.

During the investigation, criticism of the EOC mounted within its own walls and outside. As in the American EEOC, early relations between staff and commissioners were strained over policy directions and priorities. The staff wanted to go further and faster than Commissioners and resignations were threatened. But by the end of 1977, it was clear that commissioners were reassessing their use of available enforcement powers and in the next two years they initiated five more investigations into employment and other matters.[68]

At the same time, the EOC stepped up legal assistance in cases involving important principles and precedents. Once, it had been argued that the NCCL did more than the EOC by helping individuals and training trade unionists in bringing cases. The EOC guide to the preparation of tribunal cases was the subject of internal dispute for four years but was brought out in 1979. Until funds were diverted in 1984 to the WISE project, allocations for financial and practical assistance to individuals was increased. As a result, the EOC has been involved more regularly in important submissions to precedent setting bodies like the Court of Appeal and the House of Lords. In addition, it has been influential by backing submissions to the European Court of Justice which, because of the EEC, can influence British law. This has become of special interest as the European Directive on equal pay has become more generous than British provisions, mainly because it now embodies the idea of work of equal value. The EOC's legal experience at home and in Europe has enabled the Commission to draw up a list of amendments to the British laws which it urged the government to introduce as soon as possible. It has been obliged to point out that, had such advice been acted upon, the first set of EEC infringement proceedings in 1982 could have been avoided and that EOC recommendations could pre-empt further arraingments in the pipeline in 1983 and 1984. Lack of serious commitment among political leaders has always been of concern to the Commission which argues that concerted efforts are needed at all levels by all institutions. Because of this and its advisory responsibilities, Commissioners have had continuing discussions with Chancellors of the Exchequer, the Departments of Education, Employment and Health, the Home Office, the Manpower Services Commission, the Central Arbitration Committee and ACAS. Often these have had disappointing outcomes, whatever the government in power.

Departments and agencies dealing with training and employment[69]

In 1974, the Department of Employment commissioned a study of the implementation of the Equal Pay Act directed by Baroness Seear, then in the London School of Economics. The new EOC became a joint sponsor and the study extended to the new Act and to tribunal applications. Fruitful co-operation has continued on the whole, although the Department, together with that of Education, disappointed the EOC in 1977 by its limited proposal for training school leavers for new employment destinations. The Department of Education and the Training Service Agency persist in dissatisfying the EOC, particularly because of failures to use the enabling positive action provision for training. The latter body is part of the Manpower Services Commission which, despite 'mutually beneficial liaison' has refused to adopt 'a more coordinated and planned programme for increasing training opportunities for women . . .'.[70]

Other bodies that enforce employment laws[71]

According to the Commission, the Central Arbitration Committee (CAC) and the Advisory Conciliation and Arbitration Service (ACAS) were helpful in the development of the draft Code of Practice on employment. But, in general, the CAC has actively encouraged women's equality while ACAS has not. From the beginning, the CAC was severe on employers who sought to avoid discriminatory collective agreements by relabelling grades in a 'unisex' manner more or less as Electrolux did. The Committee went beyond its specific instructions to eliminate structures overtly labelled 'male' and 'female' because 'it did not take the legalistic view that, because the rate looks unisex, it must be'.[72] For this it was congratulated by the EOC but its broad approach was ended by the Courts in 1979. One of the EOC's proposed amendments is intended to allow the Committee to act, as it cannot now, when neither employers nor unions are willing to refer matters to it.

The first duty of ACAS is to assist in the obtaining of settlements that eliminate the need to go to tribunal. But research into the role of ACAS in 1978 reveals that more than half of women who had withdrawn tribunal applications had been given unhelpful advice and most of the others had been given inaccurate information. One quarter of them withdrew with no settlements and others with derisory ones. Despite instructions to officers to inform individuals as a matter of course about the EOC, only one did so. However, it may be that an institution designed to produce conciliated solutions or compromises is an unsuitable vehicle for bringing about standards expected under legal rights.[73]

Courts and tribunals[74]

Tribunals. While America has its over-arching constitutional principles, Britain has its own distinctive institutions; precedents set in the European Court of Justice and industrial tribunals in the domestic legal system. Industrial tribunals were invented in 1965 to enforce redundancy and employment laws informally, rapidly and expertly through presiding officers with legal experience assisted by representatives of the two sides of industry. It was thought that employees, inexperienced in the law and with insufficient resources for legal representation, would be able to seek justice in an unintimidating forum from people who, because of their background, would have a broad and intelligent knowledge of industrial relations. Such knowledge is of the type that might in principle, be presented as formal evidence in American *amicus curiae* briefs. If help were needed, trade union officials would participate and the chairperson could assist in ensuring that the right questions were asked.

Tribunals have not lived up to their promise, at least for women. Applications, always higher under the Equal Pay Act than the Sex Discrimination Act, have dwindled dramatically for the former and more slowly for the latter. These trends may reflect the fact that the Equal Pay Act, as it stands, has been used as far as it can be. But there are other important factors. Between 1979 and 1982, the rate of unemployment for women rose nearly three times faster than it did for men. Even if women still have jobs, they appear to the EOC to be increasingly reluctant to take the risk of insisting on equal pay.

Discouragements also exist that are independent of the recession. It was clear before 1979 that plaintiffs lost cases more often than employers at all levels of the judicial system. Inconsistent rulings appeared in different geographical areas. And legal representation was becoming more necessary while, at the same time, it continued to be difficult to obtain. Speed in resolving disputes has been affected by rising case-loads.

Presiding officers have become accustomed, because of a larger than anticipated number of middle management cases, to professional defence. Representation for working-class plaintiffs is difficult. No legal aid is available and, for some time, trade union representation was not always possible. This was because tribunals were associated with other unwelcome state intrusions into industrial relations and were boycotted. Substantial assistance by the EOC was restricted to cases with important general consequences and pressure groups or feminist lawyers have too few resources to help in large numbers of cases. All the same, EOC assistance has become more extensive and trade unions have relented towards tribunals[75] but these changes coincided with the onset of the recession. Because early evidence of regional irregularities and apparent failures by some tribunal officers to understand the laws, the EOC in 1976 offered training but this was never taken up by the Central Office of Industrial Tribunals.

Legal developments in courts and tribunals. Broadly speaking, tribunals and courts in Britain have been more conservative than their American counterparts of the last days of the liberal ascendancy. But, although the effects of the British Acts have been limited by the courts, some positive developments have also taken place.

Like work. Most tribunals at first construed 'like work' in the Equal Pay Act strictly, even where anomalies resulted, such as confirmation of lower pay for a more senior female member of staff.[76] The Employment Appeals Tribunal (EAT), however, began in 1977 to overrule lower decisions, using arguments that are familiar in the United States. Trivial differences between jobs are to be disregarded and contractual obligations to perform extra duties can only count if they are actually done to a significant extent. Mr Justice Phillips has argued that the time of day should make no difference to basic payments for actual tasks.[77] But it is less easy for British judges than American to be definitive about the indirectly discriminatory effect of employment practices that deny women access to premia for shiftwork obligations or to night-time training because legal restrictions still exist on the hours during which women may work. British employers, however, can apply for exemptions which are usually granted.

Justifiable exceptions. British judges have been stricter than their American counterparts about the circumstances in which 'red-circling' is lawful under the 'material difference' section of the Act.[78] In other respects, as Byrne and Lovenduski point out,[79] the material difference clause is the biggest loophole in equal pay law, especially because the EAT differed from American courts by admitting 'market forces' as a defence. In two cases, EAT judges 'undercut the very foundation on which the Equal Pay Act is based' by agreeing that higher pay could be offered to attract male employees from other posts. The Court of Appeal rejected this argument but a new loophole has been created. In a case heard in Europe that was a victory for part-time workers, the Court referred to the economic circumstances of employers and this has been argued in the EAT to mean that reduced profits of an employer might be taken into account in decisions about whether there is a material difference between employees.[80] The 1984 Government Order aiming at compliance with European provision for equal pay for work of equal value explicitly allows judges now to accept 'market force' defences.

Indirect discrimination. There have been two 'land-mark' indirect discrimination cases in the British courts. The first is that of Ms Belinda Price who disputed the age bar of 28 in the recruitment of executive officers to the civil service. Having lost at tribunal, she appealed to the EAT where Mr Justice Phillips applied analogous criteria to those he had used in equal pay cases. The important point was not whether someone could in theory do something but whether the requirement would be met in practice.[81] The second involves criteria for redundancy, which is of increasing importance as unemployment rises. The EOC has assisted in redundancy cases to test whether the principles of 'last in first out' and 'part-timers first' constitute forms of indirect discrimination. The EAT agreed in 1982 in the case of two part-time workers, *Clark and Powell* v. *Eley (IMI Kynoch Ltd)*, that a redundancy scheme based on part-time workers first could constitute indirect sex discrimination.[82] Because of the European Court, indirect discrimination may become relevant in certain equal pay cases head in the British courts. This is discussed later.

Less favourable treatment based on stereotypical generalisations. The meaning of less favourable treatment under the Sex Discrimination Act was controversial in several cases involving stereotypical views of womanhood that are unlawful in the United States.[83] In 1977, a male employee, Mr Peake, of Automotive Products Ltd argued that he was less favourably treated than women because they could leave work five minutes earlier than men. The company argued that they and disabled men left early for safety reasons 'to avoid being bowled over in the 4.30 rush'. Mr Justice Phillips overruled a lower tribunal and pointed out that the concession amounted to a loss of two and a half days pay a year. But, in the Court of Appeal, Lord Denning sided with the employers and thought

> it very wrong if the statute . . . were to obliterate the differences between men and women or to obliterate all the chivalry and courtesy which we expected mankind to give womankind, or that the courts must hold that the elemental differences of sex must be disregarded in the interpretation of an Act of Parliament.[84]

Had such a case been heard in the United States, concern by employers for safety would have been respected but it is likely that some other, less arbitrary method of achieving it would have been ordered. The House of Lords declined to hear an appeal, supported by the EOC, on the ground of *de minimus*. But the case was not trivial for reasons to be discussed later.

Procedural and evidential matters. On procedural and evidential issues, the initial onus of proof remains firmly on the plaintiff in cases of direct discrimination, although, as in America, British judges said at first that there was a strong burden on the respondent to produce convincing evidence, after which the burden returns to the plaintiff.[85] But a plaintiff's ability to produce convincing evidence was circumscribed in 1978. A county court judge rejected a questionnaire designed by the EOC to assist applicants to elicit relevant information; and Lord Denning, in the Court of Appeal, denied applicants right of access to confidential information about other candidates, except in very restricted circumstances. He believed that the EOC and Commission for Racial Equality already had inquisitorial powers and pointed out that respondents had a right not to incriminate themselves. However, in 1980, it was ruled that a combination of the questionnaires and reasonable rights of access to information were necessary for plaintiffs. But re-establishment of plaintiff's rights was followed in 1981 by an easing of the burden on respondents when it was decided that the reasons for their decisions were justifiable if they were 'acceptable to right-thinking people as sound and tolerable . . .'.[86]

On other evidential matters, it is important that British judges cannot, like Americans, refer to Parliamentary deliberations to augment their understanding of legislative intentions. A drafter of the Sex Discrimination Act pointed out that the consequences of Lord Denning's personal interpretation of Parliament's intentions established 'the dangerous principle that the Act does not necessarily mean what it says';[87] he meant its ambiguous statement that provisions applying to women should be read as applying to men. To disregard this, he argued, 'gravely impaired protection for both sexes. It has also been argued that the new, less rigorous standards applied to employers justifications ignores Parliamentary intentions by not requiring reasons to outweigh the adverse impact of decisions.[88]

The absence of provision for *amicus curiae* briefs in British courts makes it difficult to present statistical evidence of patterns and practices of discrimination. However, the *Price* case is important because the EAT ruled that the industrial tribunal had been wrong to dismiss the claim because of inadequate statistical data. Moreover, the respondent, the Civil Service Commission, was ordered to assist in the provision of statistics for a re-hearing.

The European Court of Justice. British case law has been modified in several important respects by the European Court. In the first equal pay case to go in 1980 to the European Court, a major obstacle was removed from some equal pay applicants.[89] Court of Appeal judges had been unable to agree about whether tribunals had been wrong to dismiss a case because a comparison had been made with a predecessor. But they did agree that a strict interpretation might conflict with Community law. They were proved right for the European Court decided that not only could a predecessor be used but also a 'hypothetical' man. Such a possibility might have made a difference to the terms of application of an early unsuccessful part-time case heard in a British court in 1971.[90]

The earlier case failed because of difficulties over the relationship between the Equal Pay Act and Sex Discrimination Act. Part-time work generally carries lower hourly rates than do full-time posts. One part-time clerical officer, unable to apply under the Equal Pay Act because she had no male comparator, applied under the Sex Discrimination Act. She argued that full-time work was a necessary condition for the higher rate, that the rule was not related to performance, and it disproportionately affected women. Citing *Griggs* and accepting her statistical evidence, the tribunal chairperson agreed with her principle but dismissed the case because it was about pay and, therefore, excluded from the Sex Discrimination Act. In a similar case brought in 1978, it was argued that Article 119 of the Treaty of Rome could be construed as recognising the concept of indirect discrimination in equal pay cases. This was rejected by Mr Justice Slynn, successor to Mr Justice Phillips. But a third case was referred to the European Court of Justice where *Griggs* was again cited.[91] In 1981, the European Court ruled that victims of indirect discrimination leading to unequal pay were protected by Community law and entitled to remedy in British tribunals, provided employers could not show lawful economic or business reasons for the inequality. Of the nearly four million part-time women workers in Britain, many may be eligible depending on how seriously British judges incorporate European rulings: the EAT, in this case, decided only 'with considerable reluctance' to send it back to the industrial tribunal for a new hearing. One of the EOC's proposed amendments is to include indirect discrimination in the Equal Pay Act.

Benefits relating to retirement and death are excluded from the Acts but these and other fringe benefits have been considered in the European Court which has ruled that, under certain circumstances, differences contravene the Equal Treatment Directive. On the other hand, European judges have said that the EEC cannot influence statutory retirement ages and, if these are the cause of different benefits, there are no directly enforceable European remedies.[92]

Of particular importance is that infringement proceedings have been or are to be brought by the EEC through the European Court against the British government for failing to comply fully with Directives on Equal Pay and Equal Treatment. It remains to be seen how seriously the British government will seek to meet its treaty obligations.

Pressure groups and policy implementation[93]

An important contrast between Britain and the United States is the difference in the involvement of feminist and civil rights pressure groups in policy implementation. Springing into the political foreground after the Civil Rights Act was passed, American feminists have put strong pressure on the EEOC and other institutions and, through their ability to submit *amicus curiae* briefs, have influenced judicial developments. This contrasts with the distance maintained until the 1980s, by the EOC between itself and women's groups.

American feminist campaigns

As Freeman points out, very many women's rights groups exist in the United States; professional associations and trade unions contain women's caucuses; religious organisations have women's rights sections; and the American Civil Liberties Union counts female equality as one of its concerns.[94] An important point to note about them all is that, as Randall and Freeman suggest, it is a mistake to dismiss them as reformist simply because they aim at improvements in the law.[95] The charter of the National Organisation for Women (NOW), which has become an 'umbrella' group, for example, would transform society if implemented. Because it is an 'umbrella' group and because it is of special interest in its relationship with the EEOC, co-operating with it and challenging it, it necessarily has an important place in the campaigns discussed here.

NOW was created when the Citizen's Advisory Council on the Status of Women failed to shake the first chairperson of the EEOC out of his reluctance to do more for women than insist on a narrow interpretation of the bona fide occupational clause of the Civil Rights Act. Such anxieties were shared by some administrators in the EEOC, who discreetly began to encourage women outside government to form an organisation like the National Association for the Advancement of Coloured Peoples. When officials in charge of the third National Conference of State Commissions on the Status of women refused to allow a motion to be put about EEOC priorities, notes were circulated which led to the creation of NOW. Betty Friedan became its first President and Richard Graham, a disgruntled former EEOC Commissioner, its Vice-President.

Affirmative action for women. One of its first campaigns was not, however, against the EEOC but at President Johnson to include women in contract compliance regulations and, after a series of meetings with him in 1966, a revised Order appeared the next year. Enforcement was slow but when guidelines eventually appeared in 1970 and 1971, NOW filed complaints against 1300 corporations receiving Federal Funds. The Women's Equity Action League (WEAL) initiated a campaign in the universities. Dr Bernice Sandler and women in other universities brought charges in 1970 against a collection of universities and colleges with contracts totalling over $3 billion. NOW brought similar actions against Harvard and the whole state education system of New York. Although the Department of Health Education and Welfare believed the charges would die a natural death, the campaigns mounted with Congressional lobbying and picketing. As a result, the Department decided to include sex discrimination in all investigations as a matter of course, although it continued to be poor, as other line agencies were, in securing proper implementation. University suits cover manual, clerical and administrative staff as well as academics. Equality for working class women is the special objective of groups like Women Employed and Women Working in Construction. The former succeeded in getting the Treasury and the General Services Agency to improve their affirmative action plans and the latter was one of the main groups involved in charges against the OFCCP for not including women in construction contracts. All groups find the targeting of specific companies a productive tactic and NOW, and its Legal Defense Fund, persisted in a long campaign against Sears Roebuck. Action included lobbying the OFCCP and EEOC, picketing of shops and co-operation with the women's division of the Methodist Church, a shareholder in the company. When the company lost, it appealed on the ground that an EEOC attorney was too closely involved with NOW but this was rejected in 1979. Since the late 1970s, women's groups have been engaged in persuading the EEOC to keep its promise about patterns and practices of discrimination. This would have the positive outcome of more affirmative action. But, at the same time, they have increasingly had merely to defend affirmative action as it exists from attack from a variety of quarters. Not least among their concerns has been the growing effects of redundancy on gains won through affirmative action.

Job advertisements. Although NOW was happy with the EEOC's early, narrow definition of the bona fide occupational clause (BFOQ), the two organisations clashed over the question of job advertisements. The then newly formed NOW threatened to take the EEOC to court and began direct action and legal charges against newspapers and publishers. The EEOC capitulated in 1967 and 1968 and, although their new guidelines were suspended by the courts, most newspapers are now either legally banned or, for other reasons, have desisted from listing men's and women's jobs separately.

Stereotyping and protective legislation. At the same time, NOW ensured that EEOC guidelines on the BFOQ would be as strict in practice as in principle and urged the Commission to resist the special pleadings of airline companies that it was a business necessity to employ young female attendants. The result of this has already been noted. It will be recalled that the EEOC held back in the question of whether protective legislation was a BFOQ. Many women's groups believed that it was being used by employers as an excuse for lower wages. The AFL-CIO and American Civil Liberties Union (ACLU) thought that protective legislation should remain and that there was no evidence that women wanted extended overtime opportunities. NOW's position on the issue temporarily lost it the support of the Union of Auto Workers, which had provided it with office services and facilities. In the meantime courts were ruling that, where possible, protection should be extended to men and, where not, protective laws should fall. By 1970, unions, the ACLU and feminist groups were more or less united in their agreement that where no other solution was possible, protective laws should be brought to an end.

Institutional matters. Throughout the 1960s and 1970s, civil liberties and feminist groups through legal defence funds, legal rights groups (sometimes funded by the EEOC) and public interest law firms were closely involved in important judicial judgments involving, for example, the BFOQ and stereotypical views of womanhood. This has been done both by *amicus curiae* briefs and by direct legal representation, especially in class actions. NOW also persuaded the EEOC to consult it before signing consent decrees and to allow it to help in monitoring settlements.

Women's groups have also been active in trying to secure the appointment of sympathetic people to important public positions. Proposals for middle level appointments were rebuffed by Presidents Johnson and Ford and the records of President Carter and President Reagan do not differ much. But two of President Nixon's nominees for the Supreme Court were defeated by the Senate as a result of combined lobbying by civil rights and feminist activists of Senators. President Carter acknowledged the unanimous views of women's groups, shared with a section of the black civil rights lobby when he asked Eleanor Holmes Norton to head the EEOC.

On questions of institutional reform, feminist displeasure at the caution of the Department of Justice contributed to the transfer of some of its powers to the EEOC in 1972. Between 1976 and 1978 women and civil rights groups were closely

involved in President Carter's attempt to fulfil his election
pledge to improve civil rights institutions. His proposal to
transfer equal pay to the EEOC was the only important
contentious issue. President Carter and Eleanor Norton met
women's demands, however, that the EEOC would be given
special allocations for equal pay; that the law would be
administered separately so that it would not get bogged down
in the EEOC backlog; that EEOC staff would be trained by the
Department of Labor; and that ways would be devised to
reinforce and expand the idea of equal pay for different work
which could be construed as of equal value. President Carter
also agreed to introduce legislation about pregnancy to miti-
gate the effect of the *Gilbert* decision. Other compromises were
reached over eventual responsibility for contract compliance
and whether or not the EEOC should have 'cease and desist'
powers. Pressure group views about the former and enforcement in the civil service were upheld by President Carter over
opposition from other quarters.

Starting with a massive strike in 1970, women confounded
the Department of Justice view that the laws could not work for
them because 'they were not out on the streets'. Demonstra-
tions were held and business corporations in States that had not
ratified the ERA were boycotted. Robinson argues that under
dint of intense pressure from women's groups the EEOC and
the courts made Title VII into a 'magna carta' for working
women[96] and according to an official in the Department of
Labor, civil rights laws in the late 1970s, if they worked for
anyone, did so for women, because they were making them do
so.[97] The rise of the moral majority, already obvious in
opposition to the ERA, led by a woman Phyllis Schafly – also a
member of the John Birch Society – and in back tracking in the
Supreme Court, culminated with the election of President
Reagan. He has tried to speak with several voices, arguing
rhetorically in favour of equality, appointing the first woman
Supreme Court judge but, at the same time, opposing affirmative action and reducing allocations for employment, training,
welfare and social policies, all of which affect the precarious
improvements made by women in the preceding ten years.
Anger and renewed activity has begun among feminists, even in
his own party. Membership of NOW has been doubling[98] and

dissatisfaction has been sufficiently vocal to make the President give his daughter responsibility for persuading women that their rights are safe.

Concerns of British feminists

Relations with enforcement institutions. British pressure groups, although the recipients of EOC grants to educate and publicise, have not been allowed to become directly involved in the development of Commission policy. Even in grant-giving decisions, some Commissioners have been reluctant to establish relationships with radical women's groups. Some relaxation of 'the armslength' relationship has occurred, however, in the 1980s, but before this women's groups had to develop their own policy demands in isolation and were obliged to lobby the government about dissatisfaction with the Commission. Criticisms expressed between 1976 and 1979 were about EOC timidness, secrecy, unaccountability, its inadequate use of formal investigations, its decisions not to issue Codes of Practice and the absence of Commissioners with a feminist viewpoint. While two feminist Commissioners were appointed, governments failed to respond very positively to other representations made through Labour women MPs or directly to the Home Secretary. British feminists cannot like Americans become involved in legal developments through the submission of *amicus curiae* briefs. From time to time, suggestions have been made that more women be appointed to industrial tribunals but this would not necessarily lead to the presence of women fully committed to the aims of the legislation.

Relations with central government. Among others, Women in the Media, the Equal Pay and Opportunities Campaign (EPOC), the National Women's Farm and Garden Association, the National Council for Civil Liberties (NCCL), and the Fawcett Society all recommended wide ranging improvements in enforcement. On 27 November 1980, a day of action was held, organised by the Fawcett Society and Women in the Media and attended by 67 other groups. A copy of its agenda was sent to the Prime Minister. Mrs Thatcher replied that her government was in favour of equal opportunities because:

More than ever we need to mobilise the skill and ability of all
our citizens if we are to revitalise the currency and increase
prosperity in this country.[99]

At the same time, however, institutions like the EOC and CRE
were suffering from reduced budgets and staff. Unemployment
was reinforcing inequality and, as in President Reagan's
administration, cuts in health and social services, were being
considered that would force women to resume traditional roles
with less help than before.

Policy issues. In such an unfavourable climate the EOC, having
been described as a potential force for good but 'constantly
disappointing',[100] began at last to adopt policies already well
established in women's groups.

Between 1975 and 1979 various calls had been made for
improvements in maternity arrangements, parental leave and
childcare facilities. These are difficult issues in Britain because
of differences in opinion about whether child-rearing is a
private pleasure or public investment and the consequent
partisan division of whether provision for childcare should be
public or private. According to Coussins, feminist thinking on
it is 'muddled and remiss'.[101] The National Labour Women's
Advisory Committee and the TUC asked for better local
authority facilities. EPOC produced a guide for work-place
agreements, praising those negotiated by employers and
unions in Camden Borough Council, Norfolk Capital Hotels
and *Time Out*. The TUC produced a charter in 1979 that closely
resembled the EPOC guide. The EOC did not publish its own
discussion document until that year, but, at the same time, as
interest also grew among the Central Policy Review Staff, it lent
support to Parliamentary campaigns. Improvements in these
matters were recommended in the document sent to Mrs
Thatcher in 1980. But, while the NCCL and the Child Poverty
Action Group persuaded her to drop changes in maternity
grants, her government persisted in introducing more complicated procedures for the return to work after childbirth.

The lateness of a draft Code of Practice on employment was
mitigated by its contents. EPOC recommended only small
changes to the 1981 draft. These were: a statement about its

legal status; greater specificity about the size of firms; a more positive description of what small firms would have to do; greater explicitness on pensions and benefits; and more encouragement of the provision of crèche facilities and better maternity leave.

In Chapter 3, it was noted that some individuals and groups had hoped for some kind of contract compliance and stronger positive action provisions. An experiment in scrutinising government contractors was started by the CRE and the Home Office in 1978 and EPOC asked the Home Secretary to instruct the EOC to do the same. He prevaricated. Jean Coussins of the NCCL tried, with limited success, to develop voluntary positive action schemes with selected unions and employers. A number of Industrial Training Boards, however, succeeded in co-operating with employers unions and Brunel University, to institute positive action in production engineering and management. By 1981 the training boards were thought to be the 'leading innovators'[102] in the use of positive action. But at the same time the government was threatening to close them down. Thames Television, the only organisation to respond to Ms Coussins in the late 1970s, launched a pioneering project on positive action with the NCCL. The EOC took an interest, helping financially and at meetings with other bodies about the possibility of similar projects elsewhere. In 1981, the Ford Foundation and the German Marshall Fund underwrote a conference by the NCCL about the experience so far. Positive overtures were made by several other firms. The EOC also reports interest in positive action among a number of banks, industries, including Electrolux and British Steel, and governmental organisations.

Proposed reforms. As early as 1977, Ms Coussins had produced a list of 35 amendments thought by the NCCL to be necessary to the two Acts.[103] These covered: pensions; the role of the CAC; problems of comparison where there was no suitable colleague of the other sex and where segregation existed without job evaluation schemes; the absence of indirect discrimination in the Equal Pay Act; specific difficulties for single women; and the burden of proof under the Sex Discrimination Act. At the end of that year Women's Liberation began a campaign for such amendments and, more particularly, to equalise pensions, social security and taxation. Although the EOC agreed then that the scope of the Acts needed to be extended, their own proposals did not appear until 1981. These are intended to harmonise the two Acts and to strengthen them. The most important recommendations are: to make indirect discrimination unlawful in pay; to extend scope of the Acts to include, for example, part-time work in the Equal Pay Act and stronger positive action in the Sex Discrimination Act; to make them compatible with European law in the above respects and by dealing with equal pay for work of equal value; and to strengthen various administrative and enforcement procedures. Since then the EOC and women's groups have been at one in their disappointment at the absence of immediate governmental interest and, in 1983, by the half-hearted and unnecessarily complicated way in which the government intends to comply with European infringement proceedings.

PART FOUR

The Product of
Comparison

5

The Comparative Politics of Policy Implementation

As Chapter 4 shows, no definitive judgment can be made about whether equal opportunity laws have a bigger impact on the labour market of one country than the other. However, until the rise of a right-wing Republican majority, American institutions seem to have been more assertive than the British. America also appeared to lead ideologically. Opinion polls of the 1970s showed majorities among men as well as women in favour of ending sex inequality and in 1978, although Phyllis Schafly's anti-ERA Campaign was active, people still believed that 'to declare oneself against women's rights was to place oneself on the unacceptable fringe of politics along with the John Birch Society and the Ku Klux Klan'.[1] In Britain 'an entire audience laughed' when told that Virginia Novarra had used her Winston Churchill Travelling Scholarship for research on equal opportunities for women.[2] Newspaper commentaries on the Belinda Price case scorned this victory for women and Lady Howe was attacked on several occasions in the respectable conservative press for being associated with the EOC. American exchange students are bemused by the lack of legitimacy accorded to women's rights in Britain and by the way it is still possible to belittle the idea that women have a public role. In order to understand how it is that women's rights in one country were high on the political agenda for ten years and then lost that place and, in the other, have flourished hardly at all, it is necessary to consider the influence of wider political differences between them.

135

Regulatory agencies and non-departmental bodies: the EEOC and EOC

Institutions responsible for policy implementation which are not Departments or Ministries are new in neither the United States nor Britain.[3] The Interstate Commerce Commission is one of the oldest in America. In Britain, until the nineteenth century triumph of the twin ideas of ministerial responsibility and neutrality in a meritocratic civil service, independent boards were common. A professionalised civil service also developed in the United States from the end of the nineteenth century, although less fully than in Britain. In both countries independent boards that continued into or were created in the twentieth century became objects of criticism. In the United States unease was commonly expressed during the New Deal. In Britain objections have been most vocal during the last decade.

Nevertheless, despite some reforms resulting from the criticisms, non-departmental or regulatory agencies are an established feature of the machinery of government in both countries, operating alongside conventional administrative departments. Just as differences exist in the histories of each country's civil service, so are British independent boards sometimes less similar to American than they might seem. The weaker establishment of the American civil service in the upper echelons coexists with powerful regulatory agencies with policy-making responsibilities. The number of British non-departmental bodies has been placed as high as 3000.[4] But, on the whole, each covers a smaller policy area and does not enjoy the same range of executive powers as those in the United States.

In spite of these general differences and despite common negative opinions about their roles, such bodies are also viewed positively in both countries for similar reasons. For example, it is believed that implementation can be carried out more effectively by small uncomplicated institutions where 'clearance points' for decisions are minimised; that they provide a way of making the best use of voluntarism and expertise; and that for 'affected groups' they provide a clearly visible unit of responsibility.[5]

Jowell argues that the Equal Opportunities Commission and the Commission for Racial Equality are, in formal terms, exceptional in British government.[6] The scope of their responsibility and the extent of their powers places them closer to their American counterpart than to the usual British non-departmental body. However, the EOC began by implementing the law more in the fashion of a traditional advisory body than as a powerful law enforcement agency. Commissioners explained this approach, apparently unintended by policy-makers, by reference to the untried nature of the law and to 'teething troubles'.[7] But, since all new institutions, including the American Commission, experience initial staffing and administrative difficulties, it is necessary to move beyond this level of explanation and to seek it in the effects of different emphases in the administrative and decision-making traditions of the two countries. These are considered here under the headings of bureaucratic styles, incorporation and systems of party and government.

Bureaucratic styles

Although it is often believed that Britain is characterised by ministerial responsibility and civil service neutrality and America by a politicised bureaucracy renewed with each Presidential election, reality is more complicated than these simple concepts suggest. The simple dichotomy characterising the British system does not and cannot explain who makes policy and who does not. Up to a point, the American Federal Civil Service Commission operates with notions of meritocracy and neutrality with which any Briton would be entirely familiar; although it coexists, sometimes uneasily, with the practice of presidential appointment.[8] The stereotypes, however, do have some reality in the equal opportunity policies of each country.

The EOC may be one of the few British institutions which has tried seriously to operationalise the constitutional definition of the respective tasks of administrators and politicians. The analogy between the proper roles of EOC staff and commissioners on the one hand and civil servants and ministers on the other was made explicitly to the Commission staff during a period of tension about policy priorities in 1977. Staff were told to behave like administrators and to 'leave their feminist hats at home'.[9]

Insistence that all policy decisions be left to Commissioners created administrative difficulties at the time because of the infrequency of full Commission and subcommittee meetings. The content, too, of decisions was a source of tension between staff and Commissioners. Members of staff believed in a policy direction more akin to 'the hard and fast' knocks recommended by Byrne and Lovenduski.[10] However, the Commission's initiation of more investigations can be traced to this period and, with changes of personnel on both sides, it seems that there is a more realistic appreciation that the evolution of policy involves both administrators and politicians.

The idea that bureaucrats can and should wear two hats is less well established in the United States. The old idea of a politicised bureaucrat is one that has worked to the advantage of women in that country, although its uncomfortable partnership with ideas about meritocracy and neutrality has been evident. The EEOC, too, was wracked once by disputes about the distribution between staff and Commissioners of policy-making functions, yet it continued to be regarded as normal for staff in it and related institutions to maintain personal contacts with political groups and cooperate discreetly to stimulate decisions favourable to women.[11] Examples of the consequences of this style have been mentioned already and others will be discussed in Chapter 6. They include discreet encouragement by officials in the creation of the National Organisation of Women; the stimulation by staff of complaints in order to persuade Commissioners of the seriousness of their responsibilities towards women; and encouragement of officials of Southern female textile workers to become unionised. In general, it means that pressure groups were kept informed about proposals for changes in regulations that affected women, so long as government staff were sympathetic.

On the other hand, the interests of sectional economic groups have been better represented than those of feminists on the British Commission; and, despite insistence that feminist staff adhere to an ideology of neutrality 'economic hats' are not left at home by Commissioners.

Incorporation of interest groups into the formal structures of implementation

Tendencies towards corporatism in policy-making have been noted in almost all advanced industrial societies. Considerable dispute exists about precisely what the concept means and what empirical observations might be expected in a system that is corporatist. A widely quoted description of a corporatist society is that of Panitch:

> corporatism ... connotes a political structure within advanced capitalism which integrates organised socio-economic producer groups through a system of representation and cooperative mutual interaction at the leadership level and of mobilisation and social control at the mass level.[12]

Because of the chimerical nature of the concept and the disputes surrounding it, Byrne and Lovenduski describe the representation of the Confederation of British Industry and the Trades Union Congress on the Equal Opportunities Commission as tripartism.[13] Although they can be sympathised with over the conceptual problem, their choice of concept may not describe adequately what is going on. Tripartism is also used to describe the frequent practice of British governments of discussing legislative proposals with the CBI and the TUC in advance of their becoming law. But implementing laws also counts as policy-making and, as Richardson and Jordan point out, groups whose activities are to be regulated may succeed in eroding policy after the passage of legislation.[14] Success in controlling the impact of policy is even more likely to be the case if such groups are actually represented on the body that is to do the regulating than if it is merely the case that consultations continue.

Incorporation of interest groups into the American EEOC did not in the 1970s lead to the representation of major producer groups. On the face of it, this is surprising. The United States is often seen as the most advanced capitalist society with a marked transition from interest group liberalism to corporatism. The paradox becomes more understandable if the notion of 'agency capture' is broken down. Early American regulatory agencies were notorious for being 'captured' by the very interests they were to regulate. For example, the Interstate Commerce Commission, created to regulate passenger and freight transport across the States, became dominated by railway magnates. Organised labour in America, by nature of its history, is less often involved than in Britain in the process of agency capture. The growth of concern, however, about race relations and poverty during the 1960s was accompanied by worries about policy delivery. Demands for appointments to counter the 'capture' of an agency by the regulated community became widespread.[15] By the middle of the 1970s, the EEOC was in the hands of leaders committed to expanding rather than eroding equal opportunity policies.

Responses to demands that those in charge of agencies should be those who wanted policies to work probably did not arise simply out of a humane concern for increasing equality. The belief that women were not a source of social disruption and then fear of a powerful alliance of radical blacks and women have been mentioned. By the 1970s, women were 'out in the streets demanding their rights' and some attention was being paid to their preferences in political appointments.

The system of appointments to the British Commission follows the usual pattern. Although there have been proposals to reform the system – from the civil service itself – selection to non-departmental bodies generally institutionalises the existing organisation of interests. Whitehall nominations to the EOC therefore represent party, region and the two sides of industry. One expectation of this method is that it will introduce individuals into decision-making who are experts in a field and who may, therefore, be able to deliver policies more effectively than a government. Women's interest groups were opposed three times over suggestions for appointees known to be knowledgeable about female employment and at the same time to hold feminist views. However, later appointments included women with more obvious personal commitment than their predecessors to the intentions expressed in the law.[16]

Despite these concessions, the contrast with what happens in the United States is sharp. The British list of public appointments has its larger counterpart in the American 'plum book'. But appointees are not taken from a list of 'the great and the good'. It is necessary for American presidents to distribute commissionerships equally to the two parties, and to seek the advice and consent of Senate for some appointees. Beyond that, the main concern is to secure qualified personnel who will also satisfy the protected lobby; in this case, for liberal Presidents, the civil rights and women's constituency. According to Heclo, great efforts were made during the Kennedy and Johnson administrations to seek out suitable appointees outside the normal political channels. He also argues that the old systems of partisan spoils and ethnic patronage became adapted to suit the new pattern of minority group politics.[17] It is also important to note that a President cannot always immediately replace people on accession to office, but may have to wait until his predecessor's appointees finish their terms or retire.

It is difficult to be precise in comparing different policy consequences following from these different systems of interest group integration because official proceedings, particularly in Britain, are confidential. American Congressional hearings and those of other bodies, revealed the early corruption and mismanagement that stemmed from minority group rivalries on the Commission. They also show that these new appointees, both efficient and committed to equality for all protected groups, seemed to be resolving these problems. One example of the extent to which the structure of decision-making integrates political leaders, agency leaders and protected instead of regulated or producer groups, was President Carter's Civil Rights Reorganization Program, discussed in Chapter 4, and there are other examples that will be referred to later. Problems of access to information about public affairs in Britain mean that there is very little material with which to examine hypotheses about the influence of corporate interest groups.

Both labour, as presently organised, and capital have interests that, at least in the short term, conflict with the aims of legislation; that is, to protect 'male' jobs and to maintain stability in the primary sector of the labour market. And, as has been mentioned, it is possible that social-psychological reasons exist for male resistance to anti-discrimination laws. Despite long-term arguments about the quality of life and the most rational distribution of person-power, the employers and male trade unionists may have short term interests in colluding with each other to limit the effects of equal opportunity laws, whatever they may say in public about them. The shreds of evidence available suggest that representatives of capital and labour on the EOC indeed have acted to erode the Equal Pay Act and Sex Discrimination Act. If they have, it is serious because, as Byrne and Lovenduski point out, equality could be impeded by their dominance on a Commission that it is supposed to be the focal point of change.[18]

Although staff have been sacked for breaches of confidentiality, it is routine for employers and trade union representatives to refer Commission discussion documents to their 'parent' organisations.[19] At the end of its first year, Coote reported that the Commission had initiated a survey of employers but not trade unions because trade unionists 'were reluctant to let the EOC into territory traditionally occupied by the TUC'.[20] Other voluntary Commissioners and the two full-time Commissioners apparently were either unsure of their functions or too 'lady-like' in style to counteract the dominance of employer and trade union representatives. This did not necessarily stem from lack of knowledge or opinion about women's employment. One of the then voluntary Commissioners, Margaret Allen, was economics correspondent for *The Times* and the first chairperson, Betty Lockwood, had been involved in persuading Labour Party leaders of the need for action. In the month after Ms Coote's report, another journal noted that it was 'an open secret that difficulties' were being caused by the conflicting interests of representatives of both sides of industry between the work of the EOC and their parent organisations.[21] In the same article it was reported that TUC representatives tried to deflect action on complaints received from women that their unions were being unhelpful. But it was also pointed out that the TUC was worried that the existence of the Commission 'would undermine the importance of joining a union'. In the middle of 1977, questions were still being asked about whether producer groups had delegates or representatives on the Commission.[22] One employer was clear about his function. Writing to the CBI about the issuing of guidelines instead of more significant codes of practice for employment, Philip Jones said:

You will note that it is to be published in the form of guidance rather than a code of practice. I am glad to be able to tell you that this is to a great extent due to CBI influence on the EOC.[23]

In 1980 Commissioner Ms Marie Patterson told a reporter that she experienced no conflict of interest and never would because trade union policy was always best for women.[24] But the reporter noted that traditional trade union policy on part-time workers conflicted with women's interests. When jobs are scarce, the pruning of part-time work first dispropor-tionately affects women. It is only as a recession has bitten all workers deeply that trade unions have begun to discuss retaining part-time work, limiting the hours for everyone and job-sharing schemes.

A former TUC Commissioner, Ms Ethel Chipchase, was withdrawn by the TUC from the EOC for not acting as a delegate. When the Commission published its recommenda-tions for reform of protective legislation, she, having partici-pated in the lengthy consideration of the issue, did not sign a dissenting report that conveyed TUC ideas. The TUC allowed her neither another term of office on the EOC nor to continue as TUC Women's Officer.[25]

On the other hand, employers and personnel managers were not expecting to be protected on the Commission. It seems that they were waiting for 'hard and fast' knocks in the first year and only later began to feel free to ignore the law.[26] And, even while Mr Jones was a Commissioner, it was planned that codes of practice would be published eventually. Moreover, it may be that British Commissioners, like their American counterparts, are being 'educated' by the process of implementing the law into a belief that there is a serious problem for them to solve. In view of newspaper comments in 1976 and 1977 it seems implausible that Ms Chipchase would have acted as she did five years earlier. But the extent to which the American and British enforcement bodies come to follow similar paths to the same policy goals may be limited by the fact that they operate within very different systems of party and government.

Regulatory agencies and systems of party and government

An institutional factor that might influence the British EOC is suggested by Byrne and Lovenduski to be the consequence of a system of adversary politics. Following Finer, they argue that, in a system of alternating parties in government, any institution has to keep an eye open to avoid displeasing a future government.[27] Commissioners cannot have failed to notice that all governments of recent years have tried to solve continuing problems by institutional reorganisation. The Commission could well have worried about a future under a Conservative government that was not likely to favour interventionist institutions. Throughout the 1970s the Commission was criticised, in effect, for pursuing its goals in a fashion more akin to original Conservative proposals than to the American-inspired ideas of Mr Jenkins.

A corollary of the point made by Byrne and Lovenduski is that where the system of party and government is different, agencies like the EOC would be able to be less cautious. President Reagan enjoys the unusual privilege of a majority of his own party in the Senate, and a strong conservative, but not necessarily Republican, following in the House of Representatives. On accession to office, he hinted that civil rights institutions were at risk and, while he has not disbanded civil rights institutions, he has reorganised welfare bodies and has curtailed Federal responsibilities for economic and social policy. Severe though the effects of this are, he has not been able to dismantle the public sector as much, or as quickly as he promised, despite stronger than usual support on Capitol Hill. Depending on the strengths in Congress and Senate, the complete abolition of civil rights institutions might not be within his power, although at the same time, he has been able to begin to attenuate their impact through new appointments, reduced allocations and denials of political access. For example, it has taken him until January 1984 (and a number of rows) to be able to secure a right wing predominance on the Civil Rights Commission.

When, as is usual, there are not the same partisan majorities in the Presidency and Congress, it seems more unlikely that civil rights institutions could be disbanded. Beyond that, the implication is unclear. In principle, the result could be 'immobiliste'. On the other hand, an activist and astute agency could play off a favourable Congress against a reluctant President and vice versa. For example, pressure groups frustrated President Nixon through a Democratic Senate by ensuring that two of his Supreme Court nominees were not ratified. Greater complexity in American institutions extends to those through which agencies are normally publicly accountable. A variety of other bodies are responsible for examining the EEOC to ensure not only that it spends money correctly, but that it is managed effectively and that it deals with complaints properly. For example, indictments by the Civil Rights Commission, Congressional Committees and the General Accounting Office of the EEOC spurred President Carter into fulfilling his intention to do something about enforcement of civil rights policies.

In contrast, the scrutiny of British non-departmental bodies is very imperfect. Like the EOC, they may have to lay Annual Reports in Parliament and may be financially accountable through the Comptroller and Auditor General. But that office is not interested in the same wide management audit as the American General Accounting Office, although a recent Select Committee report has recommended reforms that would increase the similarity of their functions, at least in respect of departments.[28] Questions in the House of Commons about the EOC and other non-departmental bodies are often deflected by Ministers because of lack of knowledge or because it is thought they ought to be addressed directly to the body concerned. It has also been suggested recently that the reformed Select Committees take on responsibility for inspecting non-departmental bodies as well as departments.[29] This would mean that, as in the case of the American Congressional Committees, staff and commissioners could be called upon to describe successes and explain failures. But problems of confidentiality have been evident already in investigations by Select Committees of departments and the same problem would affect scrutiny of the EOC. It is no coincidence that most proposals for reform of procedures of accountability see different regulations about official secrets as complementary.[30] In this issue area, too, the American Freedom of Information

Act is invoked as an exemplar. But even if this could be resolved, partisan cohesion in Britain and the importance of cross-party alliances in the United States would limit the similarities of Select and Congressional Committees.

Judiciaries

On the face of it, the responsibilities placed on the judicial systems in Britain and America for clarifying equal opportunity laws are similar. But the course of judicial developments must be expected to run differently because of dissimilarities in the roles of the judiciaries in their respective societies. The contrasts are fourfold. First, there are differences in procedure. Secondly, there is the British division of responsibility between courts and tribunals. Thirdly, citizens have different beliefs about the use of litigation to secure rights. And fourthly, partly in corollary of the third aspect, the judicial incumbents in each country have different constitutional positions and understandings of their functions.

Procedures

So far as equal opportunity policies are concerned, the most important procedural differences concern: the rules of evidence; the interpretation of legislation; the authority to award damages; and the distribution of legal costs. Most have been referred to already and are summarised or compared more systematically here. The potentially large impact of class actions need no further discussion.

One of the most important evidential differences is the existence of *amicus curiae* briefs in the United States and their absence in Britain. Rendel discusses their values, pointing out that these may be used to put forward 'wide ranging general evidence relevant to the purpose and principles of the legislation, but not tied specifically to the case before the court'.[31] A precedent for the form and content of such a brief was won by Louis Brandeis and Josephine Goldmark in the Supreme Court when they filed a document containing sociological, psychological and medical data about women in suport of protective laws in the State of Oregon in 1908. Under current practice, individuals or organisations who are not parties to an action may apply for court permission to submit similar briefs as 'friends of the court'. Trade unions, women's groups and the EEOC have used this device frequently in cases where it would be difficult for a complainant herself to collect and submit certain kinds of evidence. Ironically, briefs of this kind have been used to overturn the objectives of Brandeis and Goldmark by invalidating older generalisations about female frailty and vulnerability and by demonstrating patterns of discrimination based on 'romantic notions'. The important point that Rendel makes about *amicus curiae* briefs is that they reduce the likelihoods that an outcome will be determined simply by the relative skills of counsels for each side. This is not so in Britain where no such evidence is permitted.

Another important difference is the recourse permitted in America but not in Britain to legislative records. This led to the expansion in America of the meaning of discrimination, although reference to Congressional intentions is now being used to limit the laws in some respects. British judges sometimes seem compelled into flights of fancy about Parliamentary intentions and, in so doing, Lord Denning contradicted a clear statement in the Sex Discrimination Act. Parliamentary discussions on equal pay referred especially to what might be construed as like work but it took a year and the EAT for tribunals to give substance to such ideas. Because reference to Parliamentary records is not allowed, drafters of British legislation have to try to cover every possible eventuality in statutes. This means that British laws are more incomprehensible to lay people than is the case in the United States. Moreover, drafters of law are not infallible and not all eventualities might be covered. Such an omission in the Employment Protection Act was dramatically highlighted in the Grunwick case, discussed by Rogaly.[32]

On the question of damages, provision for damaged feelings was made by the British Government in equal opportunity laws. Inspiration came in part from the Rent Act and also from the United States. British judges have exercised discretion in this respect less freely than Americans. When added to the greater impact in terms of remedies in the American courts – especially in large class action cases – this means that American plaintiffs can probably secure more significant benefits by going to law than the British.

So far as costs are concerned, parties in the United States usually pay their own whether they win or lose. Sometimes attorneys take a percentage of damages if the case is won and nothing if it is lost. In Britain the whole costs of both parties is usually awarded against the loser. As Rendel points out, this means that, in a system that is in any event very expensive, the possibility of using British law as an instrument of reform is limited.[33]

Division of British equal opportunity jurisdiction between courts and tribunals

Tribunals exhibit two particular problems. One, discussed by Rendel, relates to procedures.[34] She points out that 'informality' does not mean that there are no procedures. It means rather, that because tribunals are intended to be informal, procedures are not formally set out. Therefore, those who are accustomed to the system will apply unconsciously rules, albeit informal ones, which are not known or understood by those who appear before them. This places the latter at a disadvantage in presenting their cases. The other problem is described by Byrne and Lovenduski.[35] This is the same British practice of tripartism that has been a problem in the EOC. Each of the 60 regional tribunals and the Employment Appeals Tribunal is chaired by a legally qualified person who is assisted by two lay members. One lay member is nominated by the CBI, the other by the TUC. Few lay members are women and attempts to expand their numbers have been resisted by the TUC for fear that the increase would be at the expense of trade unionists – although one-third of trade unionists are female.

It is not clear that expertise in shopfloor practices necessarily means expertise in elucidating rights under discrimination law. Issues arising under the Sex Discrimination Act are often seen by employers as involving managerial prerogatives and by trade unionists as aspects of collective bargaining.

Because of the inhibiting structure of tribunals, Byrne and

Lovenduski have more, but not much more, confidence in the formal courts. The procedural risks discussed above and the values of citizens and judges discussed below may add limits to their already cautious optimism.

Citizens' beliefs about the use of litigation to secure rights

Rendel argues that citizens in the United States and Britain have different attitudes about the propriety of using the law. She draws attention to a diffuse attitude in Britain of deference to government bodies.[36] Whether it is deference or whether it is knowledge that they are unlikely to win, working-class citizens may not believe that they have real rights of access to the courts or that they will be treated equally once there. On the other hand, Rendel argues that a stronger sense of legal equality in the United States may encourage an expectation that the parties will be on equal footing in litigation to resolve conflict. Thus, if women in Britain find that their interests are not being pursued by traditional protectors, they, because of general social attitudes, may be less willing than their American sisters to use the judicial institutions at their disposal.

Pervasive attitudes among the populace about the roles of the two judiciaries must be connected to their respective constitutional positions and to how judges have interpreted their functions in respect of public policy in general and rights in particular.

The constitutional positions of judges

Caution among British judges in dealing with equal opportunity cases is attributed by Byrne and Lovenduski to their natural conservatism. They cite Griffith's view that the British judges tend to reflect social prejudice in matters where they have discretion.[37] Thus, they are probably uncomfortable when responsible for enforcing ideas embodied in the Sex Discrimination Act that could encourage radical change. The relative optimism of Byrne and Lovenduski stems from the observation that a *slow* adjustment in the judiciary to new policies is normal. Griffith attributes judicial conservatism to the class origin of judges. But the class position of American judges is not fundamentally different from British judges, and yet American judges began boldly when dealing with sex discrimination legislation. Therefore, there must be wider reasons for initial activism in one country and caution in the other. These can be found in both the constitutional position and the politics of the American Supreme Court and the comparatively limited role of the British Judiciary combined with an absence of public law.

Although Americans are accustomed to speaking of the separation of powers, Neustadt argues that the system is more accurately described as one of separate institutions sharing powers of policy-making.[38] Among other things, this is because the Supreme Court in its function of judicial review, may actually change or modify policy. The most famous example is the shift from the nineteenth-century doctrine expressed in *Plessy* v. *Ferguson* that separate treatment of blacks and whites was *not* unequal to the ruling in *Brown* v. *Board of Education* in 1954 that separate treatment is inherently unequal.[39] After the New Deal and the judicial changes of 1936, the Supreme Court consistently upheld the social and political rights of ethnic minorities. Of course, implementation of them depended on government allocations and policing. But paradoxically, given an association of a *laissez-faire* ideology with America and welfare-statism with Britain, the New Deal court, without organised pressure, came closer than British courts to accepting the idea that economic rights for the poor have a similar status to traditional and political liberties.[40] Consequently, the idea of equal employment rights for classes of persons could easily be assimilated by what was, by the 1960s and 1970s, the beginning of the end of the New Deal court.

The paradox is not as extraordinary as it seems. The doctrine of rights for the underprivileged does not entail equal economic outcomes for all individuals. It means that the law may intervene to perfect the market or, in other words, to establish equal rights to become unequal. Nevertheless, the point is that economic rights, if at a minimal level, became accepted by a liberal court with a recognised policy role as a proper area of judicial intervention.

In Britain, the pursuit of economic rights for underprivileged classes has been the prerogative of politicians. The courts have, of course, played a part in economic affairs. Traditionally the main interest has been in protecting property rights of individuals, although Lord Scarman has indicated his dissent from the norm by stating that he finds 'nothing illogical or surprising in Parliament legislating to override a property right if it be thought to be socially necessary'.[41]

The constitutional position of the British judiciary is, of course, unlike that in America. British courts, according to Lord Scarman;

> do not, as a general rule, interfere with government. Only exceptionally would our courts scrutinise the propriety of executive action: and they would never question the validity of a statute. This tradition has developed since 1689 when the supremacy of Parliament and the independence of the judges were assured by the Bill of Rights.[42]

It is not, however, the case that British courts play absolutely no role in the policy-making process. Even strictures about interpreting only the words of statutes leave room for discretion over ambiguities. Moreover, as Lord Scarman points out, the standing of judges and the climate of the time affect interpretations of statutes. In a case involving social rights conferred on classes of persons (racial minorities), Lord Diplock stated that the Race Relations Act was a statute 'which, however admirable its resolves, restricts the liberty which the citizen has previously enjoyed at common law to differentiate between one person and another in entering or declining to enter into transactions with them'.[43]

In so far as equal employment conditions for women are concerned, uneasiness about the rights of classes is less obvious in equal pay. This may be because the facts are easier to ascertain and because such disputes involve the equity principle which is well established in jurisprudence. The facts in sex discrimination cases may be less tangible and judges, with notable exceptions in the Employment Appeals Tribunal, may share the view that non-contractual elements of employment are part of managerial prerogatives. Consequently, they may believe that a law about them is an unnecessary intrusion into personal relationships. Lord Denning's ruling in *Peake* v. *Automotive Products*, discussed in Chapter 4, is similar to some extent to Lord Diplock's in that, despite the rules governing the relationship between the courts and government and which insist on analyses of the words of statutes, he felt able to state what he thought the Act did or did not intend to achieve. His conclusion departed from the intentions of legislators.

The ambiguity between constitutional theory and some practical applications of anti-discrimination laws would be changed, according to Lord Scarman, by the presence of a stronger concept of public law. He recommends the clear formulation of general guiding principles, like those that exist in written constitutions, accompanied by specific statutes based on them.[44] The statutes would provide criteria to facilitate the exercise of the general principles. As a result, he argues, judges would be able to avoid both the courses of action open to them now. One is to retreat behind observations that the matter is one for ministers to decide. The other course presently available is for judges to 'exercise discretion, unguided and untrammelled by anything other than the judge's own sense of what is appropriate'.

The unwritten constitution of Britain is augmented by the accession to the Treaty of Rome, which, with its directives, embodies principles about the economic rights of women. Thus it may be that the concept of public law, common in Europe, is being brought into Britain by the 'back door' as it were, and European 'guiding principles' of equal pay and opportunities have influenced British Courts.

Despite the apparent rationalism and fairness of a democratically established constitutional framework and set of guiding principles, within which judges may exercise reasoned and reasonable discretion, such a solution can have uncomfortable implications. These are discussed in Chapter 6. But first it is necessary to consider general aspects of interest group politics that facilitate involvement by groups in implementation and enforcement in the United States and discourage it in Britain.

The relative importance of groups and parties in British and American politics

The arguments of the pluralist democracy school in the United States are too well known to be rehearsed in detail. Briefly, the central point is that democracy is protected by a myriad of shifting coalitions of groups, enabling citizens to participate in decisions on issues that are important to them. Parties, too, are loose coalitions, less controlled by leaders than those in Britain. In Britain, there has been a tendency to think of pressure groups as anti-democratic. Their importance is often downgraded relative to a cohesive (until 1980) party system.[45]

Arrangements of political actors in both countries look broadly similar in so far as pressure groups and parties appear in both. But closer examination reveals differences. For example, despite criticisms of theories of pluralist democracy in America, it is the case that the configuration of influential pressure groups in the United States is not the same as in Britain. Relatively speaking, the group system in the United States may indeed be more democratic than in Britain.

However, so far as producer groups are concerned, organised business and labour are less equitably represented in the American decision-making sphere. The traditional pattern of agency capture, discussed earlier, benefited business rather than labour. Organised labour is not linked constitutionally to the Democratic Party and in 1972 the relationship was tenuous enough for the AFL-CIO to withhold endorsement of the party's presidential candidate, Mr George McGovern. In Britain, business and labour are both relatively closely involved in government. In part this is connected to party links, but Richardson and Jordan attribute present arrangements to the relationships established during the Second World War to keep up production of essential goods.[46]

So far as 'cause' groups are concerned, success in affecting policy, albeit limited, may be easier to achieve in the United States than in Britain. Gelb and Palley accept, to some extent, Schattschneider's view that success depends on accepting social 'bias'.[47] But they also find that where groups are cohesive and broad-based they can secure reform that is, in the long run, redistributive provided they can present the proposed change as merely distributive. Cohesion and representativeness are also sources of legitimacy for groups in Britain. But it may be easier in the United States than in Britain to acquire the approved characteristics for at least two reasons. One is the different systems of funding in each country and the other is the different relationship between groups and parties. In addition, a specific contrast in respect of women is a different relationship to black civil rights movements.

Sources of funds for pressure groups are in general more numerous and more generous in the United States than in Britain. This benefits both sides in any dispute, a factor evident in anti-ERA and anti-gun control campaigns. Novarra states that individual groups in favour of women's rights like the National Organisation for Women and the Women's Equity Action League have smaller memberships than several British organisations.[48] But she also points out that the gap between subscriptions and their large expenditure is filled, for particular programmes, by grants from large foundations and from the government. For example the Ford Foundation gave $106 000 to the National Council of Negro Women for a leadership training programme, $140 000 to the Ohio Women's Law Fund for a litigation and education programme, and $91 000 to NOW's Legal Defence and Education Fund. The Kellogg and Sears Roebuck Foundations gave $300 000 apiece to groups promoting the training of women and the maximisation of their employment. The government, through the National Commission on the Observance of International Women's Year, gave WEAL $32 000 to publicise federal laws on equal opportunities.

Groups in Britain experience a problem that arises in general from the creation of new non-departmental bodies. This is the possibility that old sources of funds dry up as new ones appear when the intention may have been to increase resources. The Voluntary Service Unit of the Home Office, for example, became reluctant to grant funds to women's groups after the creation of the Equal Opportunities Commission.[49] But, in its first year, the Commission could allocate only £40 000 to *all* groups with an interest and competence to pursue activities similar to American counterparts. Private foundations of the type referred to above have not been customary donors to women's groups in Britain, although underwriting by the Ford Foundation and the German Marshall Fund of NCCL Conference on positive discrimination may be a sign of change.

The mistake of crudely classifying American feminists by 'right' or 'left' labels has been mentioned. Nevertheless, there are groups which, in practice, tend towards modifying existing society and others, less interested in piecemeal reform, concerned to alter it radically. And the issue of sexuality has been a source of bitter disputes among different components of the women's movement. But on specific issues, groups with different philosophies work jointly through both political parties.[50] In Britain women's groups are more irreconcilably fragmented. Co-operation among women's groups in America is compatible with the prevailing American ideology that links group politics with democracy. In Britain, dominance on the left of the idea that the end of class inequality is the main tenet of democracy is one of the reasons for fragmentation among women on key issues. Divisions along party lines on class-type issues that affect women's lives, like state provision and cuts in public expenditure in the social services, engender sufficient mutual suspicion among the various elements of the women's movement to frustrate co-operation of the kind found in the United States. Cracks were papered over in 1973, however, and subsequent issues, like the Nationality Bill, inspired unity among those against legal restrictions. Press treatment does little to foster the growth of unity. Disputes are usually reported, but when almost seventy disparate groups did come together for the day of action on 27 November 1980 to discuss and deliver to politicians a policy programme for women's employment, education and domestic life, the event went almost unnoticed by the press.[51] This contrasts with the 'newsworthiness' of women's co-operation, as well as disagreement, in the United States.

Division between even the 'left' of the women's movement and the left-wing in politics generally is still evident in Britain, partly because of a continuing suspicion that feminism is a diversion from the class struggle.[52] Conventional party politics are alike in both countries in that women are poorly represented in the major parties of their respective legislatures.

At the Federal level in America there are even fewer women

than in the British Parliament. But the looser party system in America may make it potentially easier for women to break the pattern from time to time. One example of the contrasts between the relative cohesiveness of respective major parties and control by them of the political agenda, is the fate of women who have tried to defeat the system. In the United States, democratically-minded Elizabeth Holtzman defeated the official Democrat incumbent and candidate for New York, Emanuel Cellar, solely on the issue of the Equal Rights Amendment.[53] Una Kroll failed in her attempt to win an election standing as a women's rights candidate in Britain. Most of the few women in Congress belong to the National Women's Political Caucus and collectively work for most issues of interest to women's groups.[54] The aim of the recently formed all party 300 Group in Britain is to assist women to become elected representatives in the major Parliamentary parties. But the group has attracted opprobrium for its treatment of homosexual women and radical feminist issues. There are, too, doctrinal objections to a 'Parliamentary (or any other "elitist") road to feminism' which are discussed in Chapter 6.

Fragmentation and suspicion are, of course, not absent in the United States; they are submerged for particular purposes. Attitudes similar to those characterising the relationship between the British left and feminism can be found in the relationship between the black civil rights and women's movements in the United States. On the other hand, the connection between the two movements has also been a source of strength. In the early 1960s, black women saw feminism as a diversion from the more important struggle to undo racial oppression. Ten years later, black women (and white female civil rights activists) were prominent in the women's movement.[55] Like British radical feminists, they discovered that many radical men still held conservative views about the role of women. And like nineteenth-century American feminists, they found analogies too glaring to resist. In addition, the problem of 'double discrimination' was causing a serious anomaly between levels of education and occupational destinations for black women.[56] An alliance between the two movements was a powerful one for liberal political leaders to risk dissatisfying. Such a combination is almost completely absent in Britain.

Black American women, however great their oppression, share at least some American cultural characteristics, by virtue of centuries of inhabitation of the United States. Despite the black power movement, the 'Americanisation' of blacks was obvious when it was fashionable in the early 1970s for them to visit Africa to seek out their roots.[57]

Immigrants to Britain were brought to an alien and often hostile environment mainly in the 1950s to cure labour shortages in occupations that were badly paid with low status. It is difficult to see how they could feel attached to a Britain that promised much and gave little. It is not surprising that young British citizens of West Indian origin often prefer the political ideas of the American black power movement or that women of Asian origin may prefer to retain a custom of seclusion from public life.

But the relationships in both countries may come to resemble one another. White feminists in Britain have stopped ignoring the lives of black women. More members of ethnic minorities are British by birth, have footholds in two cultures, and speak and write of their own experiences of racial and sex discrimination. Economic recession in the United States, even by the middle of the 1970s, was beginning to reactivate suspicions of feminism because of fears that the women's movement was succeeding at the expense of ethnic minorities and a belief that acknowledging analogies belittled the origins of racial oppression. Nevertheless, the extent of co-operation in the United States that still exists and its comparative absence in Britain have implications for the seriousness with which political leaders treat demands for proper implementation of anti-discrimination laws.

A combination of differences in the significance of interest groups in the politics of the two countries, the greater permeability of the American bureaucracy than the British, the relatively greater equality of a set of institutions with policy-making functions in the United States, and the more hierarchical nature of government in Britain all affected the development of equal rights for women. So long as the liberal political philosophy dominated, it was possible for a well rounded anti-discrimination policy network to exist in the United States. By the same token, it has become possible for the policy network to be taken over by the new 'moral majority'. In Britain, it is extremely difficult for any new, weakly established movement to take over anything. The significance of policy networks is discussed in the final chapter.

6

Insights of Comparison

This final chapter is headed 'insights' deliberately instead of by 'lessons' or some other equally definitive sounding word. This is because, although policies may be defined similarly and even, as in this case, consciously used as exemplars, they operate in different political contexts which cannot be transplanted along with the policies themselves. For example, tribunals are specifically British while the Supreme Court is not. Parties seem similar on the face of it, but operate differently. In some ways, therefore, only negative lessons are possible that indicate institutional advantages in one country that do not exist in the other or that it may not be worth expending as much effort in quite the same ways in the two systems. On the other hand, comparisons can reveal how characteristics that seem to be unique to each country may be used for similar ends. For example, on the face of it, the EEC has no equivalent in the United States but, on closer examination, Britain's relationship to it means that certain tactics which seem peculiarly suited to the American system may be of relevance to British women. Despite the opening proviso, some specific policy insights do exist precisely because of the similarities described in Chapter 1 in the position of women in the two labour markets. These will be discussed in this chapter. But it is important to remember that the pursuit of solutions will need to take account of different institutional strengths and weaknesses.

The creation of 'policy networks'

From the institutional point of view, the works of Edelman and Freeman on 'policy networks' are important and should be of interest both to activists and administrators.[1] Edelman suggests that laws purporting to protect 'victim' groups or extend rights to them may be but symbolic reforms. By the mere passage of laws or the creation of new institutions, governments may be seen to be concerned about 'victims' without necessarily enforcing any material changes. The 'victims' may be satisfied with symbolic success, in which case, governments increase their legitimacy at very little cost. But, if tangible benefits are to follow from legal symbols, organisation and collective action are necessary. Organised groups among those protected by the law must take an informed interest in its administration and bargain for benefits.

Edelman's treatment of the administration is mainly concerned with the relationship between enforcement agencies and groups whose activities are supposed to be controlled. This is because his main interest is in why real changes seldom follow legal reforms. Freeman is more concerned with the conditions necessary for protected groups to secure the tangible benefits promised in the legal symbols. She grounds her analysis of the politics of women's rights in the literature on social movements. In her account, several characteristics have to be present for 'victims' to secure both symbolic reforms and tangible benefits. First, there must be a sense of deprivation felt by politically skilled members of the 'victim' group. And there must be a pre-existing communications network of others amenable to being organised. For American women this was provided by political groups in the universities and the State and Federal Commissions on the Status of Women. A catalytic event, like the passage of the Civil Rights Act, followed by poor enforcement for women, is needed to spur them all into political action to remedy the deprivation. Finally, Freeman also argues that collaboration between interest groups and institutions is necessary to give substance to the law. But she concentrates more than Edelman on positive possibilities. Her analysis shows that the administration may have to do more than react to the demands of already established groups; that is, sympathetic 'insiders' have to help in the creation of coherence out of an amorphous mass of individuals and small groups of 'victims'.

At a formal level, this is difficult for institutions like the EEOC and EOC because of the impartiality expected in democratic systems of constitutional bureaucracies and law enforcement bodies. But, according to Blumrosen, an academic lawyer and once a senior member of staff at the EEOC, it is necessary for equal opportunity administrators to go beyond a 'bland neutrality' in order to counteract pressures from groups that are to be regulated and to do so by involving participants from the beneficiary class.[2]

Networks in America

Examples of productive network orchestration by 'insiders' in American equal opportunity institutions have been referred to several times in this book. Other examples include the encouragement and information given by a member of the Department of Health, Education and Welfare to Dr Sandler in her efforts to bring universities within affirmative action law. Members of government departments have also worked with groups like Wider Opportunities for Women and the Coalition of Labor Union Women to open up new training opportunities. The New York Contract Compliance Officer, referred to in Chapter 4, encouraged the creation of two pressure groups to act in ways that would not have been permissible for a public servant. One is an information centre and a source of mutual moral support for actual and aspiring female construction workers. The other is a group of distinguished New Yorkers who lend their eminence in high-level lobbying of employers and public bodies.

But it is also important for the network to spread through a range of institutions beyond those that are directly responsible for the enforcement of equality laws. This is obvious in the account by Gelb and Palley of four different policy interests of women's groups.[3] They point out that attempts in Congress to limit 1972 legislation on equality in education were restricted by the 'leaking' of new draft set of regulations which was sent to President Ford. Official bodies and interest groups were equitably integrated into President Carter's reorganisation proposals and, as noted earlier, his staff stimulated a lobbying campaign to ensure that Congress accepted the proposals agreed by all of them. Blumrosen argues that Congress, too, has facilitated the integration of members of the 'protected' groups into the administrative process by introducing rules about the award of costs in court proceedings during the last ten years which have the effect of 'encouraging private litigation to achieve public purposes'.[4] In addition the form of accountability and the process of 'advice and consent' for Presidential appointments to the Supreme Court and Executive Agencies, discussed in the previous chapter, provide a variety of access points through which groups may initiate or be invited to take part in bargaining for benefits in terms of personnel or policy development.

An incomplete network in Britain

The British EOC has tried to develop fruitful relationships with other governmental bodies. But, at least until 1979, its policy-network, unlike that of the EEOC, seems to have concentrated on the upper level rather than on the grassroots as well. The results of consultations with non-departmental bodies do not satisfy Commissioners completely. It has been noted already that they were disappointed by the Committee of Industrial Tribunals and the Manpower Services Commission. In 1978 the EOC was forced to ask the Prime Minister to instruct the latter to do more about female school leavers.[5] In 1977, the Commission reported that two nationalised industries, despite EOC comment, continued to provide training only at night, hence denying women the possibility of apprenticeships.[6] Only ACAS and the CAC have escaped Commission censure.

Relations with central departments and ministers are notable for both failures and modest gains. The Department of Education and Science, reluctant from the start to be covered by the Act, has been particularly difficult so far as the EOC is concerned. Towards the end of 1977 a supposedly confidential report by the Home Office stated that there was no need for an education section in the EOC. Its duties could be split between the Goods Facilities and Services section of the EOC and the Department of Education and Science. The department itself has done little to publicise the relevant provisions of the Act in circulars. The proposed transfer was vigorously opposed by the Commission in discussions with Mrs Shirley Williams. Dr Byrne of the EOC's education section was dismissed for discussing the matter with the press, although a tribunal later held her sacking to have been unfair.[7] More recently, thirteen departments were criticised by the Commission for not setting an example by seeking qualified women to serve on public bodies.[8]

Since the EOC is expected to advise governments on taxation and social security, and because of its view that change requires concerted action, Commissioners have continually pressed Chancellors of the Exchequer and Secretaries of State for Health and Social Security to end discriminatory regulations.[9] Modest improvements have been made particularly in connection with children. But, in 1979, social security benefits still discriminated against women, particularly married women caring for invalid dependents. Initial changes in taxation were regarded as cosmetic by the EOC and a Green Paper published in December 1980 discourages (on grounds of cost) the EOC aim for an early separation of the taxing of wives and husbands. The EOC's proposed amendments to the Sex Discrimination Act, released in January 1981, call for the ending of discrimination in tax and social security legislation within ten years.

It is not surprising that civil servants and junior ministers might not take the views of the EOC seriously given that leading politicians do not seem to set the pace. At the start there were suspicions that the Sex Discrimination Act, whatever Mr Jenkins' personal commitment, was a 'test-run' for the 1976 Race Relations Act.[10] Later Labour Ministers were evasive in response to questions, suggestions and criticisms.[11] Mrs Thatcher tried to reassure Women in the Media and the Fawcett Society but she is better known for her general opposition to State intervention into economic and social affairs and her lack of enthusiasm for the women's movement. Moreover, unlike American politicians, British political leaders have little incentive to espouse the cause of women's rights because of the less cohesive grassroots element of the British policy-network on equal opportunities.

It is only recently that the Equal Opportunities Commission has begun to take an interest in actively stimulating co-operation with women's groups. To begin with, the Commission invited pressure from women.[12] But, as noted in Chapter 4, subsequent EOC overtures to women's groups were confined to grants to promote research and publicity and even this invoked disagreement about whether funds should be allocated to radical women's rights groups.[13] As a law enforcement agency (rather than an advising or educative body) the EOC has conducted relations with pressure groups in the 'arms length' manner that is thought constitutionally proper. In November 1979, however, a one-day conference with women's groups was held to discuss 'Barriers to Full Equality' but became preoccupied by the pressing issues of the day; possible erosions of the employment conditions of pregnant women workers and the status of women's nationality rights. The Commission acknowledged then that if government proposals to narrow existing rights were to be resisted, a concerted campaign was necessary.[14] In 1979, while stressing its need not to appear like a pressure group, the Commission began to try to instigate a united campaign by pressure groups for its proposed amendments to the Equal Pay Act and Sex Discrimination Act. Nevertheless, there was little evidence in 1983 of co-operation between the Commission and groups in lobbying for Jo Richardson's Sex Equality Bill which would have covered many of the concerns of the EOC and EEC.

A comparison of factors affecting the representation of feminist interests in policy-making in the two countries

The creation of a network extending through non-departmental bodies, government departments, parties, legislatures and to positions of political leadership is more difficult in Britain than in the United States. Heclo argues that bureaucratic and political institutions in the United States are more permeable than those of any other country and that permeation by interest groups increased with the growth of governmental intervention in the 1960s and 1970s.[15] The previous chapter discussed the effects of bureaucratic styles, systems of public appointments and the variety of scrutinising bodies that are influential in the United States and which provide a greater number of worthwhile access points for American feminists. Here, some political considerations need further discussion.

Political leadership. First, there is the question of commitment by political leaders which, except under Presidents Nixon and Reagan, was obvious and important in the United States and is almost entirely absent in Britain. But American presidential candidates do not become presidents because their parties win in Congress in the way that party leaders become prime ministers when they and their parties gain a majority of seats in a British election. There is no single party machine working for members of Congress and presidential candidates. Nor can presidential candidates depend as much as British politicians have been able to on traditions of class-based electoral support. Consequently, presidential candidates have to foster their own electoral bases. The electoral system is biased towards populous areas and all of these factors have made it possible for an urban-based civil and women's rights alliance to be the most important bedrock of support for liberal candidates.

Britain on the other hand has a system that, until the 1980s, appeared to rest on a relatively stable coincidence of class and party divisions which had a habit of providing rotating majorities for the Conservative and Labour parties. As a result it would have been and may still be folly for party leaders to risk traditional party loyalties by fostering their own particular electoral bases among groups of voters that span existing partisan boundaries. The advent of the Social Democratic Party and its alliance with the Liberals is a symptom of underlying changes. With its particular kind of middle-class base and with leaders who include Roy Jenkins, anti-discrimination policies and a Bill of Rights occupy the centre of its approach to equality in place of socialist solutions and conservative attachment to traditional forms of rights. In this sense, the SDP has an American flavour. At the present, however, it is not in a position of national leadership and the 300 Group is right to acknowledge the strong roots of existing

institutions as avenues to leadership positions by encouraging
greater female representation in parties which, for wider
political reasons, continue to attract women differently.

Representation of feminist interests in legislatures. A second political
factor influencing the extent to which leaders can be forced to
take women's rights seriously is the interest shown among
members of legislatures in the subject. In Britain, the idea of
increasing the number of women members of Parliament is
often criticised. In one view, Parliament is part of a system
either of male or of class domination and that women members
are no different from men who subordinate other women or
classes. Some support for this proposition is provided by
Vallance, who describes an ethos and a career pattern that
made older women MPs chary of adopting the cause of
women's groups.[16] A second view is that Parliament is now one
of the 'dignified' parts of the constitution; that its legislative
programme is virtually controlled by the government; and that
there is, therefore, very little point in electing feminists to it.
Thirdly, it is observed that the strength and cohesion of
class-based partisan loyalties, reinforced by the 'whip' system
prevent effective co-operation among women members. Some
evidence for these propositions exists in the recent work of
Drewry and Brock who argue that women peers are consistently more partisan than feminist.[17] In contrast, a national
party organisation in the United States, mainly geared to
presidential elections, leaves members of Congress largely
beholden to their State bases. And the Congressional
'whipping' system is weak. These factors make cross-party
alliances on some issues by liberals and conservatives sensible
(see Chapter 3). Thus the similar behaviour of the bipartisan
National Women's Political Caucus is traditional and therefore
normal. Moreover, not only the weaker whip system but also
the Constitutional separation of powers mean the Congress and
its committees have real powers to make, modify or overturn
domestic policies.

However, British objections to improving the representation
of women should not be maintained rigidly. Vallance also
points out that younger women members, whose politicisation
has coincided with and been affected by the growth of

feminism, are more aware of responsibilities to other women and have been able to influence the ways in which the House of Commons thinks about women's roles. And, although it cannot be denied that Parliament is weaker than Congress, women members do affect feminist policy issues. Vallance argues that abortion debates were important, not only because of the effect on the thinking of women members about other women and of male politicians about women colleagues, but because proposed restrictions were defeated by women. In the 1930s and 1940s Parliamentary upsets on equal pay occurred because women (and male sympathisers) defied party divisions. Joyce Butler found a difference in attitudes about equal opportunities with the arrival of new women members of the kind described by Vallance. And in the House of Lords, too, discussion of an anti-discrimination law *was* characterised by bipartisan co-operation.

If more women were encouraged to become representatives these changes could become permanent features of British political life. As acknowledged in ideas about affirmative action, 'token' women cannot be expected to do other than take on the characteristics of men in any organisation and that a 'critical mass' is needed to ensure not only that equality is more than symbolic, but also that female participation and women's rights are as normal and legitimate as other public concerns.

The first difficulty for women in both countries is getting involved in established party machinery, traditionally dominated by men to return male legislators. In the United States, however, where party organisation is less uniformly cohesive, women have been able to become better represented in the Coventions which select Presidential candidates and to influence the electoral fortunes of Congressional candidates who opposed the Equal Rights Amendment. In the end, however, a President was elected who ended his party's support for the Amendment. But amending the Constitution is an enormous task, requiring ratification by two-thirds of the States and women's campaigning in party politics at all levels almost brought it off. British women are becoming much more active in the management of constituency parties and this needs to continue and expand. Vallance describes an early example; it was to militancy among female party workers that Barbara

Castle owed her selection. But it is often easier to create than to reform institutions and SDP women have a golden opportunity, which they have shown signs, however, of missing, to make an organisation in which their equal participation is the norm.

Appointments to public bodies. A third political consideration in ensuring that feminist interests are represented in policy-making structures is the question of appointments to public bodies. It is important for it to be made normal for women to be appointed, not only to public bodies dealing with so-called 'women's issues' like consumer affairs and ancillary social services, but also to those that are responsible for their basic economic rights and for matters like transport, employment, defence and foreign policy, and trade and industry. Chapter 5 described how political factors specific to the United States forced presidents to enlarge conventional pathways to public office and showed that such pressures are less strong in Britain. However, feminist protest has resulted in some concessions in EOC appointments, and, if feminists are to expand their influence, it is necessary to exploit existing avenues. Trade unions and professional associations are customarily consulted in the compilation of the list of suitable persons. Pressure groups thought by governments to be 'respectable' are also asked for suggestions. It is therefore important for advocates of women's rights to be active in such organisations even if, in general, they do not always find them sufficiently radical.

Group–class alliances. Although 'cause' group politics is a surrogate for class politics in the United States, and less influential than class-based politics in Britain, British radical feminists cannot afford to discount group politics altogether and more conservative feminists ought not to be too pessimistic about its possibilities. At the same time, feminists in both countries need to think carefully about intergroup relations. In the United States, this is particularly important in respect of relations between women's groups, civil rights groups and trade unions. In Britain, relationships between different kinds of women's groups also need more serious attention.

From 1965 until the late 1970s, the strengths of the American civil rights–feminist alliance were undeniable. From the centre to the left in British politics a growing interest is obvious in the interconnections of various forms of discrimination and inequality and in how present fissiparous tendencies might become a more cohesive force for a fairer and more civilised approach to race relations and the position of women. But British institutional traditions make it more difficult than in America for women whose thinking is based on a materialist analysis of society to work with women, like Ann Robinson of the EOC, who are deeply concerned about women's rights and Conservative. That fundamental disagreements can be put aside for the sake of specific, urgent issues, as commonly occurs in the United States, was shown in the lead up to the Sex Discrimination Act and in the opposition to recent racist and sexist amendments to British nationality law. Deliberate selection of issues which can transcend deeper differences ought to be extended and there are opportunities for doing so in improving the equal pay and opportunity laws. On the other hand, British leftist strategies and ideas should not be discounted by American women simply because they operate in a political system that is less class conscious. The civil rights–feminist alliance is not now, it will be recalled, without its problems. When, because of high levels of unemployment, equal opportunity policies do not simply distribute an expanding pool of opportunities but appear to redistribute a declining number of them, rivalries are bound to break out among groups for which co-operation was once thought natural but which now may see themselves as competitors. This may make it more important to nourish links with trade unions.

But, as in Britain, American groups and trade unions need to define objectives in such a way that natural allies do not necessarily threaten one another. This is because, while Americans are less class-conscious than the British, the United States is also a class based society in materialist terms and unemployment makes this more obvious. Although the traditional emphases on who are natural allies is different, women in neither country can formulate policies that will be applied on the shopfloor if they do so in isolation from organised labour and if they produce solutions which male colleagues in trade unions will refuse to adopt as negotiating issues. This is not to say that women's rights should be subordinate to traditional radical minority or male trade unionist concerns but that, in specific circumstances, ways must be found of articulating demands that promote women's equality but which can be construed as improving the quality of life for black or white men. For example, rethinking criteria for selection or promotion in the United States benefited women and racial minorities. All men as individuals enjoy higher family incomes if their wives get equal pay. Widespread practices of parental instead of maternity leave and allowances enable men to enjoy the pleasures (and pain) of family responsibilities without appearing to be 'deviant'.

The European dimension in Britain

Domestic politics mean that it is easier for what can be made to appear a women's movement to have permeated bureaucratic and political bodies in the United States and to reappear as a thorn in the flesh of unfavourable political forces. However, institutional and ideological complications in Britain do not mean that the ideas of Edelman and Freeman are of but limited relevance. This is not just because there is room, as it were, for group politics alongside what is conventional in Britain but also because Britain's membership of the EEC introduces elements of an 'American' policy network. First of all, EEC Directives on equal pay, opportunities and social security are an equivalent of a set of guiding constitutional principles and the European Court of Justice acts rather like the Supreme Court when it decides whether or not British statutes are adequate or defective within a European framework. And, as shown in Chapter 5, its judgments are enforceable right down the line to regional industrial tribunals. Moreover, as Hoskyns and other members of Rights of Women point out, European officials behave more like pro-feminist administrators in America than British civil servants. Adopting 'a much more overt and publicly visible political role',

> they can be heard at consultative meetings openly seeking pressure-group support against recalcitrant national ministries and revealing details of controversial negotiations in a way which would be quite unthinkable in Whitehall.[18]

Hoskyns *et al.* also note that British pressure groups have been slow, especially in the field of social policy, to take up opportunities afforded by the openness of the EEC. The lesson is obvious for feminists who are in favour of remaining in the EEC. Those hoping for British withdrawal – mainly in the Labour Party but also some Conservatives – need to think carefully about their priorities. For the right, the basic issue is the general principle of reduced sovereignty of British institutions over British affairs. For the left there is a specific issue of sovereignty. This is that ceding power to an institution that embodies the principle of the free market precludes freedom to introduce collectivist and socialist solutions to inequality in Britain. Given what has been said in this and other chapters about class and politics, about the limits of resolving inequality through individual cases and about the need to co-operate with trade unions to secure collective, non-discriminatory agreements and positive action plans, it may be argued that a court is indeed a poor vehicle for altering deeply entrenched employment practices. But it has also to be said that judicial declarations can be of considerable symbolic and practical significance. The Supreme Court declaration in *Brown* v. *Board of Education* shook political consciences about racial segregation. The *Griggs* ruling was important symbolically because of its definition of discrimination but it also had a large practical impact on a wide range of practices and on procedure in later cases. Immediately practical effects of judgments in the European Court were noted in Chapter 4. Its criticism of British equal pay law means that it is obvious that it is not 'freakish' to believe that the law needs to be changed.

A different body of European law – the European Convention on Human Rights – has been adopted by the Social Democratic Party. It wants to incorporate the Convention into British law, thus directly providing Britain with a written Bill of Rights which would be protected by a new legal institution. While it can indeed be argued that such American and European arrangements have extended women's rights, it has to be said that the constitutional approach can have uncomfortable implications for civil libertarians. First, the content of the 'guiding principles' is problematic. It might be relatively easy to secure agreement about procedural and institutional matters. But the substantive content of what are to count as rights is fraught with difficulties. It has already been noted that disputes exist about the status of property rights and whether welfare needs and employment conditions are equivalent to constitutionally recognised civil liberties. These were sub-merged, but not fully resolved, by signatories to the UN Declaration on Human Rights, the late New Deal alliance in the United States and in support from the right for welfare and anti-discrimination policies in Britain. Curious alliances on both sides of the argument about a Bill of Rights for Britain exist between those most attached to property and legal rights and those for whom welfare rights are of primary importance. Behind the confusion is the question of how significant class structures would be in determining who would guard the constitution and what consequences this would have for substantive interpretations of it.[19]

Political opportunism

From a general institutional point of view, what may be an uncomfortable conclusion for feminists cannot be avoided. This is that a certain amount of political opportunism is necessary. It is no good maintaining ideologically pure posi-tions in the hope that existing male or class dominated institutions will go away. If they are ignored they will stay. And it is no good ignoring potential allies because of an inexact coincidence of ideas and aims. In both countries, feminists have to make informed political judgments about which existing institutions can be used to advantage at particular times and neglected when they seem immutable or have served a purpose. And similar political skills need to be applied to making productive alliances for particular ends. At the same time, theoretical honesty can be maintained. Indeed, it is necessary *not* to become submerged by the prevailing ideologies of hierarchical or male dominated institutions. Women's branches of unions, parties and professional associations exist in both countries formally and informally alongside the conventional. These are used and can be used more for developing confidence and skills and for planning demands and tactics in co-operation, where appropriate, with other women's groups. That it is possible to modify the ways in which institutions treat women or think about their role in society is evident in the successes of the American Coalition of Labor Union Women and in American university and professional women's caucuses. It is also evident in Vallance's account of the House of Commons and in the seriousness with which some trade unions are engaged now with the NCCL, EOC and women's groups in the development of positive action programmes. It is no use dismissing this because it is reformist. Randall's observation has been noted already that reforms can be part of a revolution for women. Revolutionary theorists – notably Gramsci – believe that elements of pre-revolutionary ideology and social forms persist in post-revolutionary societies.[20] If sex and racial discrimination exist, then, in our present society, they will do so in whatever type of social organisation succeeds it. While improvements in the economic position of women in the Soviet Union have been made, women are by no means as liberated as its Socialist Constitution proclaims. In Britain, an important start in exploring the influence that feminism can have on left-wing political organisation and practice can be found in *Beyond the Fragments*.[21]

Policy development

It has been noted already that laws about equal pay in its most straightforward form have probably been used to their limits. With some improvement to existing British law, however, women's earnings could be increased through greater use of job evaluation and by more use of the positive action clause of the Sex Discrimination Act. In the United States, women's earnings might be expected to improve if affirmative action continues.

However, the precariousness of women's gains even in the United States highlights one of the major difficulties of equal opportunity legislation. This is that the policy rests on an assumption of economic growth which provides an expanding pool of opportunities. In both countries such an assumption can now be seen to have been over-optimistic. In periods of stability without growth, occupational distribution can still be

altered without too much political cost because of voluntary
turnover in the labour market. But when there is a declining
pool of opportunities, equality policies stop being distributive
and involve the politically problematic task of redistribution.
This means that it can be difficult to reduce resistance to
solving the main continuing cause of women's inequality in pay
and opportunities; that is, job segregation. However, it is
possible to argue that segregation has adverse effects on
individual family incomes, the quality of life and the probable
future of industry and that equality for working women is not
only a question of justice, but is in the interests of society as a
whole. The next part of this chapter considers in more detail
how the existing laws and institutions might be used or
modified to reduce segregation.

Reducing segregation involves widespread general changes
and solutions that affect whole firms and industries. American
legal procedures and legally imposed affirmative action policies
go a long way towards adapting a legal system that is based on
individual rights, remedies and sanctions into a suitable vehicle
for solving collective problems. And the British may be able to
use European law in some similar ways. But, given the nature
of the legal system, the collective bargaining and voluntary
co-operation that are characteristic of Britain are also necessary. Nevertheless, it is the view even of the TUC that these
cannot take place without a background framework of law and
legal sanctions.[23] Consequently, a careful combination of
recourse to existing law, campaigning for better laws and
work-place negotiation is needed in both countries.

Job segregation and low pay

Although segregation is declining faster in the United States
than in Britain, it continues in both countries to be a principal
cause of unequal earnings. American law has no parallel to the
British provision for equal pay for jobs rated as equivalent
under an evaluation scheme. But as it stands, the British job
evaluation clause is not helpful and, on the contrary, allows no
effective remedy against schemes with in-built biases based on
traditional stereotypes. Consequently, there is no way of
getting at strategies adopted in the 1970s by some employers

and trade unions to minimise equal pay obligations by using job evaluation schemes to manipulate grading systems so as to restrict eligible equal pay applications. Some American cases were cited earlier that granted equal pay for different work, yet efforts by, for example, the American Civil Liberties Union to assault widespread segregation have come to nothing. European and American rulings mean that the effects of segregation are mitigated for individual women by the fact that they need not find a contemporary male colleague with whom to compare themselves. But they probably still need to find a predecessor or successor. Pressure groups in both countries might do well to consider demands like that of the British TUC for a concrete measure giving effect to the 'notional' man mentioned in the European Court. This is the New Zealand idea of considering what an employer would have had to have paid a male recruit to do the job. Other aspects of equal pay policies that need special attention are: recognition of indirect discrimination, equal value, job analysis, and, in Britain, the jurisdiction of the CAC.

European and American rulings have reduced some of the effects of segregation in some equal pay claims by incorporating the idea of indirect discrimination. Such a development is important enough to warrant specific recognition in the statutes of the two countries. Specific amendments to equal pay laws are necessary. This particular harmonisation of the Equal Pay Act and Sex Discrimination Act is one of the most important of 22 amendments proposed by the EOC in 1981 about which the government has done so little so far. Difficulties, however, should not be underestimated. Such a provision would affect all contractual terms and conditions of employment and might include merit and seniority systems which have become so contentious under American civil rights and affirmative action law. In Britain, there is the added complication of the status of protective legislation. Job scarcity has made these issues divisive in the United States and campaigns for an indirect discrimination amendment to equal pay laws need careful planning and meticulous attention to aspects that may increase fragmentation when political and economic circumstances mean that co-operation is most important.

However, in Britain, indirect discrimination in pay has been overtaken for the time being by the broader question of equal pay for work of equal value. In 1982, the European Court decided that the British government had neglected to fulfil Council Directive 75/117/EEC because

> it had not made provision for all employees who consider themselves wronged by failure to apply the principle of equal pay for work to which equal value is attributed and for which no system of job evaluation exists to obtain recognition of such equivalence.[24]

The American Civil Liberties Union and the EEOC which is responsible for eliminating 'systemic' causes of segregation may or may not be able to use this lead to shame, as it were, an American government into introducing an equal value clause into its equal pay law.

But Britain should be avoided as a model for the precise form of such a measure. Fredman points out that remarkably little attention has been paid to British government proposals for compliance from 1984 which place so many obstacles in the way of applicants that the measure will be severely restricted and the law will probably still infringe treaty obligations.[25] Lord Denning believes the new regulations to be so complex as to be incomprehensible, even in the Court of Appeal. Their acknowledgement of market forces as a justifiable defence, referred to earlier, runs counter to American judicial views on the matter. A third main objection is that equal pay for work of equal value is couched as a residuary, not primary, right for use only if the like work and job evaluation clauses are inapplicable. By definition, equal value applicants will not be able to apply under the like work clause. But, if a job evaluation scheme exists, it is, as noted earlier, very likely to embody discriminatory assumptions and yet, in Britain its existence may mean that no further claim can be made.

Moreover, this is a difficult problem for judicial resolution, despite the outcomes referred to earlier in some American courts. Claims under an equal value heading have large implications for and repercussions on practices throughout a firm and for collective agreements between employers and trade unions of which several may be involved. Such claims also entail detailed expert analyses of a whole range of jobs which may be entirely different from one another. But expertise does not mean that job evaluation is a 'scientific' or objective exercise. The British government intends it to be done for tribunals by equality officers designated by ACAS. American experience in investigating equal pay and in drawing up affirmative action plans shows that special training in sex discrimination is essential. No provision in law for this has been made so far in Britain. The EOC and Incomes Data Services have produced advice about good practice in reducing sex bias in job evaluation. Government action makes the publication of an EOC Code of Practice a matter of urgency. Moreover, given the implications for collective agreements, EOC earlier recommendations for extending the jurisdiction of the Central Arbitration Committee beyond overtly discriminatory agreements take on a new significance. Involvement of the CAC in equal value cases already has the support of the TUC. It could be productive for this to be made a joint action issue by the EOC, feminists and trade unionists.

Segregation and job opportunities

Occupational segregation also generally confines women to jobs with poor prospects for promotion and personal satisfaction. In order to eliminate employment practices causing such restrictions, it is not enough to eliminate formal barriers. It is not enough to rely on new legal expressions of a norm of equality. It is not enough for a few individual women, with or without the law, to become judges and engineers and a few men to become secretaries and nursery nurses. Indeed it is dangerous to rely on limited innovations like these. The likelihood of token women behaving like men will be accompanied by complacency because the law exists and by the belief that, if one can do it, so can all. Smug satisfaction ignores the fact that the strength of past or present, unconscious discrimination continues to deny chances to the majority of women who are unexceptionally but as adequately qualified as the majority of men. And it ignores the effects this will have on women in judging whether it is worthwhile persisting in unconventional ambitions. What is necessary is a pattern of employment where it is as normal for women as for men to be found in a wide range of occupations. This means that women can develop an expanded set of expectations that is also realistic. In addition, the 'demonstration effect' of a new pattern of employment is likely to reduce irrational prejudice amongst others. For these reasons, positive steps need to be taken to encourage substantial numbers of women and men into untraditional occupations. These must involve the law and voluntary action.

Although the operation of such positive steps in the United States reveals pitfalls, officials in that country and pressure groups in Britain agree that the faster American rate of desegregation owes a good deal to *enforceable* affirmative action policies. And it is agreed that numbers, which were to start with small in absolute terms, cannot be enlarged overnight. Affirmative action is a generational process involving schools, further education institutions, work-place training and not simply the points of recruitment and promotion. There are genuine worries in the United States about the appropriateness and legality of particular imposed affirmative action plans. There are also difficulties about whether voluntary, not imposed, affirmative action policies are lawful because of the restricted circumstances in which race can legally be taken into account. Failure in Britain of reliance on voluntary implementation of small enabling clauses on training should be used in the United States to resist attacks on the imposition of good affirmative action plans. At the same time, although organised labour is weaker in the United States than in Britain, the recession means that Americans, too, should acknowledge the NCCL's observation that affirmative or positive action needs voluntarism and co-operation with trade unions. This is because of its effects on merit, seniority systems and the like, over which trade unions have gained some control and which have become more important as redundancy becomes more common.

In 1981, the NCCL published an excellent document about how the British law might be used, as it stands, to better advantage by trade unionists within their own organisations and in negotiating agreements with employers.[26] This is based on examination of the American experience and consultations with relevant British organisations and ought to be read by all feminists, trade unionists, employers and public officials.

Many measures that are legal obligations in the United States could be negotiated in Britain to modify patterns of recruitment, training and promotion, etc. These include the collection of detailed and accurate information about recruitment patterns and procedures, careful analysis of it, consideration of goals and targets for future employment, proper training for employees and trade union officers involved in personnel work, publicity about equal opportunity policies and, perhaps above all, monitoring of any negotiated agreements.

The NCCL analysis of voluntary positive action possibilities in Britain also reveals shortcomings in American plans that need to be corrected. One of these is failure to foresee the effects of continuing hurdles and the consequent need for high targets to counteract drop-outs. Another object lesson is the identification, cited earlier, by the Civil Rights Commission of significant regional variations in existing female participation rates in different trades.

Thirdly, Americans should also protest about, and the British avoid, the minimising strategies identified by the NCCL. For example, statistics are sometimes whitewashed by redefining jobs so that when secretaries become described as executive employees, it looks as though great advances have been made. It is essential, therefore, for regulatory bodies like the EEOC and EOC and for equality officers in trade unions to be meticulous in scrutinising proposals and monitoring their implementation. A fourth problem to be overcome in one country and avoided in the other is the discovery by the Department of Labor that endless delays can ensue from disagreements about what counts as a reasonable catchment area.[27] For some jobs, like airline pilots, this might be expected to be unarguably the whole country. But, for recruitment to factories, employers can postpone action by arguing about whether cities of distance apart such as Richmond and Washington or Bath and Bristol are catchment areas for one another. This is perhaps of less importance to white women who are evenly spread geographically than for different racial groups who often inhabit distinct areas. However, combining various protected groups in comprehensive affirmative action plans is common in America and steps need to be taken to minimise such delays.

Despite the difficulty, the divisive consequences of the recession may mean that it would be politically sensible in Britain to try to foster a common interest in the development of voluntary positive action programmes that cover more than one category of worker. But this needs to be planned carefully in Britain and reforms are necessary in the United States so as to acknowledge differences, as well as shared interests, among women and the various minority group workers. For example, while white and black women share some interests, they also have different problems. And the interests of black women are not always those of black men. It has been mentioned already that, in America, the discrepancy between educational achievement and labour market rewards was particularly acute for black women and more so for them than for white women and black men. Americans need to resist unthinking affirmative action plans which, for example, apply similar remedies for American Indians and Americans of Asian origin when one group has the poorest educational chances and the other, like black women, has a high rate of academic achievement without appropriate employment.[28]

As the Supreme Court did in the *Griggs* case and the Department of Labor does in its instructions, it is important to resist the charge that affirmative or positive action means treating protected groups more favourably and to remind opponents that it compensates for past discrimination and expands the pool of qualified applicants. In this respect, what the NCCL recommends for publicity and education and what is called the 'outreach' component of American affirmative action are important. This means encouraging members of the agreed catchment area to consider it worthwhile to become suitable candidates. It may involve special relationships with local schools, publicising company policy on equality, ensuring that job advertisements encourage applicants from the relevant group and, where appropriate, advertising in journals or newspapers that reach a wider audience. Lest it be thought that such activity is unnatural to Britain, it is worth remembering that special relationships have always existed between some public schools and some universities and some universities and some employers. And, in recent years, it has not been thought unreasonable for some universities to counter the prevailing networks by creating new ones with state schools in deprived areas. Moreover, extra public resources have sometimes been allocated as a compensatory measure to areas of special deprivation.

In so far as employers are rational in believing that investment in training women is less profitable than for men, it is right that public intervention should take place. Consequently, it is important for the British government to agree to requests made possible by the Sex Discrimination Act for new centres to be designated, like Brunel University, as special training centres for women wishing to adopt unconventional careers. For the same reason, the reinstatement of the lost Industrial Training Boards ought also to be a priority in feminist and trade union campaigns. New affirmations by the MSC about the training of women and girls need to be monitored. And more extensive public help like the Wider Opportunities for Women Courses could be given to married women who want to keep up with developments in their field or to take refresher courses. The importance of this kind of intervention in America is recognised by Lady Platt, the new Conservative chairperson of the EOC. She is impressed by such schemes in Wisconsin, where, it will be recalled, particular efforts were also made in respect of apprenticeships. However, employers should not be allowed to use arguments about the returns on investment in training women to get away with too much. Apart from the observations of American managers discussed earlier, a British banker told Lady Platt that the solution was not to deny training opportunities for women but lay in making it worthwhile for them to remain employed. Such an observation is another corroboration of dual labour market theories.

The NCCL deals mainly with what can be achieved by existing British laws because it is felt that the political climate does not favour improvements to them. But, if only to pre-empt the common argument that silence denotes satisfaction, it is important for feminists, trade unionists and the EOC to continue their campaigns to encourage reform of existing legal provision for positive action. First, voluntary or agreed schemes are limited by the fact that the law at present only allows employers to take positive steps in training schemes. At the selection stage, it is unlawful not to choose the then best qualified candidate. Consequently, it is often difficult to actually employ the very people for whom special training becomes lawful *after* recruitment.

Secondly, there is the related question of contract compliance, resisted by the 1975 Labour Government and reopened by the Commission for Racial Equality, the Equal Pay and Opportunities Campaign and the NCCL. In the United States, it and affirmative action are inextricable. But in Britain no special scrutiny is required of compliance by government contractors with existing law, let alone of any voluntary positive action. In 1975, it was argued that cutting contracts could not be contemplated because most contractors were in areas where unemployment would be high were it not for government funds. But the idea of contract compliance already existed in regulations about fair wages and the 1975 argument was not allowed to prevail later when a non-statutory pay policy was broken. In the present, there is a glaring discrepancy in government thinking. Mrs Thatcher's government claims that it is not a direct public responsibility to minimise unemployment and that it is a governmental obligation to spend tax-payers' money with propriety. Since governments must also believe that laws should be obeyed, to reject the idea of contract compliance is to contravene all these canons. Logically speaking, the unemployment argument should be irrelevant and firms receiving public funds should be required to act lawfully. At the very least, the government ought to be made to set its own house in logical and ideological order. But beyond that, it ought to set an example. It is happy to do this in other aspects of public sector employment through cash limits. Senior American officials are amazed that no British government has thought it right to set the pace of good equal employment practices in the whole public sector.[29]

If the law were to be changed, attention would have to be paid to enforcement problems. As the NCCL points out, most British employers fail to obey the law requiring them to discriminate in favour of a small number of disabled people. In the United States, contract compliance institutions were reformed because sanctions were rarely applied. In the British provision for the disabled, the problem seems to be unwillingness to enforce monitoring provisions which lead to prosecution. In the United States supervision exists but it seems too often to be thought that the sanction applied must be the ending of a contract and that this would have unmanageable consequences, possibly of the type envisaged by the British government in 1975. In general, the relationship between crime and punishment is delicate and needs careful consideration. The Utilitarians argued that it was no good punishing sheep stealing by hanging if judges refused to convict because of the severity of the punishment. There may indeed be legitimate economic, political and administrative reasons for not imposing its equivalent on governmental contractors. But there are less immediately disruptive possibilities which may be effective in the long run. For example, it is possible under American law to allow one contract to be completed while insisting that no further agreements can be reached with one or all government departments if disobedience persists. These intermediate sanctions are not used enough in the United States and, if given proper consideration in Britain, could allay genuine political fears of the idea of contract compliance.

Dispelling myths

Action specifically aimed at reducing segregation through the law and collective bargaining needs to be accompanied by continuing persuasion and education. Employers' perceptions of womanhood, of what jobs women can or cannot do and of their attachment to the labour market have been discussed several times in this book. These beliefs are often still shared by trade unionists and even by women themselves. This is a common characteristic of dominant ideologies. Indeed, they can only dominate if they are accepted by their victims. And they are strongest when they appear, even to their victims, to have some basis in reality. It is of course true that there are women who conform to stereotypical assumptions about their family roles and the secondary significance of jobs held by wives. But they may not always do so because they believe this to be right but rather because there seems no worthwhile alternative. Evidence that supports the understanding of ideology in dual labour market theories is becoming overwhelming. Public statistics, research by the TUC itself, the EOC and independent academics show more and more of what has been acknowledged in the United States since the 1960s: that wives' incomes are not a luxury; that, in any case, the number of single parent families is rising dramatically, that women with paid jobs work regularly for most of their lives; and that, in any case, men are no longer conforming to what employers describe as the pattern of employment that is rewarded by higher pay and better opportunities. More and more women believe the present state of affairs to be unfair, even if they are not prepared to go or cannot go to the law. It appears increasingly obvious that the consequences of these perceptions are that employers can recruit women, who often have to be exceptionally well-qualified, to jobs for which they can be paid badly. This is particularly evident in part-time work which, whatever the sex of the job holder, is characterised often by higher productivity but which, as it happens, is mostly female and usually paid at lower hourly rates.

The EOC is right in saying that much humdrum work needs to be done to correct prejudice and misperceptions. This is all the more true if positive steps are to be taken by employers and trade unions like the 'outreach' components of American affirmative action plans. The EOC's own research reports and those commissioned by it are useful adjuncts to legal and voluntary action and in challenging employers' attitudes. Employers' assertions that it is inappropriate for the law to regulate working practices should be treated sceptically. Apart from evidence in Britain that the Commission's gentle approach has caused complacency, the attitudes of American corporate managers are enlightening. Facing a far bigger panoply of regulations, they feel obliged to protest in public about the administrative costs of unnecessary and complex governmental intervention. But at least some are prepared to admit in private that, irritation over details apart, the laws have forced them to modernise structures and procedures and that, in the long run, this reduces labour costs.[30]

Ultimately, however, equality at work depends not solely on anti-discrimination policies, but on wider social considerations that go beyond existing or modified equal opportunity laws.

The future

The relationship between paid employment and family

Chapter 1 referred to the view of Chiplin and Sloane that changes may be taking place in the conventional division of private and public spheres. Recently, researchers have been prepared to argue that in both countries the extensive increase in labour market participation by women is accompanied by an equally dramatic rise in men wishing to be more involved in family life.[31] Laws about equal rights at work do not deal systematically with family issues. The British Sex Discrimination Act bans discrimination because of marital status and American case law does not allow motherhood to be a justification on its own for different treatment. Moreover, other laws – dealing with taxation, social services, and families – actively discourage the equal rights and duties for men and women in the private sphere that are necessary for equal rights at work. Although only 5 per cent of British families conform to the supposed norm of a husband in paid employment, a wife at home and two children,[32] these laws, despite some changes, continue in important respects to assume that men are legally heads of households, are the only or main economic supporters of them and that women are primarily 'carers'. Similar changes in family structure are also evident in America. And some States, which are the main law-makers in family policy, have removed discrimination in laws about custody of children and their maintenance. However, federal law which assists families with dependent children was criticised in the 1970s because its eligibility criteria actually encouraged the break-up of families. In effect, this increased the numbers of poor women rather than men with dependent children.

In the 1980s, cuts in the allocation of such aid, granted through states, is imposing further burdens on single parent families. In the 1970s and 1980s, reduced expenditure on health and social services has forced people in need of care 'out into the community'. As in Britain, this often means into the care of female relatives. Improvements have been made in Britain in some aspects of social security and in allowances for dependent children but harrowing accounts exist of the

hardship and humiliation imposed by the workings of regulations about invalid housewives and the care of disabled
relatives, which appear to assume that women do not need paid
employment, are able to care for themselves in the home and
are available to look after relatives in need.[33] The EOC has
protested about this and women's groups and the TUC have
expressed concern. For EOC suggestions – which is all they can
be under existing law – to be shown to have some force, serious
campaigns are needed.

British tax regulations, as they stand, assume that, unless
otherwise requested, wives earnings belong for tax purposes to
husbands and that there are no automatic rights of privacy or
separate treatment for women.[34] The secondary status
attached to wives earnings exists even where a husband is
unemployed. The problem is not simply one of wording and
dignity. Higher allowances for married men mean that single
people and married women, even if they have won equal pay,
will take home less than married men. What is to count as a tax
deductable expense is also a problem for women in Britain,
where a single mother cannot claim the costs of child care as a
legitimate deduction from her taxable income. In the United
States, working parents can claim such an expense in Federal
tax assessments. In Britain, there are widespread demands for
reform, of which this might be one. But in neither country can
such a provision remove the problems of poor families and
poverty is one of the principal objections to eliminating the
married man's allowance in Britain. But it is not impossible to
devise a scheme that is sexually fair and which protects
children. Income gained from giving married men the same tax
relief as single people and married women could be used, as the
NCCL and others recommend, to increase allowances paid
directly to those responsible for the care of children and
dependent relatives. Women in the Conservative Party are as
concerned as others, who include men disadvantaged by the
present system, and, although favoured solutions vary at
present, it might well be possible to develop a cohesive
campaign.

It is even possible to consider direct action. In 1983, some
members of British religious organisations which are pacifist
argued for a right to withhold that amount of tax that is

estimated to be spent on defence. In the United States, where welfare provisions embody even more than in Britain the idea of personal responsibility for 'failure', it will be extremely difficult for a restoration of benefits to be part of a tax package. But even the middle classes were alarmed by the consequences of their tax revolt in California, which led to sudden reductions in public services. A proposed Constitutional amendment requiring all States to balance budgets has lost its initial appeal. Nevertheless liberal Democrats and Republicans have an uphill struggle to reinstate both benefits and services.

Arrangements for childbirth and child-care also need attention if equality in both spheres is to be realised. In Britain, state benefits and employment rights in respect of *maternity*, dealt with in the Employment Protection Act, are inflexible. In contrast, American judicial rulings insist on flexibility in dates of departure from employment. On the other hand, they have also limited the provision of benefits provided by insurance schemes. In both countries interest exists in *paternity* provision. In Britain a recent report shows that this interest spans classes but that present arrangements mean that it costs working-class men proportionately more than middle-class men to take time off at the birth of a child.[35] The report also shows that a vast majority of men favour a negotiated paternity leave agreement which would not lead to excessive losses of pay or annual leave. The TUC is campaigning for statutory provision but there is nothing to stop individual unions from carrying out what many members would like at individual places of employment.

Child-care is, of course, a longer term business than childbirth and it is clear that a mixture of provision is necessary for different children at different stages. At present this is coped with in Britain, as in America, by a mixture of private arrangements, flexible attitudes to employment by women when children are young, some work-place provision and by the education system.[36] Negotiated arrangements need to be an important component of any agreed positive action programme and may be more forthcoming than campaigns for better public provision of crèches and nurseries. If fathers are concerned to be available at the time of birth, then it might be reasonable to assume that they would be prepared, too, to share responsibility in later family difficulties like sickness or school holidays.

Such a provision might also be worked into paternal leave agreements. But, if equality at work cannot be achieved without equality at home, it is important to think of an undifferentiated set of *parental* responsibilities and to campaign not for better maternity or paternity leave but for agreed parental leave and benefits for *all* employees with children. Proposals for such reforms have been criticised for failing to take into account fully the way in which paternal contributions continue to be seen as 'help' rather than shared duties, that this continues to force women into being flexible about the jobs they accept and their hours and duration and that this, in turn, enables employers to exploit them as home-workers, part-time workers or seasonal workers.[37] But cause and effect are not clear-cut. While laws and employment practices relating to the family remain as they are, incentives for a radical reconstruction of public and private life are weak. Unemployment could provide a material condition for rethinking a whole range of social phenomena; but it needs careful handling.

Unemployment and equality

The argument that unemployment makes equality policies impossible has a certain simplistic appeal. Up to a point it can be rebutted by the idea that quite a lot can still be done because of turnover rates. However, involuntary redundancies, which are not followed by the employment of new people, are now widespread in both countries. At the same time, although there are fewer full-time jobs, people are being told that hard work is necessary for recovery. Employers are exhorted to modernise work processes and yet the very modernising technology that is required will itself diminish the demand for labour. It is not just factories, newspapers and railways that might be so revolutionised. It is even possible to envisage education and shopping with fewer teachers, sales assistants and bank clerks because of video equipment and computer terminals in the home. It seems likely that economic recovery will mean permanently high unemployment if work continues to be construed as it is today.

What is needed, then, in both countries is not the tired call for harder work but a reassessment of what it means to hold a job. This reassessment must be based on an intelligent understanding of what is already obvious in the labour market. At the moment, policy makers, employers and trade unions treat full-time work as normal and part-time work as deviant. But as Drew points out, apart from high unemployment, the average hours of full-time workers is declining in Western Europe while the hours of part-time workers vary up to over thirty-five hours a week.[38] Further reductions in full-time hours are being recommended by the EEC and trade unions which would make the distinction between the two even less clear. This means that the chance exists to end the supposition that part-time jobs are 'women's' jobs and that full-time workers are, and should be, primarily male. Since the idea of reduced hours for full-time workers is welcomed and since the hours of part-time work are in fact so varied, it is therefore possible to consider ways of sharing existing job opportunities that would enable men to participate equally in family life and women equally at work. Economic necessity leading to different employment patterns as well as changing values about work and family roles makes it rational to consider properly protected job sharing schemes. It may also be possible for men and women to choose to work at home in circumstances that are less exploitable than those suffered by most female home-workers today. A new approach to job holding would involve a flexible combination for either sex, of work at home of a domestic or paid nature, work outside which may vary in hours or seasonally, and special arrangements for parents.

However, considerable care is needed in ensuring that what is now going on anyway takes a form that is fair and as satisfying as possible for everyone. First of all, rising unemployment can and does induce fear, suspicion and divisiveness. Belief that protected groups compete with each other has already weakened the civil rights coalition in the United States. And there and in Britain immediate and thoughtless political reactions are that women should stay at home. This solution misses the point that work is still largely divided into 'women's' and 'men's' occupations. Nevertheless the idea that, whatever the reality, 'a woman's place is in the home' has hardly been buried and is susceptible to revival. The danger is that to reconstruct ideas about work and actual practices needs exactly that co-operation that recession is discouraging.

This is because workers in home, part-time and seasonal employment as constituted at present are vulnerable. As Drew points out, this kind of work is generally offered because it reduces labour costs. Productivity is often higher, and workers are often prepared to 'stay on for a bit' to 'help out'. Such workers are often not organised and legislation guaranteeing minimum wages and protecting terms and conditions does not cover those at home or in short term employment and often excludes part-timers. It is in the economic interests of employers to allow a restructuring of work to increase this kind of vulnerability. And this is expressed in political interest in simple job splitting schemes which do not carry the same protection of conditions and of career opportunities that are part of pressure group and trade union ideas about job-sharing. Related to a restructuring of work and family life is the question of policies to deal with social instability induced by enforced leisure. This goes beyond the immediate scope of this book but should not be ignored by those who see the possibility of a civilised society in the ashes of economic failure.

If this seems hopelessly utopian, it is not, in fact, unrealistic; because eventually the very political and economic leaders who insist that technological innovation is necessary will have to acknowledge that they cannot simultaneously extol the old virtues of work and obedience to the law and introduce changes that make it impossible to realise these values. But they must not be allowed to reconcile the contradictions in their own way. For this, the divide-and-rule consequences of depression and the re-emergence of outmoded orthodoxies must be resisted with fierceness and intelligence. There is an urgent need for cohesive and thoughtful pressure at all levels of political, economic and social life according to what is appropriate in the two countries.

Afterword

Most of the research for this book was originally undertaken for the preparation of a thesis. Although a thesis is supposed to embody material of a publishable standard, the objectives of writing a thesis and a book often diverge. Usually the conflict arises because a thesis is expected to deal with important theoretical issues while a book is intended to appeal to a wider community of readers interested in the substantive but not necessarily the academic aspects of the subject. At the substantive level, my motivations for writing the thesis and the book are the same. I am a woman and an egalitarian. My feminism commits me to what Janet Radcliffe Richards calls 'a sexually just society' (*The Sceptical Feminist*, London: Routledge & Kegan Paul, 1980). This is what made me want to find out about developments in and impediments to the political and economic emancipation of women. And this is what made me wish to try to convey to others the hopes, advances, frustrations, set-backs and possibilities that characterise one of the most important aspects of that story; women's rights at work.

As a student of politics, however, I also have an academic interest in the more general political and methodological problems and controversies that arise from a study of equality policies. In writing the thesis, I was particularly interested in apparently competing theories of how and why political change occurs in liberal democracies. And I wanted to explore rival ideas about the contributions to knowledge of public affairs that could be made by the study of public policy. On the question of political change, the conventional wisdom is that

reforms in liberal democracies are the culmination of a long,
drawn-out process involving discussion of ideas among isolated
individuals and their popularisation through pressure groups
and parties. Eventually representative and responsible
governments acknowledge public opinion by passing new laws
and instructing administrations to put them into practice.
'Diffusion of Innovation' theorists like J. Walker (*American
Political Science Review*, vol. 63, no. 3, Sept. 1969) challenge this
by pointing out the frequency with which political leaders,
looking for innovations for whimsical reasons, 'borrow' reforms
from other political systems. The hasty and ill-considered
manner in which this happens is thought to preclude discussion
of different circumstances and this is expected to lead to
ineffectiveness in the system to which solutions are transplanted. The prediction in the model invites a comparative
study of implementation of 'borrowed' policies. But, although
America is often posited as a 'leader' in legally protecting civil
rights and although British politicians self-consciously
'borrowed' when framing the Sex Discrimination Act, the
evidence in this policy area is too contradictory to be used to
support or to undermine the theory. Nevertheless, comparing
implementation is not pointless from the academic point of
view. This is because of the growth from political science of
policy analysis. By its stress on implementation, policy analysis
can help to break down the conventional distinction between
politics and administration, the artificiality of which is evident
in enforcement of equality policies. For some policy analysts,
however, the main justification for comparing policies is that it
can provide a substitute for the controlled experimentation that
is the methodology of the natural scientist. In this way, policy
analysis is thought to be a tool for improving the technical
efficiency of public innovations. But this approach can be
criticised because it often assumes too narrow a conception of
rationality in which, as T. Lowi points out, political considerations and values are defined as irrational. (In S. Nagel
(ed.), *Policy Studies and the Social Sciences*, Lexington: D. C. Heath
& Co., 1975 and in D. Ashford (ed.), *Comparing Public Policies*,
Beverley Hills and Sage, 1978.) However, another impetus to
comparative study is that those very values and the power
relations between holders of competing values can be illumi-

nated by examining the processes of policy formation and implementation across states (D. Ashford, ibid).

Sustained discussion of these academic controversies has been excluded from this book because they are perhaps too esoteric and distracting for readers who are primarily interested in the substantive question of women's rights. I am grateful, therefore, to colleagues for having given me the opportunity to discuss the theoretical and methodological issues in a paper at the Public Administration Committee Conference at York University in 1982.

Many of those to whom I am indebted in the preparation of the thesis are also those to whom I owe thanks for assistance in writing this book. The then Social Science Research Council granted me a three-year Studentship award and, in times of hardship, generously funded fieldwork in Britain and the United States. Additional fieldwork funds were provided by the American Politics Group of the Political Studies Association. My research in the United States would have failed had it not been for the help of innumerable individuals in the corporations, pressure groups, trade unions, parties, agencies and departments that are discussed in this book. I am also grateful to staff and students in the City University of New York, Columbia University, Smith College, Wellesley College and the Wellesley College Center for Research on Women. So many gave so generously that they cannot all be named. Nor would I wish to embarrass any of them. Most are cited in this book in their institutional locations and I ask them and others to accept my thanks through the following: E. Bloomfield, A. Callan, M. Cunliffe, D. and B. Coleman, M. Eisenstein, J. Goldstein and his family and friends, D. Green, R. S. Ratner, S. and R. Ross, B. Sheppard, T. Straub and S. and Z. Wing. Above all, I should like to thank Elizabeth Durbin and Florence and Bob Perman for their generosity, assistance with and continuing interest in my work. I am also grateful to Joyce Gelb and Connie Myers for their assistance on my return to Britain.

In Britain, too, fieldwork would have been impossible without the co-operation of members of many of the companies, pressure groups, trade unions, parties and public institutions which feature in the book. For reasons of confidentiality not all individuals can be thanked personally. But I should like especially to thank the Equal Opportunities Commission through Christine Jackson and Lady Elspeth Howe who introduced me to Florence Perman. I should like to thank the Commission through Ethel Chipchase and also to convey my thanks to trade unions through her and Anne Gibson. I also owe thanks to British parties and parties in the European Parliament through Joyce Gould, Caroline Jackson and Baroness Seear. I would also like to thank the staff of the National Council for Civil Liberties, the Women's Research and Resources Centre and, through Catherine Dennis, the Fawcett Society. I am also grateful for the sources I have had access to as a member of these bodies and of the Equal Pay and Opportunities Campaign. I should also like thank J. Airey for showing her private papers.

In both countries, the courtesy and helpfulness of librarians and archivists responsible for special collections of papers was of considerable importance. In particular, I should like to thank the keepers of the Sophia Smith Collection in Smith College, of the papers of the National Council for Civil Liberties in Hull University and of the Fawcett Society papers in the City of London Polytechnic.

Academic guidance, practical help and moral support were given unstintingly during the preparation of the thesis by the Warden, Fellows, students and all staff of Nuffield College. I extend warm thanks to them all through my supervisors, D. E. Butler and L. J. Sharpe and through C. Bliss, K. Hope, W. McCarthy and P. M. Williams. Developments in my ideas for the thesis and the book also occurred because of opportunities to discuss my work with staff and students in other universities, especially at Sussex, Bath, Bristol and the Research Unit on Ethnic Relations at Aston. I should like to convey my thanks to them through R. J. Benewick, M. David, B. C. Smith and J. Solomos. I am particularly grateful to Claire Callender, who was kind enough to give me a copy of her own dissertation submitted at Bristol University and to Alan Butt-Phillip of the Bath Centre for European Industrial Studies for passing on European sources.

Members of various academic groups collectively and singly also invited me to discuss my research, opportunities for which I am grateful. I should like to thank everyone in the American

Politics Group and Women and Politics Group of the Political Studies Association, the South West Women's Caucus of the British Sociological Association and the Oxford University Sexual Politics Group and Women's Studies Group. Miriam David, Joni Lovenduski, Margherita Rendel and Sandy Fredman were particularly generous in helping with sources arising from their own research or in commenting on my work or in both. I owe a special debt of gratitude to Vicky Randall, not only for the same reasons, but also for her readiness to show me her own draft manuscript for *Women and Politics* recently also published by Macmillan.

In the final stages, colleagues and friends were again prepared to read my manuscript and I extend warm thanks to Brian Smith and John Cullis for doing so. I have also been blessed by the extraordinary fortune that brought Alice Leonard to Bath and to its Centre for Applied Social Policy. She, too, paid close attention to my manuscript. Moreover, she was prepared, amidst her own preoccupations with research into industrial tribunals to feed me with up-to-date sources on legal issues in both countries and to discuss their implications. Most of the secretarial staff in the School of Humanities and Social Sciences at Bath had a hand in typing bits of the thesis and the book. I should like to thank them all through Nicky King. She shared with two others – Joyce Adam and Julie Swinburne – the main part of the burden. To the three, I am especially grateful. Needless to say, none of those to whom I owe such immense debts of gratitude bears any responsibility for my own shortcomings. Mistakes and misinterpretations are entirely my own doing.

Finally, many friends have made life easier for me during the tensions that inevitably accompany such an undertaking as this. I should like to thank them all. But, in particular, I have been glad of the friendship of my politics colleagues, Roger Eatwell, Brian Neve and Brian Smith. And I have been sustained by the moral and practical support of Bob Benewick, Edward Horesh, Suzanne Skevington and Julie Swinburne.

Appendix 1
List of Groups Involved
in Equality Campaigns

Britain

List of organisations revealed in research to have participated to a greater or lesser extent in campaigns for equality at work. Some are trade unions, sections of political parties, or politically funded bodies. Others are pressure groups, some of which are 'umbrella' organisations to which others, sometimes listed, sometimes not, are affiliated for specific purposes. The list contains 108 organisations. At least another 100 women's organisations exist, some of which espouse feminist issues; others are anti-egalitarian; most are engaged in cultural, religious or sporting activities.

Actresses Franchise League.
All Party Equal Rights Group.
Amalgamated Union of Engineering Workers.
APEX.
Associated Countrywomen of the World.
Association of Broadcasting and Allied Staff.
Association of Headmistresses.
Association of Assistant Mistresses in Secondary Schools.
Association of Moral and Social Hygiene.
Association of Scientific Staffs and Engineering Technicians.
Association of Scientific Technical and Managerial Staff.
Association of Teachers of Domestic Subjects.
British Commonwealth League of Women.
British Federation of University Women.
Campaign for Financial and Legal Independence.
Co-operative Women's Guild.

Concert Artistes Association.
Confederation of Shipbuilding and Engineering Unions.
Conservative Women's National Advisory Committee.
Council for the Single Parent and Her Dependants.
Council of Women Civil Servants.
Cruse Organisation for Widows.
Electrical Association for Women.
Equal Pay Campaign.
Equal Pay Coordinating Committee.
Equal Pay and Opportunities Campaign.
Fawcett Society: Formerly London Association for Suffrage, London and
    National Society for Women's Service.
Federation of Soroptimist Clubs.
General and Municipal Workers Union.
Guild of Insurance Office Staff.
Housewives Register.
Institute of Qualified Personal Secretaries.
International Alliance of Women for Suffrage and Equal Citizenship.
International Alliance of Women.
Inter-Organisational Committee sponsored by Fawcett Society.
Josephine Butler Society.
Legal Action Group.
London and National Society for Women's Service.
Married Women's Association.
Medical Women's Federation.
Mineworkers Federation.
Mothers' Union.
National Advisory Centre for Careers for Women.
National Association of Local Government Employees.
National Association for One Parent Families.
National Association of Probation Officers.
National Association of the Self Employed.
National Association of Women Citizens.
National Association of Women's Clubs.
National Council for Civil Liberties.
National Council for Social Service.
National Council of Women of Great Britain.
National Federation of Business and Professional Women's Clubs.
National Federation of Women's Institutes.
National Joint Committee of Working Women's Organisations.
National Labour Women's Advisory Committee.
National Organisation for Women (London chapter of US organisation).
National Union of Journalists.
National Union of Public Employees.
National Union of Students.
National Union of Teachers.
National Union of Townswomen's Guilds.
National Union of Women Workers.

Open Door Council.
Over Forty Association of Women Workers.
Post Office Engineers.
Rights of Women.
Royal College of Midwives.
Royal College of Nursing.
Runnymede Trust.
St Joan's Alliance: Formerly The Catholic Women's Suffrage Society.
Six Point Group.
South Wales Miners.
Standing Conference of Women's Organisations.
Status of Women Committee.
Suffragette Fellowship.
Tailors and Garment Workers Union.
TASS.
Trades Union Congress and its Women's Advisory Committee.
Transport and General Workers Union.
Union of Shop Distributive and Allied Workers.
Union of Women Teachers.
Wages for Wives.
Women in Building.
Women's Engineering Society.
Women's Farm and Garden Association.
Women's Forum: Formerly Women's Group on Public Welfare.
Women's Freedom League (Breakaway from Women's Social and Political
    Union).
Women's Gas Federation and Young Homemakers.
Women's Guild of Empire.
Women's Human Rights Movement.
Women's Information and Study Centre.
Women's International League for Peace and Freedom.
Women's Liberal Federation.
Women's Liberation Workshop.
Women's Lobby.
Women in the Media.
Women's National Commission.
Women in Parliament.
Women Public Health Officers Association.
Women's Publicity Planning Association.
Women's Report Editorial Collective.
Women's Research and Resources Centre.
Women Solicitors Group.
Working Women's Centre.
World Association of Girl Guides and Scouts.
Young Women's Christian Association.

America

List of organisations revealed in research and by Freeman (The Politics of Women's Liberation) that participated to a greater or lesser extent in promoting equality for working women; or that supported President Carter's Reorganisation Project. The list is very selective. It does not include all unions, etc with women's rights programmes, nor does it include all of the many of groups thought to exist, especially locally based organisations of national organisations.
(Examples of these are Chicago Women's Liberation, New York Radical Women, Seattle Radical Women, all the chapters of the National Organisation for Women)

Amalgamated Clothing Workers.
American Civil Liberties Union.
American Council of the Blind.
American Federation of Government Employees.
American Federation of Labor – Congress of Industrial Organizations.
American Federation of State County and Municipal Employees.
American GI Forum of the United States.
Anti-Defamation League of B'Nai B'Rith.
Asian-American Legal Defense and Education Fund.
Asociacion Nacional Pro Personas Mayores.
Center for Law and Social Policy.
Center for Women's Policy Studies.
·Church Women United.
Cleveland Women Working.
Coalition of Labor Union Women.
Commissions on Status of Women (Federal and State).
Communication Workers Union.
Congress of Cities.
Congressional Black Caucus.
Dayton Women Working.
Disability Rights Center.
Federally Employed Women.
Federation of Organizations for Professional Women.
Gray Panthers.
Human Rights for Women.
International Association of Official Human Rights Agencies.
International Ladies Garment Workers Union.
Lawyers Committee for Civil Rights Under Law.
League for Academic Women.
League of American Working Women.
League of Women Voters.
Legal Research Services for the Elderly.
Martin Luther King Center for Social Change.
Mexican American Legal Defense Fund.
National Alliance of Postal and Federal Employees.

National Association for the Advancement of Colored People and NAACP
Legal Defense and Education Fund.
National Association of Retired Persons.
National Bar Association.
National Black Caucus of Local Black Elected Officials.
National Black Feminist Organization.
National Business League.
National Catholic Conference for International Justice.
National Coalition of American Nuns.
National Coalition for Women and Girls in Education.
National Conference of Puerto Rican Women.
National Council on the Aging.
National Caucus on the Black Aged.
National Council of Negro Women.
National Council of Senior Citizens.
National Education Association.
National Federation of Federal Employees.
National Federation of Independent Business.
National Indian Council on Aging.
National Organization for Women and NOW Legal and Education Defense
Fund.
National Retired Teachers Association.
National Small Business Association.
National Student Association.
National Urban League.
National Urban Coalition.
National Women's Party.
National Women's Political Caucus.
Operation Push.
Opportunities Industrialization Center.
Professional Women's Caucus.
Project on the Status and Education of Women.
Puerto Rican Legal Defense and Education Fund.
St Joan's Alliance (US counterpart of British organisation).
Southern Christian Leadership Conference.
A. Philip Randolph Institute.
Retail Clerks International Union.
Teamsters Union.
United Automobile Workers.
Wider Opportunities for Women.
Women's Action Alliance.
Women's Board of Methodist Church.
Women's Caucus of American Political Science Association.
Women's Caucus of American Psychological Association.
Women's Caucus of American Sociological Association.
Women Employed.
Women's Equity Action League.
Women Inc.

Women's Legal Defense Fund.
Women's Lobby Inc.
Women Office Workers.
World Committee of Islam in the West.
Young Women's Christian Association.

Appendix II
List of Major Cases Cited

Britain

Albion Shipping Agency v. *Arnoly* [1981] IRLR 525
Capper Pass Ltd v. *Lawton* [1976] IRLR 366
Clarke and Powell v. *Eley (IMI Kynoch Ltd)* [1982] IRLR 131
Clay Cross (Quarry Services Ltd) v. *Fletcher* [977] IRLR 258; [1978] IRLR 361
Dick v. *University of Dundee* 1983 EOC Case Note 4
Dugdale v. *Kraft Foods Ltd* [1976] IRLR 368; [1976] IRLR 204
Electrolux Ltd v. *Hutchinson and Others* [1976] IRLR 410; [1976] IRLR 289
Garland v. *British Rail Engineering Ltd* [1978] IRLR 8; [1979] IRLR 244; [1982] IRLR 247
Handley v. *H. Mono Ltd* [1979] IRLR 534
Jenkins v. *Kingsgate (Clothing Productions) Ltd* [1980] IRLR 6
McCarthy's Ltd v. *Smith* [1979] ICR 785
Meeks v. *National Union of Agricultural and Allied Workers* [1976] IRLR 198
Nasse v. *Science Research Council* [1978] IRLR 201; [1978] IRLR 352; [1979] IRLR 465
Ojutiku v. *Manpower Services Commission* [1981] ICR 515
Oxford v. *DHSS* [1977] IRLR 225
Peake v. *Automotive Products Ltd* [1977] IRLR 366; [1979] ICR 968
Pointon v. *University of Sussex* [1977] IRLR 295; [1979] IRLR 119
Price v. *Civil Service Commissioners* [1976] IRLR 405; [1977] IRLR 291; [1978] IRLR 3
Snoxell v. *Vauxhall Motors Ltd* [1977] IRLR 123
Sorbie and others v. *Trust House Forte Ltd* [1976] IRLR 371
Waddington v. *Leicester Council for Voluntary Service* [1977] IRLR 32

United States

Albemarle Paper Co v. *Moody*, 422 US 405 1975
American Tobacco Co v. *John Patterson*, 80 US 1194 1982
Brush v. *San Francisco Newspaper Printing Co*, 9th Circuit 1972
Cleveland Board of Education v. *La Fleur*, 414 US 632 1974
Corning Glass Works v. *Brennan*, 417 US 188 1974
County of Washington v. *Gunther*, 101 US 2242 1981
Defunis v. *Odergaard*, 416 US 312 1974
Diaz v. *Pan American Inc*, 5th Circuit 1971
Fernandez v. *Wynn Oil Co*, 9th Circuit 1981
Franks v. *Bowman*, 74 US 728 1976
Frontiero v. *Richardson*, 411 US 611 1973
General Telephone Co of Southwest v. *Falcon*, – US – 1982
Gilbert v. *General Electric Co*, 429 US 125 1976
Green v. *Waterford Board of Education*, 2nd Circuit 1973
Griggs v. *Duke Power Co*, 401 US 424 1971
Hodgson v. *Brookhaven General Hospital*, 5th Circuit 1970
Hodgson v. *Daisy Manufacturing*, 8th Circuit 1971
Hodgson v. *Fairmont Supply Co*, 4th Circuit 1971
Hodgson v. *Security National Bank*, 8th Circuit 1972
Hodgson v. *Golden Isles Convalescent Home Inc*, 5th Circuit 1972
Hodgson v. *Behrens Drug Co*, 5th Circuit 1973
Leisner v. *New York Telephone Co*, 358 F. Supp. 359 SDNY 1973 (5 FEB cases 732)
McDonnell Douglas Corp v. *Green*, 411 US 792 1973
Meadows v. *Ford Motor Co*, 62 FRD 98 WDKy 1973 (5 FEP cases 665) 510 F2D 939
Morrow v. *Mississippi Publishing Corp*, SD MISS 1972
Phillips v. *Martin Marietta Corp*, 400 US 542 1971
Pittsburgh Press Co v. *Pittsburgh Commission of Human Relations*, 98 US 5/5 1973
Regents of University of California v. *Bakke*, 438 US 265 1978
Rosenfeld v. *Southern Pacific Co*, 9th Circuit 1971
Shultz v. *First Victoria National Bank*, 5th Circuit 1969
Shultz v. *Wheaton Glass*, 3rd Circuit 1970
Shultz v. *American Can Co*, 8th Circuit 1970
Sprogis v. *United Airlines*, 7th Circuit 1971
Wilson v. *South-West Airlines*, 131 N.D. Texas 1981

End-notes

See 'Books, Articles and Unpublished Research', p. 234, for full references to the works cited.

Chapter 1

1. J. Walker, 'The Diffusion of Innovations Among the American States', *American Political Science Review*, vol. 63, no. 3 (September 1969). D. P. Moynihan, *SSRC Newsletter*, No. 10 (1970).
2. R. Goodin, 'Banana Time in British Politics', *Political Studies*, vol. xxx, no. 1 (March 1982) pp. 42–58.
3. S. Nagel (ed.), *Policy Studies and the Social Sciences* (Lexington: D. C. Heath & Co, 1975).
4. D. Ashford (ed.), *Comparing Public Policies* (Beverley Hills: Sage, 1978) especially pp. 12–14, 82, 83.
5. G. Routh, *Occupation and Pay in Great Britain 1906–1960* (Cambridge University Press, 1965).
6. W. Creighton, *The Development of the Legal Status of Women in Employment in Great Britain*, Doctoral Thesis (Cambridge University, 1973).
7. *Department of Employment Gazette* (London: December 1976) 1396. The Equal Pay Act had been passed in 1970 but compliance was voluntary until 1975.
8. J. Kreps (ed.), *Women and the American Economy* (New Jersey: Prentice-Hall, 1976) p. 13. United States Department of Labor, *1975 Handbook on Women Workers*, Bulletin 297 (Washington, 1975) p. 156.
9. The Equal Pay Act was passed in 1963 and the Civil Rights Act in 1964.
10. L. Mackie and P. Patullo, *Women at Work* (London: Tavistock, 1977) p. 41. Department of Employment (1976) *Gazette*, 1396.
11. Office of Manpower Economics, *Equal Pay Report* (London: HMSO, 1972) pp. 51, 67–83.
12. C. Hakim, *Occupational Segregation*, Research Paper No. 9 (London: Department of Employment, 1979) pp. 3–4, 8–13.

13. United States Department of Labor, *Bulletin* 297, p. 1.
14. Hakim, *Occupational Segregation*, ch. 3.
15. Routh, *Occupation and Pay in Great Britain*, pp. 44–8. Census data 1961, 1966 (10 per cent sample). Department of Employment (1976) *Gazette*, N. Seear, Research Paper 11, *Royal Commission on Trade Unions and Employers' Associations* (London: HMSO, 1968) 2, 3.
16. The following paragraph is a summary of information gathered from: Census data 1961 and 1966 (10 per cent sample). Seear, Research Paper 11, p. 3. New Earnings Survey Data, Office of Manpower Economics, *Equal Pay Report*, p. 51.
17. United States Department of Labor, *Bulletin* 2080, pp. 10–11.
18. Discussed by Hakim, *Occupational Segregation*, p. 46.
19. B. Chiplin and P. Sloane, *Sex Discrimination in the Labour Market* (London: Macmillan, 1976).
20. R. Barron and G. Norris, 'Sexual Divisions and the Dual Labour Market', in D. Barker and S. Allen (eds), *Dependence and Exploitation in Work and Marriage* (London: Longmans, 1976) pp. 47–69.
21. Confederation of British Industry and Engineering Employers Federation, *Minutes of Evidence and Proceedings of House of Lords Select Committee on Anti-Discrimination Bill* (London, 1972/3). Report of the Committee on Private Employment, President Kennedy's Commission on the Status of Women (Washington, 1963) 34–9.
22. United States Department of Labor, *Bulletin* 297, pp. 204–7.
23. L. Thurow, *Generating Inequality* (London: Macmillan, 1975). Hakim, *Occupational Segregation*, argues that, depending on different historical circumstances, gender, region, race or religious affiliation may come to service as screening devices in differentiation between groups.
24. Seear, Research Paper 11, p. 6.
25. Labour Party, *Discrimination Against Women* (London, 1972).
26. United States Department of Labor, *Bulletin* 297, p. 232. United States Department of Labor, *Women in Apprenticeship – Why Not?*, Manpower Research Monograph No. 33 (Washington, 1970).
27. Chiplin and Sloane, *Sex Discrimination in the Labour Market*. They also provide a useful review of 'demand side' explanations.
28. Barron and Norris, 'Sexual Divisions and the Dual Labour Market'.
29. Some useful sources for the following paragraphs are as follows: P. Dunleavy and K. Hope, *Social Mobility Study*, Nuffield College, 1974. M. Fogarty, A. Allen, I. Allen and P. Walters, *Women in Top Jobs* (London: PEP, Allen & Unwin, 1972). M. Fogarty, R. Rapoport and R. N. Rapoport, *Sex, Career and Family* (London: Allen & Unwin, 1971). A. Hunt, *Survey of Women's Employment* (London: HMSO, 1968). A. Hunt, *Management Attitudes and Practices Towards Women at Work* (London: HMSO, 1975). P. Jephcott, N. Seear and J. Smith, *Married Women Working* (London: Allen & Unwin, 1961). J. King, *Sex Differences and Society*, Manpower Paper No. 10 (London: HMSO, 1975). N. Seear, V. Roberts and J. Brock, *A Career for Women in Industry* (London: LSE, 1964). Seear, *Royal Commission on Trade Unions and Employers' Associations, Women and Work: A Review*, Manpower Paper No. 11 (London: HMSO, 1975).

Minutes of Evidence and Proceedings of House of Lords Select Committee on Anti-Discrimination Bill (London, 1972/3). United States Department of Labor, *Bulletin* 297. United States Department of Labor, *Bulletin* 2080.

30. Hunt, *Management Attitudes*.
31. Ibid.
32. For example, the author has seen heavy equipment that has been converted so as to operate more easily with air pressure. Once lighter, but now comparatively more complicated machinery has not. The former continue to be operated only by men, the latter by women.
33. It is worth noting here that careers for men in management are now characterised, not by long service within one firm, but by considerable mobility between firms in the early stages.
34. Creighton, *The Development of the Legal Status of Women*.
35. J. O'Sullivan and R. Gallick, *Workers and Allies* (Washington: Smithsonian Press, 1975) p. 11. W. H. Chafe, *Women and Equality* (OUP, 1977) p. 14.
36. R. Sennett and R. Cobb, *The Hidden Injuries of Class*, discussed by M. Best and W. Connolly, *The Politicized Economy* (New York: D. C. Heath & Co., 1976) pp. 82–3.
37. Dunleavy and Hope, *Social Mobility Study*. Jephcott, Seear and Smith, *Married Women Working*.

Chapter 2

1. The main sources of information for this section are: O. Banks, *Faces of Feminism* (Oxford: Martin Robertson, 1981). S. Bruley, *Women's Organisations in the UK: A Short History* (London: National Council of Voluntary Organisations, 1980). E. Cary and K. W. Peratis, *Women and the Law* (New York: National Text Book Co./ACLU, 1977). W. H. Chafe, *Women and Equality: Changing Values in American Culture* (Oxford: University Press, 1977). W. H. Chafe in Kreps, *Women and the American Economy*. W. O'Neill, *The Woman Movement: Feminism in the United States and England* (London: Allen & Unwin, 1969). J. O'Sullivan and R. Gallick, *Workers and Allies: Female Participation on the American Trade Union Movement 1824–1976* (Washington: Smithsonian Institution, 1976). V. Randall, *Women and Politics* (London: Macmillan, 1982). A. Sachs and J. H. Wilson, *Sexism and the Law* (London: Martin Robertson, 1978).
2. Brief biographical details about the women referred to in the following paragraphs and suggestions for further reading can be found in O'Neill, *The Woman Movement*.
3. Section 2 of the amendment orders a reduction in State representatives in Federal institutions if States deny voting rights to male citizens over the age of 21.
4. O'Sullivan and Gallick, *Workers and Allies*, p. 13.
5. O'Neill, *The Woman Movement*, p. 95.
6. Chafe, in Kreps, *Women and the American Economy*, p. 7.

7. Letter from Beatrice Webb to Carey Thomas, President of Bryn Mawr College from 1894 to 1922. The letter is undated but Professor Norman Mackenzie who gave the author a copy, estimates it was written in March 1934.
8. Randall, *Women and Politics*, p. 140.
9. War Cabinet Committee on Women in Industry presided over by Mr Justice Atkins (London: Cmd 135, 1918).
10. Randall, *Women and Politics*, pp. 141–2.
11. Thelma Hunter, *Manchester Guardian*, 22 March 1957.
12. Firestone's view, reported by Randall, *Women and Politics*, p. 146.
13. Fogarty, Rapoport and Rapoport, *Sex, Career and Family*, pp. 20–5. Creighton, *The Development of the Legal Status of Women*.
14. Lady Pakenham, *Spectator*, 16 January 1953. Mr Justice Denning, *The Times*, 13 May 1950.
15. J. Bowlby, *Child Care and the Growth of Love* (London: Penguin, 1953), in which he linked mental retardation with maternal deprivation.
16. This is compatible with the view of political sociologists that any social failure in the United States is personalised instead of seen as a consequence of exogenous arrangements over which the individual has little control. See S. M. Lipset, *The First New Nation* (New York: Basic Books Inc., 1963) pp. 268–73.
17. B. Friedan, *The Feminine Mystique* (London: Penguin, 1963) ch. 1.
18. One of the first was by S. Finer, *Anonymous Empire* (London: Pall Mall, 1966).
19. J. Jeffreys, *The Story of the Engineers* (London: Lawrence and Wishart, 1946) pp. 56–7. Most other information on trade union activity is taken from: Creighton, *The Development of the Legal Status of Women*. National Council for Civil Liberties, files housed in Library of University of Hull. A. Potter, 'The Equal Pay Campaign Committee: A Case Study of a Pressure Group', *Political Studies*, vol. 5, no. 1 (February 1957). Trades Union Congress Women's Conference Reports.
20. *Catholic Citizen*, August/September 1963.
21. *Daily Herald*, 1 May 1964.
22. *Daily Telegraph*, 12 July 1967.
23. J. Morton, *New Society*, 8 August 1968.
24. M. Allen, *The Times*, 6 November 1968.
25. Randall, *Women and Politics*, p. 152.
26. See Chapter 3.
27. Allen, *The Times*.
28. *Daily Express*, 3 May 1974.
29. M. Snell, 'The Equal Pay and Sex Discrimination Acts: Their Impact in the Work Place', *Feminist Review*, no. 1 (1979).
30. Page Smith, cited by J. Elshtain, 'Moral Woman and Immoral Man: A Consideration of the Public-Private Split and its Political Ramifications', *Politics and Society*, 1974, p. 460.
31. P. Richards, *Parliament and Conscience* (London: Allen & Unwin, 1971) p. 205.

32. For example, according to US Department of Labor, 'civil rights legislation works for women because they make it do so'. Interview, Washington, 1978.
33. J. Barr, *New Society*, 17 December 1964.
34. *The Sunday Times*, 11 June 1967.
35. Barr, *New Society*.
36. C. Callender, 'The Development of the Sex Discrimination Act, 1971–75', dissertation, University of Bristol, 1978.
37. A. Coote and P. Hewitt, in P. Moss and N. Fonda (eds), *Work and the Family* (London: Temple Smith, 1980).
38. A fuller account of this is provided by Potter, 'The Equal Pay Campaign Committee'.
39. M. Faulkener, *The British Federation of Business and Professional Women: An Appreciation*.
40. *The Times*, 15 March 1962. One writer points out that Mrs Cazalet-Keir occupied a very secure place in 'the establishment' which meant that her letters to *The Times* were regularly published. Potter, 'The Equal Pay Campaign Committee', p. 62.
41. *Daily Herald*, 31 January 1963.
42. *The Woman Journalist*, spring 1963.
43. These aims were given weight by the Reith Lecturer, Professor Carstairs, in the winter of 1962–3. His argument about women in British society was that their supposed equality had little reality. *The Sunday Times*, 21 January 1963.
44. *The Times*, 20 June 1963.
45. S. Delaney, *The Sunday Times*, 16 December 1962. R. Stone, *Daily Worker*, 12 March 1964.
46. *Daily Telegraph*, 17 March 1965.
47. Some of its findings are referred to in Chapter 1. The comment on it appeared in the *Observer*, 10 December 1967.
48. See Chapter 5.
49. Randall, *Women and Politics*, pp. 152–4, 166–8.
50. For example, J. Tweedie, *Guardian*, 13 March 1972.
51. Callender, 'The Development of the Sex Discrimination Act, 1971–75', p. 32.
52. Including Fawcett Society, NALGO, Soroptimists, Women in the Media, Women's Liberation, National Advisory Centre for Careers for Women, Women's Group on Public Welfare, Royal College of Midwives, National Union of Students, National Union of Journalists, National Labour Women's Advisory Committee, Women's Liberal Federation, National Federation of Business and Professional Women's Clubs, National Federation of Women's Institutes, National Union of Townswomen's Guilds, Conservative Party Women's Advisory Committee, Institute of Qualified Personal Secretaries, National Society for One Parent Families, Women's Gas Federation and Young Homemakers, Women's Engineering Society, Women's Report, Union of Women Teachers.
53. Betty Lockwood (Labour Women's Advisory Committee and National

Joint Council of Working Women's Organisations) was one who said that she could not campaign on the basis of the whole of 'What Next?'.

54. *The Sun*, 24 July 1974; *Daily Express*, 24 July 1974; *Daily Telegraph*, 24 July 1974; *The Times*, 24 July 1974.
55. *Guardian*, 24 July 1974.
56. Interview, July 1977.
57. Potter, 'The Equal Pay Campaign Committee', p. 51.
58. R. Crossman, *Diaries of a Cabinet Minister*, vol. III (London: Hamish Hamilton and Jonathan Cape, 1977) pp. 27, 790.
59. *Covernote*, September 1969.
60. House of Lords, Official Report 310, col. 137.
61. *Guardian*, 6 July 1967.
62. Randall, *Women and Politics*, p. 152.
63. S. Rowbotham, 'The Beginnings of Women's Liberation in Britain', in M. Wandor (ed.), *The Body Politic* (London: Stage 1, 1972) p. 96.
64. J. Freeman, *The Politics of Women's Liberation* (New York: David McKay & Co., 1975) pp. 59–61.

Chapter 3

1. J. S. Mill was consoled by a supporter in 1867 by the information that there was a British statute which stated that references in law to men should be taken to include women unless otherwise specified. Disraeli felt confident that judges would interpret 'men' and 'male' in the Reform Act literally. He was right. And judicial rulings in both countries over suits involving the vote, and access to higher education provide explicit statements of public attitudes about women. See Sachs and Wilson, *Sexism and the Law*. Cary and Peratis, *Women and the Law*. Randall, *Women and Politics*.
2. In America, State laws about child custody, social security, jury service and criminal offences often differentiate between men and women. The ERA lobby believes that it would be difficult for this to continue if a new norm was set in the Constitution. See Cary and Peratis, *Women and the Law*, ch. 11. Randall discusses this in respect of Britain welfare policy, *Women and Politics*, p. 98 and the EOC has shown that such differentiation persists in public statistics, social security and taxation, Research Bulletin No. 4, Manchester, 1980.
3. *Bulletin* 297, chs VI, VII.
4. Most others followed afterwards with the exception of five southern States: Alabama, Louisiana, Mississippi, North Carolina and Texas, although the last does ban discrimination in pay in the public sector.
5. Subject to favourable rulings in the Supreme Court.
6. K. Ellickson, 'The President's Commission on the Status of Women: Its Formation, Functioning and Contribution'. Unpublished paper, 1976, Walter P. Reuther Library, Wayne State University, Michigan, especially pp. 3–7.
7. Ibid., p. 67.

8. Ibid.

9. President's Commission on the Status of Women, *Report of the Committee on Private Employment*, Washington, 1963. Had later Executive Orders laid responsibilities on the Employment Services Agency some local problems in New York (see Chapter IV) might not have existed.

10. For this and succeeding information, see *Legislative Histories of Titles VII and XI of Civil Rights Act* (Washington Government Printing Office, 1964). D. Robinson, 'Two Movements in Pursuit of Equal Employment Opportunity', *Signs* (spring 1979). Freeman, *The Politics of Women's Liberation*, p. 53. B. Friedan, *It Changed My Life* (New York: Dell, 1977) p. 113.

11. Friedan, *It Changed My Life*.

12. For example, Official Report (OR) 116, col. 715; Official Report 117, col. 1811; Official Report 120, col. 217; Official Report 126, col. 2384; Official Report 129, col. 1539–80; Official Report 145, col. 1890–1947.

13. OR 302, col. 2247.

14. OR 310, cols 2014–96, 2444–566.

15. OR 398, cols 1356–90.

16. Royal Commission on Equal Pay 1944–6 Report, Cmd 6937.

17. OR 454, col. 1539; OR 489 cols 526–9.

18. OR 526, col. 211.

19. Letter to Anne Goodwin, TUC Economic Committee, NCCL file 140/5.

20. NCCL file 140/5. Report of TUC Women's Conference, 1966.

21. *Daily Telegraph*, 12 July 1967.

22. *Daily Telegraph*, 7 December 1967, 11 December 1967.

23. Public estimates of costs were from 2 per cent to 13 per cent depending on the industry (32 per cent in a few) with an average of 5 per cent estimated for the total wage bill. According to M. Corina (*The Times*, 3 October 1969) employers believed that their representatives on the CBI had colluded with the TUC to suppress information about the official estimates and the unrepresentativeness of the sample on which they were based. Given the extent of occupational segregation discussed in Chapter 1, the Treaty of Rome definition would have minimised additions to wage bills throughout industry. The CBI's other line of defence was to try to persuade Mrs Castle to delay the bill until the economy was on a sounder footing (*Guardian*, 18 September 1969). Although she would not postpone its passage, she did, against the wishes of the TUC, agree that compliance should be voluntary for the first five years, provided there was an enabling clause allowing the Secretary of State for Employment to introduce an Order, if necessary, requiring that women's wages become 90 per cent of men's by a certain date.

24. Crossman, *Diaries*, pp. 27, 790. This was wanted by the TUC who tried again in the House through Albert Booth MP; OR 800, cols 572–6; 719–21; 725–30; 736–46.

25. OR 795, cols 933–7.

26. J. Tweedie, *Guardian*, 13 March 1972.

27. OR 830, col. 1844.

28. Interview with member of the then government. His next post brought personal tragedy; as Governor of Bermuda, he was assassinated.

29. *Minutes of Evidence and Proceedings of Select Committee on the Anti-Discrimination Bill (HL) 1971–2, 1972–3* (London: HMSO, 1972, 1973). Attention was especially drawn to: the mutual reinforcement of publicity, research and legal remedies; ways in which individual remedies could be made to have a wide impact on the personnel policies of employers and unions, for example, through class actions and affirmative action; the benefits of being able to monitor compliance; the protection of plaintiffs against retaliation.

30. OR 850, col. 1886; OR 851, col. 1415; *Women's Report*, vol. I issue 3 (Feb/March, 1973).

31. OR (House of Lords), 342 cols 606–64.

32. Mrs Thatcher, who had been among Mrs Castle's congratulators, left the House of Lords in no doubt that, as Secretary of State for Education, she felt there was no need for anti-discrimination measures in this field. *Minutes of Evidence and Proceedings of Select Committee on the Anti-Discrimination Bill.*

33. Callender, 'The Development of the Sex Discrimination Act, 1971–75', pp. 14–15.

34. OR 877, cols 1296–1306.

35. *Equality for Women*, Cmd 5724 (London: HMSO, 1974).

36. Interview, 1977. D. Nandy 'Equal Opportunities for Women', Seminar, Oxford University 1979. The Parliamentary Under-Secretary of State for Employment, John Fraser, told Callender that the Home Secretary had been moved by some of the things he learned when he was in America.

37. Callender, 'The Development of the Sex Discrimination Act, 1971–75', p. 21.

38. Main sources for the information in this and the next two sections are: *Bulletin* 297, ch. 6. M. Player, *Federal Law of Employment Discrimination* (St Paul, Minnesota: West Publishing Co, 1976). Cary and Peratis, *Women and the Law. A Guide to Federal Laws and Regulations Prohibiting Sex Discrimination*, Clearing House Publication 46 (Washington: Civil Rights Commission, rev. ed., 1976). *As Compilation of Federal Laws and Executive Orders for Non-Discrimination and Equal Opportunity Programs*, HRD–78–138 (Washington: General Accounting Office, 1978).

39. See Chapter 4.

40. Other titles of the Civil Rights Act deal with, for example, political rights and are not applicable to women. Matters like credit and education, which are covered by the Sex Discrimination Act, are the subject of separate laws in the United States.

41. Player, *Federal Law of Employment Discrimination*, pp. 144–9 and ch. 4.

42. A hypothetical example of such a rule would be one which required all teachers to be taller than six feet.

43. Discriminatory student admission policies are unlawful, not under the Civil Rights Act, but under Title IX of the Education Act. The employment of staff at all levels is regulated by the Civil Rights Act. But Executive Orders on affirmative action apply to staff and students.

44. The most famous challenges which lay affirmative action open to the charge that the policy is a quota system based simply and solely on racial quotas are those of Defunis and Bakke against universities.
45. Revised Order No. 4 (Washington: 1970).
46. The main sources for this and the next two sections are: *The Equal Pay Act* (London: HMSO, 1970). *The Sex Discrimination Act* (London: HMSO, 1975). Official Reports: House of Commons, vol. 795, cols 913–1038; vol. 800, cols 505–766; vol. 889, cols 513–94; vol. 893, cols 1429–77; vol. 893, cols 1515–1611. Official Reports House of Lords vol. 310, cols 121–63; vol. 310, cols 1063–85; vol. 862, cols 95–192, 1021–1443; vol. 863, cols 979–1276. House of Commons Standing Committee H, March 1970; B, April/May 1975.
47. Mrs Castle estimated that 6 million out of 8.5 million working women would benefit: OR 795, 928.
48. It also deals with matters largely outside the scope of this book and which are treated separately in the United States; i.e. education, and the provision of goods facilities and services.
49. See Chapter 4 and fn. 60.
50. See fn. 42.
51. There are also minor enabling or temporary positive discrimination provisions for single sex schools and political parties.
52. Education complaints are dealt with first by the Department of Education and Science and then, as with other non-employment matters, the County Courts. A small but significant victory was won by Baroness Seear over the time allowed for DES investigation. It was significant because of the Department's reluctance to be covered by the Act.
53. The 'father-son' or 'word of mouth' methods of filling vacancies were common in both countries.
54. OR 800, 765–6.
55. See ch. IV for this and other judicial developments.
56. OR 889, 513. These and the following issues were raised by the Fawcett Society and the Inter-Organisational Committee, NCCL, National Labour Women's Advisory Committee, the Equal Pay and Opportunities Campaign, Women in the Media, Dr Rendel, TUC, Institute of Personnel Management, National Joint Council of Working Women's Organisations, Status of Women Group, British Sociological Association Working Party on Women's Rights. See also OR 893, 1476–7 and Callender, 'The Development of the Sex Discrimination Act, 1971–75', p. 513. Richards (*Parliament and Conscience*, p. 205) argues that, at most, women's lobbies air grievances. The Home Secretary's comments suggest they do more than this. But, according to the first reference at (57), information from the US was of more significance.
57. Interview 1977. Nandy 'Equal Opportunities for Women'.
58. As guest of honour of Fawcett Society in February 1975 to mark International Women's Year. He also referred to the present division of family responsibilities which militated against rapid full equality.
59. OR 893, col. 1459. On one point she has been vindicated. Mr Callaghan was prepared to forget Labour Party objections to contract compliance

(because most contractors operated in areas of high unemployment) when he suspended a contract with Ford Motor Co., without statutory authorisation, for breaking the pay norm.

60. In retrospect, policy-makers believe they could have pushed through a lot more. They deliberately left out pensions, taxation, social security and maternity because their complexities were expected to lengthen the passage of a bill that they were anxious to pass quickly. Nandy, 'Equal Opportunities for Women'.

61. Carr: 'It is a legitimate function of the law to put on record the judgment of the community about what is fair and reasonable. It is also a legitimate function of the law in practical terms because the law does form opinion and influence behaviour'. OR 795, 932. Gilmour: OR 889, 525–8.

62. OR 893, 1459.

63. OR (HL) 862, 146. He said he could say this since, being half American, he was saying it of himself.

64. Ibid., cols 124, 176.

65. Ellickson, 'The President's Commission on the Status of Women'.

66. Friedan, *It Changed My Life*, p. 19.

67. Crossman, *Diaries*, p. 627.

68. OR 849, col. 1851.

69. Mrs Williams, attributing the quote to Poincaré, said this when supporting Mr Hamilton in 1973. OR 1868.

70. OR 889, col. 513.

71. R. Goodin, 'Banana Time in British Politics', *Political Studies*, vol. xxx (1982) no. 1.

72. For example, Cyril Bence (Labour), OR 497, cols 1786–94, see also Ch. 2, p. 38.

73. Freeman, *The Politics of Women's Liberation*, p. 79.

74. J. Sundquist, *Politics and Policy* (Washington: Brookings Institution, 1968).

75. O. Kerner, *Report of the Advisory Commission on Civil Disorders* (New York: Bantam Books, 1968).

76. The presidential electoral system is discussed in all text books in American politics. A British observer has argued that the alliance of blacks and women is a frighteningly powerful one for American presidents, K. Whitehorn, *Observer*, 22 January 1978. It has also been argued that, as a result, the 'spoils' system came to mean the placation of civil rights groups. H. Heclo, *A Government of Strangers* (Washington: Brookings Institution, 1977) pp. 92–3.

77. A. King (ed.), *The New American Political System* (Washington: American Enterprise Institute, 1978) especially essays by S. Beer and M. Shapiro.

78. Its relationship with organised labour was evidently breaking down by the late 1960s and in 1972 the AFL-CIO withheld its endorsement of the Party's presidential nominee. Voting records show that Democratic Congressmen were becoming much less likely to vote *en bloc* on labour issues.

79. The United Nations Declaration includes economic and social issues because of the need to secure Soviet acceptance of it and in its political

philosophy these are rights without which liberal, civil and political liberties are illusory. A useful summary of the debate in the West is by D. Watson, 'Welfare Rights and Human Rights', *Journal of Social Policy*, 1 (1977).

80. A. Sen, 'On Weights and Measures: Informational Constraints in Social Welfare Analysis', *Econometrica*, no. 7 (1977). The general ideas are also discussed by J. Parker, *Social Policy and Citizenship* (London: Macmillan) ch. 9.

81. Discussed by S. Rowbotham, L. Segal, and H. Wainwright, *Beyond the Fragments* (London: Merlin, 1979) p. 35 and Freeman, *The Politics of Women's Liberation*, p. 60.

82. That women might constitute a class or be considered analogous to a working class is a major theoretical issue in feminism which does not admit agreement or compromise. For a concise discussion of the various theoretical positions, see Randall, *Women and Politics*, chs 1 and 2.

83. *Labour Weekly*, 1963.

84. Crossman, *Diaries*, p. 627.

85. Interview with J. Gould, 1977. Callender, 'The Development of the Sex Discrimination Act, 1971–75'. The study group initiated by Leadbitter produced an interim report in 1969, *Toward Equality: Women and Social Security*. Their final report of 1972, called *Discrimination against Women*, was submitted as evidence to the House of Lords Select Committee. Some members of the study group were Joyce Butler, Millie Miller, Anthony Lester and Margherita Rendel who pursued the issue elsewhere too. The group recommended that the law deal with employment, related matters, goods facilities and services (including education), advertising and contract compliance. They called for a stronger body than the Race Relations Board, for access to the courts and positive action in the civil service.

86. B. Pym, *Pressure Groups and the Permissive Society* (London: David & Charles, 1974) p. 111.

87. S. Walkland and M. Ryle (eds), *The Commons in the 1970s* (London: Fontana 1977) especially chapters by Ryle and Richards.

88. It has also been argued that in the field of race relations select committee findings helped to gain public sympathy for government action by providing a wealth of convincing evidence from a source seen to be independent of the government. See E. Rose and Associates, *Colour and Citizenship: A Report on British Race Relations* (London: Institute of Race Relations with OUP, 1969) ch. 6.

89. That there are signs of breakdown in this with the creation of the SDP–Liberal Alliance seems a predictable sequence of the sociological changes in the House of Commons discussed above, although, of course, there are many other factors involved in recent electoral changes.

90. Sen, 'On Weights and Measures'.

91. In 1952 Charles Pannell tried to defeat the old 'family wage' argument against equal pay by arguing that the welfare state meant that families did not have to rely, if they were ever able to do so, on such a component of the wage packet. OR 500, cols 1765–857. Politicians and writers on

right and left spoke and wrote in the late 1950s and early 1960s as though technology was making abundance possible. The bubble began to be seen to have burst with the publication of books like that by K. Coates and R. Silburn, *Poverty, The Forgotten Englishman* (London: Penguin, 1970).

92. Full accounts of this and legal thought can be found in E. Rose, *Colour and Citizenship*, A. Lester and G. Bindman, *Race and the Law* (London: Penguin, 1972).

93. *Daily Telegraph*, 31 October 1961.

94. Ibid.

95. *Daily Telegraph*, 26 April 1966.

96. Council Directive 75/117 Official Journal of EEC, 19 February 1975. EEC Background Report ISEC/B16/79.

97. For example, Mr Dykes, *Debates of European Parliament*, 29 April 1975, p. 59.

Chapter 4

1. *Bulletin* 297, p. 130.

2. New Earnings Surveys reproduced in EOC Annual Reports.

3. A. Malabre, *Wall Street Journal*, 28 August 1978.

4. Ibid.

5. R. Sell and M. Jackson reported in *New Society*, 6 April 1978.

6. Chiplin and Sloane, *Sex Discrimination in the Labour Market*.

7. P. Glucklich, 'Report on LSE Project on Equal Pay', *Equal Pay and Opportunities Campaign Summer Report*, July 1978, L. Mackie, *Guardian*, 27 July 1978.

8. For example, M. Snell, P. Glucklich and M. Povall, *Equal Pay and Opportunities*. Research Paper No. 20 (London: Department of Employment, April 1981).

9. Glucklich, 'Report on LSE Project on Equal Pay', and Snell, *et al.*, *Equal Pay and Opportunities*.

10. These and the following changes are documented by: Hakim, *Occupational Segregation*, p. 34, 35 and *Bulletin* 2080, p. 9 and *US News and World Report*, 4 September 1978, p. 59. *Bulletin* 297, pp. 92–3.

11. Manpower Research Monograph 33, p. 92.

12. M. Hodgson, *The Sunday Times Colour Supplement*, 29 October 1978, p. 109.

13. This and the following information comes from: EOC Annual Reports (Manchester: EOC 1976–1981). L. Owen, the *Observer*, 4 February 1979. Research funded by EOC and SSRC, carried out by IFF Research Ltd, reported in *Employment Gazette*. Dept of Employment (Nov. 1980).

14. Annual Report 1980, p. 63.

15. IFF Research. Glucklich, Report on LSE Project on Equal Pay.

16. EOC Press Notice 1745, 7 July 1981.

17. *Bulletin* 297, p. 92.

18. Interviews with equal opportunity directors and staff in two of the largest corporations in the United States, April and May 1978.

19. Manpower Research Monograph 33, pp. 7–9, 25–6.
20. *New York Times*, 12 September 1960; *Bulletin* 297, p. 92; *Wall Street Journal* 28 August, 1976; *New York Times*, 12 September 1976; *US News and World Report* 4 September 1978, p. 60.
21. IFF Research.
22. M. Walters, *The Sunday Times*, 27 February 1977. L. Owen, *Observer* quoting Gallup Poll in *Woman's Own*, 4 February 1979. M. Snell, 'The Equal Pay and Sex Discrimination Acts: Their Impact in the Work Place', *Feminist Review* 1 (1979). EOC Press Notice 1741, reporting survey of *Women* readers, 2 July 1981.
23. Glucklich, 'Report on LSE Project on Equal Pay'. IFF Research.
24. Main sources for this section are: Civil Rights Commission, *The Federal Civil Rights Enforcement Effort – 1977* (Washington: 1977), ch. 3. Freeman, *The Politics of Women's Liberation*. P. Wallace, 'The Impact of Equal Opportunity Laws', in Kreps (ed.), *Women and the American Economy*. *Spokeswoman*, December 1977, Sophia Smith Collection, Smith College, Northampton, Massachusetts. Interviews, National Organisation of Women, New York, 1978; Civil Rights Division, AFL-CIO, Washington 1978; Women's Equity Action League, Washington, 1978; Office of Management and Budget, Washington, 1978; Women's Bureau, Department of Labor, Washington, 1978.
25. Main sources of information for this section are: *The Federal Civil Rights Enforcement Effort 1977*, ch. 4; Report to Congress by Comptroller and Auditor General (Washington, Sept. 1976); Oversight Hearings by House Subcommittee on Equal Employment Opportunities (Washington: Dec. 1976, July 1977); Statement by Ms Norton to House Subcommittee on Equal Employment Opportunities (Washington: July 1977). Interviews: Office of Policy Program Implementation, EEOC, Washington 1978; General Accounting Office, Washington 1978; Office of Management and Budget, Washington, 1978; Citizen's Advisory Council on Status of Women, Washington 1978; Attorney formerly employed by EEOC, New York, 1978. A. Blumrosen, 'Toward Effective Administration of New Regulatory Statutes', pts I and II, *Administrative Law Review* (winter and spring, 1977). Interviews and correspondence with senior official of Department of Health, Education and Welfare. Freeman, *The Politics of Women's Liberation*. Robinson, 'Two Movements in Pursuit of Equal Employment Opportunity'. P. Wallace, *Equal Opportunity and the AT & T Case* (Boston: MIT Press, 1976). P. Wallace, in Kreps, *Women and the American Economy*. *Spokeswoman* (Dec. 1977). *Fortune Magazine* Report of Edonomic Committee of Congress, June 1976 (Dec. 1976).
26. According to the EEOC, posts were unpopular among the tax-paying community and did not attract individuals of high calibre. This changed when the women's movement began to put pressure on the White House and helped to make posts in the EEOC politically important. Eleanor Holmes Norton was the unanimous recommendation of all women's groups consulted and also of a substantial section of ethnic minority civil rights groups. Her commitment was never in doubt but her new

procedures were thought to open the door to the exclusion of women's groups from policy developments.

27. *Griggs* v. *Duke Power Co.*, 401 US 424 (1971).
28. *Gilbert* v. *General Electric Co.*, 429 US 125 (1976).
29. Robinson, 'Two Movements in Pursuit of Equal Employment Opportunity', p. 427.
30. Main sources of information for this section are: *Federal Civil Rights Enforcement Effort, 1977*, ch. 2; Civil Rights Commission, *A Guide to Federal Laws and Regulations Prohibiting Sex Discrimination* (Washington: Clearing House Publication 48, July 1976). Interviews: General Accounting Office, Washington 1978; Office of Management and Budget, Washington 1978; OFCCP, Washington, 1978; Department of Justice, Washington, 1978; Deputy Director New York City Office of Contract Compliance, New York, 1978; Women's Equity Action League, Washington, 1978. Interviews and Correspondence, Department of Health Education and Welfare; *AFL-CIO News* 12 September 1978. Freeman, *The Politics of Women's Liberation. Spokeswoman* (Feb. 1978).
31. An exception being the American Bankers Association which, acting with the Treasury, threatened a crisis of business confidence in Mr Carter's administration. Orchestrated lobbying in Congress put an end to the threat.
32. The Department of Justice claimed that they would take initiatives to settle inter-agency disputes only in the case of a grave national emergency.
33. Main sources of information for this section are: *Federal Civil Rights Enforcement Effort, 1977*, ch. 5; Freeman, *The Politics of Women's Liberation*. Interviews: Civil Rights Commission, Washington 1978; General Accounting Office, Washington 1978.
34. In the transition between 1972 and 1974 courts were confused about the division of responsibility in public sector cases. In 1978 President Carter confirmed that the EEOC had authority in individual charges and the Department of Justice in 'pattern and practice' cases.
35. Freeman, *The Politics of Women's Liberation*, p. 79.
36. Main sources: *Federal Civil Rights Enforcement Effort, 1977*. Interviews: Office of Management and Budget, Washington 1978; Civil Rights Commission, Washington, 1978; General Accounting Office; Washington DC Commission on Status of Women, 1978; National Organisation for Women; Women's Equity Action League; American Civil Liberties Union, New York, 1978. G. Bryner, 'Congress Courts and Agencies: Equal Employment and the Limits of Policy Implementation', *Political Science Quarterly* (Fall 1981); Blumrosen, 'Toward Effective Administration of New Regulatory Statutes'.
37. Apart from opposition cited in note 31, the other main source of dissent was the Civil Service Commission, also silenced by orchestrated lobbying.
38. Main sources: EEOC Selected Recent Developments on Title VII Law and ADEA Law, Paper prepared for EEOC-FEP Agency Sixth Annual Conference, March 1982; *US Law Week*, SOLW 4364, 4 June 1982; Cary

and Peratis, *Women and the Law*; Blumrosen, 'Toward Effective Administration of New Regulatory Statutes'.

39. E.g. *Shultz* v. *Wheaton Glass* (3rd Circuit 1970); *Shultz* v. *American Can Co.* (8th Circuit 1970); *Hodgson* v. *Brookhaven General Hospital* (5th Circuit 1970); *Hodgson* v. *Fairmont Supply Co.* (4th Circuit 1971); *Hodgson* v. *Daisy Manufacturing* (8th Circuit 1971).
40. *County of Washington* v. *Gunther*, 101 US 2242 1981.
41. Player *Federal Law of Employment Discrimination*, p. 41.
42. *Hodgson* v. *Daisy Manufacturing*; *Hodgson* v. *Brookhaven Hospital*; Player, *Federal Law of Employment Discrimination*, pp. 48–50.
43. *Corning Glass Works* v. *Brennan* (US 1974); *Shultz* v. *First Victoria National Bank* (5th Circuit 1969); *Hodgson* v. *Security National Bank* (8th Circuit 1972); Player, *Federal Law of Employment Discrimination*, pp. 55–7.
44. Player, *Federal Law of Employment Discrimination*, p. 54.
45. Ibid., pp. 144–6.
46. Cary and Peratis, *Women and the Law*, pp. 60–3.
47. *Green* v. *Waterford Board of Education* (2nd Circuit 1973); *Cleveland Board of Education* v. *La Fleur*, 414 US 632 (1974).
48. *Phillips* v. *Martin Marietta Corp.*, 400 US 542 (1971).
49. *Rosenfeld* v. *South Pacific Co.* (9th Circuit 1971).
50. For example, *Diaz* v. *Pan American Inc.* (5th Circuit 1971); *Fernandez* v. *Wynn Oil Co.* (9th Circuit 1981); *Wilson* v. *South-West Airlines*, 131 N.D. Texas 1981; Cary and Peratis, *Women and the Law*, p. 112; Player, *Federal Law of Employment Discrimination*, p. 125; Wallace, in Kreps (ed.), *Women and the American Economy*, pp. 129–30; Developments on Title VII Law, p. 19.
51. Ibid.; Player, *Federal Law of Employment Discrimination*, pp. 118–19; Wallace, in Kreps (ed.), *Women and the American Economy*, pp. 128–9.
52. *Pittsburgh Press Co.* v. *Pittsburgh Commission on Human Rights*, 93 US 515 1973; Washington citation. Freeman, *The Politics of Women's Liberation*, pp. 78–9. Player, *Federal Law of Employment Discrimination*, p. 99.
53. *Franks* v. *Bowman*, 74 US 728 1976; *American Tobacco Co.* v. *John Patterson*, 80 US 1199 1982; L. Oelsner, *New York Times*, 25 March 1976; Player, *Federal Law of Employment Discrimination*, pp. 192–4, 202–3; R. Siner, *International Herald Tribune*, 1 June 1977.
54. *Shultz* v. *Wheaton Glass*; *Hodgson* v. *Golden Isles Convalescent Home Inc.* (5th Circuit 1972). *Gilbert* v. *GEC*; Player, *Federal Law of Employment Discrimination*, p. 46.
55. *Hodgson* v. *Behrens Drug Co.* (5th Circuit 1973). British judges had to accept a European lead on this point.
56. *Corning Glass Works* v. *Brennan*.
57. Even in 1973 in *McDonnell Douglas Corp.* v. *Green* (411 US 792) restrictions appeared which seemed to do this. See Player, *Federal Law of Employment Discrimination*, pp. 147–9. For a more recent discussion, see D. Pannick, 'The Burden of Proof in Discrimination Cases', *New Law Journal*, 27 August 1981.
58. *Griggs* v. *Duke Power*, the using of agency guidelines being confirmed in *Albemarle Paper Co.* v. *Moody*, 422 US 405, 1975. But see also *American*

Tobacco Co. v. *John Patterson*; Player, *Federal Law of Employment Discrimina-tion*, pp. 145–9. Developments in Title VII Law, pp. 13–4. *Equal Opportunities and the ATT Case*.

59. *Arey* v. *Providen Hospital*, DDC 1972 discussed by Player, *Federal Law of Employment Discrimination*, pp. 217–21. *General Telephone Co. of Southwest* v. *Falcon* – US – 1982, see Developments in Title VII Law, p. 10. D. Pannick, 'Sex Discrimination and the Class Action', *EOC News*, Aug./Sept. 1981.

60. Main sources: Cary and Peratis, *Women and the Law*, pp. 29–44. M. Chase, *Wall Street Journal*, 21 September 1978. S. Wermal, *Boston Globe*, 5 October 1978. Interviews: Women's Equity Action League, Department of Health, Education and Welfare.

61. *Frontiero* v. *Richardson*, 411 US 677 1973. They were unanimous in their view that the substantive issue was discriminatory but fairly evenly divided about whether this justified declaring sex to be a 'suspect' classification.

62. Main sources: EOC Annual Reports, Press Notices and Briefings and other documents listed in the Bibliography. Report of seminar, *A New World for Women*, Women in the Media, 1977. Fawcett Society files. 'Equal Pay Today Tomorrow', *World in Action*, 2 March 1977. Newspapers, especially *Guardian*, 11 July 1977, 17 November 1978; *The Sunday Times*, 20 February 1977; *The Times*, 30 December 1977; *Tribune*, July 1978. A. Coote, 'Equality: the Curse of the Quango', *New Statesman*, 1 December 1978. P. Byrne and J. Lovenduski, 'The Equal Opportunities Com-mission', *Women's Studies International Quarterly* (vol. i, no. 2, 1978).

63. House of Commons, OR 889, col. 522.

64. Some believed that accessibility was important, that the Act was potentially more helpful to working-class than to middle-class women, that they were more numerous in the north and that Manchester was, therefore, suitable. Others believed that its location was a concession to contemporary demands for decentralisation. Others believed it was safely distant from other, London bodies that would need to be lobbied for effect implementation.

65. Annual Report 1976, para. 2.

66. The full background is provided by P. Ashdown-Sharp, *The Sunday Times*, 20 and 27 February 1977.

67. EOC chairperson, Lady Lockwood, said it would be over in a few months, *World in Action*, 2 March 1977.

68. *Guardian*, 11 July 1977.

69. Main sources: EOC Annual Reports.

70. Ibid., 1980, p. 14.

71. Main sources: EOC Annual Reports, 'The Application of Equal Pay', Paper for TUC Women's Conference 1975. J. Gregory, 'Equal Pay and Sex Discrimination; Why Women are Giving up the Fight', *Feminist Review*, no. 10, Feb. 1982.

72. 'The Application of Equal Pay', pp. 4–5. See also *R* v. *CAC* [1979] IRLR 641.

73. Gregory, 'Equal Pay and Sex Discrimination'. The role of ACAS in

unfair dismissal cases is also open to criticism, for similar reasons; see L. Dickens, 'Unfair Dismissal Applications and the IT System', *Industrial Relations Journal*, vol. 9, no. 4 (winter 1979); P. Lewis, 'The Role of ACAS Conciliators in Unfair Dismissal Cases', *Industrial Relations Journal*, vol. 13, no. 3 (Autumn 1982).

74. Main sources: EOC Annual Reports, Press Notices and Case Notes. Industrial Relations Law Reports (IRLR). NCCL Annual Reports. P. Byrne and J. Lovenduski, 'Sex, Equality and the Law in Britain', *British Journal of Law and Society*, no. 2, 1978. M. Rendel, 'Legislating for Equal Pay and Opportunity in Britain', *Signs* (summer 1978). *Guardian*, especially 18 February 1977, 10 March 1977, 16 July 1977, 27 July 1978, 4 July 1981. *The Times*, especially law reports 5 June 1977, 15 July 1977. *New Statesman*, especially 27 October 1978, 14 March 1980.

75. Hugh Scanlon, *World in Action*, 2 March 1977.

76. *Walton* v. *Wellington College* – see Rendel, 'Legislating for Equal Pay and Opportunity in Britain'. *Trust Houses Forte* v. *Sorbie* [1976] IRLR 371. *Waddington* v. *Leicester Council for Voluntary Service* [1977] IRLR 32.

77. For example, *Capper Pass* v. *Lawton* [1976] IRLR 366. *Electrolux* v. *Hutchinson* [1976] IRLR 410, IRLR 289. *Dugdale* v. *Kraft Foods Ltd* [1977] IRLR 368. *Vicker* v. *Otis Elevator Co.*, 1977, See Rendel, 'Legislating for Equal Pay and Opportunity in Britain'.

78. *Snoxell* v. *Vauxhall Motors* [1977] IRLR 723.

79. Byrne and Lovenduski, 'Sex, Equality and the Law in Britain', pp. 150–1.

80. *Clay Cross (Quarry Services) Ltd* v. *Fletcher* [1977] IRLR 258, [1978] IRLR 361. *Pointon* v. *University of Sussex* [1977] IRLR 245, [1979] IRLR 119. *Albion Shipping Agency* v. *Arnoly* [1981] IRLR 525.

81. *Price* v. *Civil Service Commissioners* [1977] IRLR 405, IRLR 991, [1978] IRLR 3.

82. A Formal Investigation into British Steel has been carried out and the EOC assisted in two cases about redundancies for part-time workers; *Dick* v. *University of Dundee* and *Clarke and Powell* v. *Eley Kynoch* (Case Note 4); the latter ([1982] IRLR 131) succeeded in the precedent-setting EAT.

83. The most celebrated were brought by A. Coote, T. Gill and other women journalists against El Vino's wine bar which insists that women may not go to the bar. It is a place where journalists need to be able to mingle freely to be able to do their jobs well. Apart from the question of whether stereotypical views about chivalry make it difficult for women journalists to carry out their work, the dispute involves disagreement about whether different or separate treatment is inherently unequal. British judges thought not. But as long ago as 1954, the American Supreme Court made a historical declaration that it was and ordered racially separate education to end 'with all deliberate speed' (*Brown* v. *Board of Education*).

84. *Peake* v. *Automotive Products Ltd* [1977] IRLR 366, ICR 968, *Times Law Report*, 5 June 1977.

85. *Oxford* v. *DHSS* [1977] IRLR 225. But also see G. Bindman, 'Proving

Discrimination: Is the Burden too Heavy?', *Law Society's Gazette*, 17 December 1980.

86. *Brown* v. *El Sombrero*, 1978. *Science Research Council* v. *Nasse* [1978] IRLR 201, [1979] IRLR 352, IRLR 465. The first was heard in a county court and not reported. Both are discussed in Byrne and Lovenduski, 'Sex, Equality and the Law'. *Ojutiku* v. *Manpower Services Commission* (1981 ICR 515) discussed by D. Pannick, 'Indirect Discrimination Under the Sex Discrimination Act', *New Law Journal*, 25 September 1982. See also G. Bindman, 'Proving Discrimination' and 'Proving Discrimination: The Importance of Discovery', *Law Society's Gazette*, 26 March 1980.

87. Francis Bennion, *The Times*, 15 July 1977. He also congratulated Justice Phillips for 'impeccable reasoning'.

88. D. Pannick, 'Indirect Discrimination under the Sex Discrimination Act', 23 September 1982.

89. *McCarthy's Ltd* v. *Smith* [1979/1980] ICR 985.

90. *Meeks* v. *Agricultural and Allied Workers* [1971] IRLR 198; see Rendel, 'Legislating for Equal Pay and Opportunity in Britain', p. 906.

91. *Handley* v. *H. Mono Ltd* [1978/79] IRLR 534. *Jenkins* v. *Kingsgate (Clothing Productions) Ltd* [1980/81] IRLR 6.

92. *Garland* v. *BR Engineering Ltd* [1978] IRLR 8, [1982] IRLR 247. *Burton* v. *BR Board* [1981] IRLR 16.

93. Main sources for this section: *United States* – J. Col, 'Women's Support Networks', paper presented at IPSA Round Table, Essex University, 1979. Freeman, *The Politics of Women's Liberation*. Friedan, *It Changed My Life*, V. Novarra 'Right on Sister', paper arising from Winston Churchill Travelling Fellowship, available WRRC. Interviews with and/or files of members of all institutions and pressure groups referred to in text. *Teamster*, March 1977. *Spokeswoman* (Feb. 1978). Round Table, Essex University, 1979. *United Kingdom* – Interviews and/or files and press releases of main groups mentioned in text. EOC Annual Reports and Press Notices. M. Bowman, *Guardian*, 22 January 1980. A. Coote, 'Equality'. J. Coussins, *Amending the Equal Pay Act and Sex Discrimination Act* (NCCL, 1977). J. Coussins, Interview in *Guardian*, 10 January 1980. L. Forgan, *Guardian*, 10 January 1980. A. Gibson, 'Women in the Trade Unions: Present and Future Policy on Equal Opportunities', PSA Women and Politics Group Conference, Bedford College, September 1980. L. Hodges, *The Times*, 2 October 1980. J. McLoughlin, *Guardian*, 31 March 1981. M. Morris, *Guardian*, 30 December 1977. Randall, *Women and Politics*. R. Taylor, *Observer*, 1 January 1978.

94. See Appendix I for a list of all those discovered to have been active in one way or another in women's equality.

95. Freeman, *The Politics of Women's Liberation*, p. 93. Randall, *Women and Politics*, pp. 152–205.

96. Robinson, 'Two Movements in Pursuit of Equal Employment Opportunity', p. 427.

97. Interview, Washington, 1978.

98. Randall, *Women and Politics*, p. 159.

99. Quoted in Fawcett Newsletter, January 1981.
100. Coussins, *Guardian*, 10 January 1980.
101. Ibid.
102. EPOC meetings 8 October 1980, 8 April 1981.
103. Coussins, *Amending the EPA and SDA*.

Chapter 5

1. Comment by Republican voter, Washington 1978.
2. Novarra, 'Right on Sister', p. 60.
3. In recent years the literature on such bodies has burgeoned. An excellent bibliography is appended to a report by the Outer Circle Policy Unit, *What's Wrong with Quangos?* (London, 1979). Particularly helpful analyses of them are: C. Hood, 'Keeping the Centre Small: Explanation of Agency Type', *Political Studies*, March 1978 and N. Johnson, 'Quangos and the Structure of Government', Editorial in *Public Administration* (spring 1978) pp. 1–12. One source on America is L. Kohlmeier, *The Regulators* (New York: Harper & Row, 1969).
4. P. Holland MP, *Quango Quango Quango* (London: Adam Smith Institute, 1979).
5. Pressman and Wildavsky, cited by J. Richardson and A. Jordan, *Governing Under Pressure* (London: Martin Robertson, 1979) p. 134. See also Fulton Committee Report (1968) and discussion of it in Outer Circle Policy Unit.
6. J. Jowell, 'The Enforcement of Laws against Sex Discrimination in England: Problems of Institutional Design', in R. Ratner (ed.). *Equal Employment Policy for Women* (Temple University Press, 1980) p. 173.
7. 1st Annual Report, pp. 1–5. A. Coote, *Guardian*, 17 December 1976. A. Erriman, *The Times*, 30 December 1977. R. Taylor, *Observer*, 1 January 1978.
8. H. Heclo, *A Government of Strangers* (Washington: The Brookings Institution, 1977).
9. Interview, July 1977.
10. Byrne and Lovenduski, 'The Equal Opportunities Commission'.
11. Interviews with officials and activists, cited in Chapter IV.
12. L. Panitch, 'The Development of Corporatism in Liberal Democracies', *Comparative Political Studies*, April 1977, p. 66.
13. Byrne and Lovenduski, 'The Equal Opportunities Commission'.
14. Ibid., pp. 143–6.
15. Blumrosen, 'Toward Effective Administration of New Regulatory Statutes', p. 92.
16. Tess Gill, Anna Coote, and Patricia Hewitt, *Guardian*, 16 September 1977 and, later, Sandra Brown, Women in the Media, and Ann Robinson, University of Wales.
17. Heclo, *A Government of Strangers*, pp. 92–3. He also suggests that where straightforward rewards for favours or party loyalty remain as the main

rationale for appointments, it is in the values of congressional or local politicians.

18. Byrne and Lovenduski, 'Sex Equality and the Law in Britain', p. 164.
19. Interviews, February 1978 and September 1980.
20. *Guardian*, 17 December 1976.
21. 'Justice for Women', *New Society*, 13 January 1977.
22. L. Mackie, *Guardian*, 11 July 1977.
23. Quoted by L. Mackie, *Guardian*, 23 March 1977.
24. P. Toynbee, *Guardian*, 10 March 1980.
25. She was a long-standing campaigner for equal pay in the TUC itself. Profile of Ms Chipchase in *The Sunday Times*, 5 March 1978. P. Toynbee, *Guardian*, 10 March 1980.
26. Findings of Equal Pay and Opportunity Campaign reported by K. Whitehorn, *Observer*, 22 January 1978 and Editorial, *Industrial Relations Review and Report*, June 1977.
27. Byrne and Lovenduski, 'The Equal Opportunities Commission', p. 132.
28. The Role of the Comptroller and Auditor General, 1st special report of Committee of Public Accounts HC 115 1980–1.
29. Outer Circle Policy Unit, p. 59.
30. J. Garrett, *Managing the Civil Service* (Heinemann, 1980) pp. 186–8, 192.
31. M. Rendel, Law as an Instrument of Oppression or Reform, *Sociological Review Monograph*, 23, 1976, pp. 151–2. Also Cary and Peratis, *Women and the Law*, pp. 22–5.
32. Lord Scarman points out that it is impossible for statutes to contain precise guidance about every eventuality. 'Public Administration and the Courts'. For an account of the Grunwick dispute, see J. Rogaly, *Grunwick* (London: Penguin, 1977) especially pp. 148–9.
33. Rendel, 'Law as an Instrument of Oppression or Reform'.
34. Rendel, 'Law as an Instrument of Oppression or Reform', p. 150.
35. Byrne and Lovenduski, 'Sex Equality and the Law in Britain', pp. 156–64.
36. Rendel, 'Law as an Instrument of Oppression or Reform', pp. 166–7.
37. J. Griffith, *The Politics of the Judiciary* (Fontana 1977) pp. 24–31.
38. R. Neustadt, *Presidential Power: The Politics of Leadership* (New York: John Wiley & Sons, 1960) pp. 32–4.
39. *Brown* v. *Board of Education*, 347 US 483 (1954), *Plessy* v. *Ferguson*, 163 US 537 (1896).
40. This is dealt with in more detail by M. Shapiro, 'The Supreme Court: From Warren to Berger' in A. King (ed.), *The New American Political System* (Washington, DC: American Enterprise Institute, 1978) p. 180.
41. *Guardian*, 10 March 1978.
42. 'Public Administration and the Courts'.
43. *Dockers' Labour Club* v. *Race Relations Board 1974*, Griffith, *The Politics of the Judiciary*, pp. 87–93.
44. 'Public Administration and the Courts'.
45. See R. Dahl, *Pluralist Democracy in the United States* (New York: Rand McNally, 1967). The British point is made by Richardson and Jordan,

Governing Under Pressure, p. 159. S. Lukes, *Power: A Radical View* (London: Macmillan, 1974) is a cogent analysis of the weakness of group theories.

46. Lukes, *Power*, p. 148.
47. E. Schattschneider, *The Semi-Sovereign People* (New York: Holt, Rinehart & Winston, 1960), and J. Gelb and M. Palley 'Women and Interest Group Policies: A Comparative Analysis of Federal Decision Making', *Journal of Politics*, vol. 41, 1979, pp. 363–71.
48. Novarra, 'Right on Sister', p. 61–2.
49. C. Hood, 'The World of Quasi-Government', SSRC Machinery of Government Project, paper presented at Public Administration Committee Conference, York University, June 1979, pp. 16–17. Ashdown-Sharp, *The Sunday Times*.
50. Examples are provided in the four case studies by Gelb and Palley, 'Women and Interest Group Policies'.
51. The event was well covered the next day in the *Morning Star*. The *Guardian*, but for a mistake, would have reported it. Mary Stott, a leading member of Fawcett, wrote about it later, *Guardian*, 18 August 1981; it passed by unnoticed by all other newspapers.
52. Rowbotham *et al.*, *Beyond the Fragments*.
53. Freeman, *The Politics of Women's Liberation*, p. 234.
54. Gelb and Palley, 'Women and Interest Group Policies', pp. 389–90.
55. The change was evident in the grassroots, too. A Louis Harris Virginia Slims poll showed that *more* black women than white favoured efforts to improve the position of women and sympathised with women's liberation groups. See Freeman, *The Politics of Women's Liberation*, p. 38.
56. Freeman, *The Politics of Women's Liberation*, p. 39.
57. The author recalls bewilderment and disappointment about not feeling 'at home' among many black American visitors to Nigeria in 1970.

Chapter 6

1. M. Edelman, *The Symbolic Uses of Politics* (University of Illinois Press, 1964) especially pp. 22–9, 37–8. Freeman, *The Politics of Women's Liberation*, especially pp. 12–43, 48–9, 54–5, 230–7.
2. Blumrosen, 'Toward Effective Administration of New Regulatory Statutes', pp. 102, 209–14.
3. Blumrosen, op cit., especially pp. 380–9.
4. Blumrosen, op cit., p. 98.
5. G. Linscott, *Guardian*, 26 April 1978.
6. Lady Lockwood, Speech to Society of Occupational Medicine. 'Protective Legislation: Who benefits – Men or Women?', 28 October 1977. Published as document with same title, p. 6.
7. *The Times Educational Supplement*, 4 November 1977. *Guardian*, 31 December 1977 and 11 January 1978.
8. Investigation into the number of women appointed to public bodies – No. 5. EOC, 1982.

9. EOC Second Annual Report 1977, pp. 35–6. EOC Third Annual Report 1978, pp. 28–31. EOC Fourth Annual Report 1979, pp. 25–7. M. Benn, 'Women Denied Equal Treatment under the New Social Security Legislation', *Rights* (NCCL Sept.–Oct., 1980). *Behind Closed Doors*, EOC, 1981.

10. Misgivings were felt by both those against a strong race relations act (*Daily Telegraph*, 13 November 1975) and those who hoped that sex discrimination legislation would be taken seriously but feared that it would not if the Sex Discrimination Act was merely a model for the Race Relations Act. Comments that this was 'the real purpose of the Act' have been made in private to the author. That is was consciously used as a model for the Race Relations Act has been confirmed (without the implications of the private comments) by M. Rendel 'Legislating for Equal Pay and Opportunity for Women in Britain', *Signs*, p. 960.

11. Byrne and Lovenduski, 'Sex Equality and the Law in Britain', pp. 161–2. An example is the reply from the Secretary of State for Employment to Mr Ashley MP, on 20 February 1979 that the operations of the EOC were for it to decide. OR 962/63 col. 99.

12. EOC Press Notice 7 July 1976.

13. Ashdown-Sharp, *The Sunday Times*, 27 February 1977.

14. EOC Fourth Annual Report, 1979, p. 29.

15. Heclo, *A Government of Strangers*, p. 17.

16. E. Vallance, *Women in the House* (London: Athlone Press, 1979) especially ch. V.

17. G. Drewry and J. Brock, *The Impact of Women on the House of Lords* (Studies in Public Policy No. 112) (Glasgow: University Strathclyde, 1983).

18. Rights of Women, 'The EEC and Women – a case study of British and European Legislation on Equal Pay', Paper presented at Conference of PSA Women and Politics Groups, Bedford College 27 September 1980, pp. 3–4.

19. P. Wallington and J. McBride, *Civil Liberties and a Bill of Rights* (London: Cobden Trust, 1976). *A New Deal for Britain: Citizens' Rights*, Green Paper 10 (London: SDP, 1982) adopted at 1983 Party Conference. Griffith, *The Politics of the Judiciary*. Watson, 'Welfare Rights and Human Rights'.

20. For example, A. Gramsci, *The Modern Prince and Other Writings* (New York: New World Paperbacks, 1972).

21. Rowbotham *et al.*, *Beyond the Fragments*.

22. M. Snell *et al.*, *Equal Pay and Opportunities*.

23. *Equality Legislation: The Way Forward*, TUC, Dec. 1982. *Women Workers Bulletin*.

24. *Commission of the European Communities* v. *UK*, discussed by S. Fredman, 'Equal Pay for Work of Equal Value', *The Law Society's Gazette*, 27 April 1983.

25. Ibid.

26. S. Robarts, A. Coote, E. Ball, *Positive Action for Women* (London: NCCL, 1981).

27. Interview, Department of Labor, Washington, 1978.

28. Correspondence with official in Department of Health and Human Resources.
29. Interviews, especially in Department of Health, Education and Welfare.
30. Interviews, ITT and Bell Systems.
31. J. Pleck *et al.*, 'Conflicts between Work and Family Life', *Monthly Labor Review* (Washington: Department of Labor), March 1980. C. Bell, L. McKee, K. Priestley, *Fathers, Childbirth and Work* (Manchester: EOC, June 1983).
32. Ibid.
33. *Behind Closed Doors*, EOC, 1981. Benn, 'Women Denied Equal Treatment under the New Social Security Legislation'.
34. *Income Tax and Sex Discrimination* (Manchester: EOC, 1982). P. Hewitt, *Income Tax and Sex Discrimination* (London: NCCL, 1979).
35. Bell *et al.*, *Fathers, Childbirth and Work*.
36. S. Yeandle, 'Women's Experience of Paid Employment', and E. Derow, 'Childcare and Employment', in K. Huidtfeldt, K. Jorgensen and R. Nielson (eds), *Strategies for Integrating Women into the Labour Market* (European Women's Studies in Social Science, No. 1) (Copenhagen: Women's Research Centre in Social Science, 1982).
37. S. Allen, 'Waged Labour in the Home', in Huidtfeldt *et al.*, *Strategies for Integrating Women into the Labour Market*.
38. E. Drew, 'Full-time Unemployment or Part-time Working?' Paper presented at Annual Conference of Development Studies Association IDS, Brighton, September 1983.

Sources and Bibliography

Official Documents

Britain

Britain in the European Community: Social Policy, Central Office of Information (HMSO, 1975), Pamphlet 136.
Women in Britain, Central Office of Information (HMSO, 1972), Pamphlet 67.
Report: A Joint Framework for Social Policy, Central Policy Review Staff (1975).
Equal Opportunities for Men and Women, Department of Employment, Department of Education and Science, Home Office – Joint Discussion Document (HMSO, 1973).

Department of Employment
    Department of Employment Gazettes (formerly *Employment and Productivity Gazette*).
    Equal Pay, What are you doing about it? (1973).
    A Guide to the Equal Pay Act (HMSO, 1975).
    Equal Pay: First Report on the Implementation of the Equal Pay Act 1970, Office of Manpower Economics (HMSO, 1972).
    Survey of Women's Employment (May 1968).
    Survey of Management Attitudes and Practices towards Women at Work. Both carried out by Audrey Hunt for Office of Population Censuses and Surveys on behalf of Department of Employment (HMSO, 1975).
    Manpower Papers: No. 9 *Women and Work, a statistical survey* (1974); no. 10 *Women and Work, sex differences and society* (1974); no. 11 *Women and Work, a review* (1975); no. 12 *Women and Work, overseas practice* (1975).
    C. Hakim, *Occupational Segregation*, Research Paper No. 9 (November 1979).

Equal Opportunities Commission
    Annual Reports – 1976, 1977, 1978, 1979, 1980, 1981, 1982.
    Research Bulletins – Nos 1–8, 1978–1984.
    Press Notices, 1976–1984.

Equal Opportunities Commission News.

Sex Equality and the Pension Age (December 1976).

Protective Legislation: Who Benefits – Men or Women? (October 1977).

Women and Low Incomes (November 1977).

Equality between the Sexes in Industry: How Far Have We Come? (October 1978).

Guidance in Equal Opportunity Policies and Practices in Employment (December 1978).

Health and Safety Legislation: Should We Distinguish Between Men and Women? (March 1979).

Fresh Start: A Guide to Training Opportunities (May 1979).

How to Prepare Your Own Case for An Industrial Tribunal (October 1979).

I Want a Baby: But What About My Job? (December 1979).

Information Technology in the Office: The Impact on Women's Jobs, Communications Studies Planning Ltd (September 1980).

Code of Practice for the Elimination of Sex Discrimination and the Promotion of Equality of Opportunity in Employment – Consultative Drafts (1981 and 1982).

Job-Sharing: Improving the Quality and Availability of Part-Time Work (August 1981).

The Role of Trade Unions in the Promotion of Equal Opportunities (August 1981).

Response to the Manpower Services Commission Consultative Document: 'A New Training Initiative' (September 1981).

Behind Closed Doors (December 1981).

The Job Splitting Scheme: Response of the EOC to the Department of Employment. Consultative Document. Equal Pay for Work of Equal Value (September 1982).

Income Tax and Sex Discrimination (December 1982).

Fathers, Childbirth and Work (June 1983).

Government Statistical Service

Social Trends (1974) No. 5.

Home Office

Equality for Women (HMSO, 1974) Cmd 572.

A Guide to the Sex Discrimination Act (HMSO, 1975).

National Economic and Development Council

Multiple Shiftwork: A Problem for Decision by Management and Labour, Monograph 1 (HMSO, 1970).

Parliament

House of Commons, Debates and Committees

Vol. 767. 479–532. Prices and Incomes Bill.

Vol. 795. 913–1038. Equal Pay (No. 2) Bill and Second Reading.

February/April 1970. Minutes of Proceedings of Standing Committee and on Equal Pay (No. 2) Bill.

Vol. 800. 505–772. Equal Pay (No. 2) Bill Report and Third Reading.

Vol. 884. 1812–44. Second Reading Debate on Anti-Discrimination Bill.

Vol. 849, 850, 1850–86, 1367–1416. Second Reading Debate on Anti-Discrimination (No. 2) Bill.
26.6.73. Special Report of Select Committee on Anti-Discrimination (No. 2) Bill.
Vol. 877. 1296–1305. Home Secretary's statement on Sex Discrimination legislation.
Vol. 884. 511–618. Second Reading Debate on Sex Discrimination Bill 26.3.75.
April/June 1975. Minutes and proceedings of Standing Committee B on Sex Discrimination Bill.
Vol. 893. 1429–1612. Report and Third Reading on Sex Discrimination Bill.

House of Lords, Debates and Committees
Vol. 310. 122–65. Second Reading Equal Pay (No. 2) Bill.
Vol. 310. 1064–86. Committee of Whole House.
1971–72, 1972–73. Session – Special Reports and Minutes of proceedings of Select Committee on Anti-Discrimination Bill (HL).
Vol. 336, 334–335, 447–448. Second Reading Anti-Discrimination Bill.
Vol. 342. 606–664. Committee of Recommitment of Sex Discrimination Bill.
Vol. 343. 2191–2209. Report on Sex Discrimination Bill (HL).
Vol. 862. 95–192. Second Reading, Sex Discrimination Bill.
Vol. 662. 1013–94, 1113–272, 1359–444. Committee of Whole House on Sex Discrimination Bill.
Vol. 863. 967–1295. Report on Sex Discrimination Bill and Third Reading.

Equal Pay Act (HMSO, 1970).
Sex Discrimination Bill (1975).
Sex Discrimination Act (1975).

Royal Commissions
Royal Commission on Equal Pay 1944–46 Report. Cmd 6937.
Royal Commission on Trade Unions and Employers Associations (1965–68) Cmd 3623 (HMSO, 1968).

Scottish Information Service
A Profile of Women in Scotland (1975).

United States

Commission on Civil Rights
Full Employment Issue, Civil Rights Digest, winter–spring 1976.
A Bicentennial Issue, Civil Rights Digest, summer 1976.
National Women's Conference 1977 Issue, Civil Rights Digest, winter 1978.
A Guide to Federal Laws and Regulations Prohibiting Sex Discrimination Clearinghouse Publication 46, Revised edition 1976.
Last Hired, First Fired: Layoffs and Civil Rights, 1977.

The Federal Civil Rights Enforcement Effort, 1977, To Eliminate Employment Discrimination: A Sequel. December 1977.
The State of Civil Rights: 1977–1978.
List of National Women's and Women's Rights Organisations, January 1978.

Congress
  Legislative History of Titles VII and XI of Civil Rights Act 1964. US Government Printing Office.
  Equal Rights for Men and Women 1971. Hearings before Sub-Committee No. 4 of the Committee of the Judiciary. House of Representatives 92nd Congress Serial No. 2. US Government Printing Office 1971.
  Report by Sub-Committee on Equal Opportunities Staff Report on Investigation of EEOC's Thirty Day Turn Around Project, Committee on Education and Labour, US House of Representatives 94th Congress December 1976, US Government Printing Office 1977.
  Oversight Hearing on Equal Employment Opportunities. Hearing before Sub-Committee on Employment opportunities of Committee on Education and Labour, House of Representatives 95th Congress, July 1977. US Government Printing Office 1977.
  Staff Report Comparing Figures for Minority and Female Employment in the Federal Government 1975 and 1977, and in 44 Selected Agencies, 1977. Prepared for Sub-Committee on Employment opportunities of the Committee on Education and Labour. US House of Representatives, 95th Congress, May 1978. US Government Printing Office 1978.
  Oversight Hearing on Federal Enforcement of EEO Laws. Hearing before Sub-Committee on Employment opportunities of Committee on Education and Labour. House of Representatives, 95th Congress, October 1977. US Government Printing Office 1978.

Department of Health, Education and Welfare
  Progress of Women in HEW, May 1972–August 1977. Data Management Center, HEW, December 1977.

Department of Labor
  Daycare Services: Industry's Involvement, Women's Bureau – Workplace Standards Administration. Bulletin 296, 1971.
  Women in Apprenticeship – Why Not?, Manpower Administration/Briggs N. Manpower Research Monograph No. 33, 1974.
  A Working Woman's Guide to Her Job Rights, Employment Standards Administration – Women's Bureau. Leaflet 55, Revised 1975.
  1975 Handbook on Women Workers, Employment Standards Administration – Women's Bureau, Bulletin 297, 1975.
  The Earnings Gap between Women and Men, Employment Standards Administration – Women's Bureau, 1976.
  Commissions for Women – Participation of Racial and Ethnic Minority Women in Membership and Program Activities, Employment Standards Administration – Women's Bureau, 1977.
  US Working Women: A Data Book Bulletin 1977, Bureau of Labor Statistics.

Perspectives on Working Women: A Data Book, Bureau of Labor Statistics, Bulletin 2080, October 1980.

Equal Employment Opportunities Commission
Annual Reports – 1965–78
Eleanor Holmes-Norton, *Overhauling the EEOC*, Commerce Clearing House Inc., 1977. Reprinted from *Labor Law Journal*, November 1977.

General Accounting Office
Report to the Congress: *The Equal Employment Commission has made Limited Progress in Eliminating Employment Discrimination*, Comptroller General of the United States, HRD-75-147, 1976.
A Compilation of Federal Laws and Executive Orders for Non-Discrimination and Equal Opportunity Programs, HRD-78-138, August 1978.

National Commission on the Observance of International Women's Year
'. . . *To Form a More Perfect Union* . . .' Justice for American Women June 1976.
National Plan of Action, 1977.

New York City Commission on Human Rights
Report on Women's Role in Contemporary Society, Discus Books/Avon, 1972.

President's Commission on the Status of Women 1963
Report of the Committee on Private Employment

President's Task Force on Women's Rights and Responsibilities
A Matter of Simple Justice, 1970.

Europe

Commission of European Communities, Council and Parliament
Women of Europe, Brussels, 1978–1981. Commission of European Communities Bulletin.
Working Document 24/75: *Report by Committee on Social Affairs and Employment on Proposal for a Directive on Equality of Treatment between Men and Women Workers*, European Parliament, Debates April 1975. PE 39.856/F.
Directive (75/117/EEC) of 10.2.75 on *The Approximation of the Laws of Member States Relating to the Application of the Principle of Equal Pay for Men and Women*, Council of European Communities, Official Journal of the European Communities L45/19, 19.2.75.
Directive (76/207/EEC) of 9.2.76 on *The Implementation of the Principle of Equal Treatment for Men and Women as Regards Access to Employment, Vocational Training and Promotion, and Working Conditions*, Council for the European Communities, official Journal of the European Communities, L39/40, 14.2.76.
Communication of Commission to Council on Equality of Treatment between Men and

Women Workers, Commission of the European Communities, COM (75) 36, 12.2.75.

European Women in Paid Employment, Commission of the European Communities. Brussels, December 1980.

Background Report ISEC/B16/79, *The Commission Moves on Discrimination Against Women*, London, April 1979.

Organisation for Economic Cooperation and Development
Manpower and Social Affairs Committee Policies for Equal Opportunity for Women in the Economy. Paris, 1978.

Documents of Parties, Groups and Individuals

J. Airey, Private Papers.

Education, Training and Employment of Women and Girls, Association of Teachers in Technical Institutions (London, 1970).

A True Balance: In the Home, in Employment, as Citizens, Conservative and Unionist Committee on Women's Questions. London: Conservative and Unionist Central Office, February 1949.

Women in Politics, E. Sturgess-Jones (ed.), London: Conservative Publicity Department, 1966.

Fair Share for the Fair Sex, London: Conservative Central Office, 1969.

European Conservative Group, European Parliamentary Papers, Brussels, 1973–76.

Discrimination Against Women (Opposition Green Paper), London: Labour Party, 1973.

Towards Equality, Women and Social Security, London: Labour Party.

Equal Pay and Opportunities Campaign Newsletters, London: 1977–1984.

Fawcett Society: London. Annual Reports, Files, Press Cuttings.

National Council for Civil Liberties: London and Hull. Annual Reports. 'Rights' and other publications listed under authors' names. Files.

Trades Union Congress: London. Annual Women's and Full Conference Reports. *The Application of Equal Pay*, Memorandum for 1977 TUC Women's Conference.

B. Webb, Letter to Carey Thomas, Bryn Mawr College 1894–1922 (undated). Estimated by Professor N. Mackenzie to have been sent in March 1934.

A New World for Women, London: Women in Media, 1977.

Women's Report – London 1974, January 1974–December 1976.

Spokeswoman 1976–1978, Sophia Smith Collection, Smith College Library. Northampton, Mass.

Seminars and Conferences

C. Jackson, Equal Opportunities Commission, University of Sussex, 1977.

J. C. Wood, The Central Arbitration Committee, Nuffield College, 1978.

J. Handler, Social Movements and the Legal System, St Cross Buildings, Oxford, 1978.

Conference on Equal Pay and Equal Opportunity Policy for Women, Wellesley College, Massachusetts, 1978.

D. Nandy, Equal Opportunities Commission, Queen Elizabeth House, Oxford, 1978.

S. Andeman, Employment Appeals Tribunal and Social Contract Legislation, Nuffield College, 1978.

M. Snell, The Equal Pay Act and Sex Discrimination Act, Queen Elizabeth House, 1979.

M. McCarthy, The Equal Opportunities Commission, Nuffield College, 1979.

R. Hepple, Industrial Tribunals, Nuffield College, 1979.

PSA Women and Politics Group Conference on Women and Public Policy, Bedford College, 1980.

N. Seear, The Equal Pay Act and Sex Discrimination Act, University of Bath, 1980.

Interviews

Britain

Conservative Party, 1979.

Equal Opportunities Commission – representatives of each section, 1977–78.

Fawcett Society, 1978.

Labour Party, 1977.

National Council for Civil Liberties, 1980.

United States

American Civil Liberties Union, New York, April 1978.

American Federation of Labor – Congress of Industrial Organizations, Washington, May 1978.

American Telephone and Telegraph Company and subsidiaries: Chesapeke and Potomax Bell; Southern Bell, 1978.

Civil Rights Commission, Washington, May 1978.

Department of Health Education and Welfare, Washington, May 1978.

Department of Justice, Washington, May 1978.

Department of Labor: Women's Bureau; Office of Federal Contract Compliance Programs, Washington, May 1978.

Equal Employment Opportunities Commission, Washington, May 1978.

E.R. America, Washington, May 1978.

General Accounting Office, Washington, May 1978.

House of Representatives Sub-Committee on the Judiciary; staff member, Washington, May 1978.

League of Women Voters, Washington, May 1978.

National Organisation for Women, B. Friedan, New York April 1978, New

York Chapter – Legal Defense and Education Fund, Washington, May 1978.
National Women's Party, Washington, May 1978.
New York City Office of Contract Compliance, April 1978.
Office of Management and Budget, Washington, May 1978.
Senate Sub-Committee on the Constitution; Chief Counsel and Executive Director, Washington, May 1978.
Universities: Columbia University, George Washington University, George Town University, New York City University, Princeton University, Smith College, Wellesley College, Washington University, St Louis.
Women's Equity Action League, Washington, May 1978.

Books, Articles and Unpublished Research

Abramson, J. (1979) *Old Boys New Women* (New York: Praeger).
Agid, S. R. (1978) *Fair Employment Litigation Manual*, Employment Rights Project (New York: Columbia Law School).
Amsden, A. H. (1980) *The Economics of Women and Work*, especially Introduction (London: Penguin).
Ashford, D. (ed.) (1978) *Comparing Public Policies* (Beverly Hills: Sage).
Banks, O. (1981) *Faces of Feminism* (Oxford: Martin Robertson).
Barker, D. and Allen, S. (eds) (1976) *Dependence and Exploitation in Work and Marriage* (London: Longman).
Barron, R. D. and Norris, G. M. (1976) 'Sexual Divisions and the Dual Labour Market', in Barker and Allen (eds), *Dependence and Exploitation in Work and Marriage* (London: Longman).
Bell, C., McKee, L. and Priestley, K. (1983) *Fathers, Childbirth and Work* (Manchester: EOC).
Beloff, M. J. and Wilson, H. M. (1976) *Sex Discrimination: The New Law* (London: Butterworth).
Benewick, R. J. (1975) 'The Civil Liberties Lobby: A Comparative Analysis', *Government and Opposition*, vol. 10 (1975) no. 4.
Benn, M. (1980) 'Women Denied Equal Treatment under the New Social Security Legislation,' *Rights* (NCCL, Sept.–Oct., 1980).
Best, M. H. and Connolly, W. E. (1976) *The Politicized Economy* (Lexington: D. C. Heath & Co.).
Bindman, G. (1980) 'Proving Discrimination: The Importance of Discovery', *Law Society's Gazette*, 26.3.80.
Bindman, G. (1980) 'Proving Discrimination: Is the Burden too Heavy?', *Law Society's Gazette*, 17.12.80.
Blumrosen, A. W. (1977) 'Toward Effective Administration of new Regulatory Statutes', parts I and II, *Administrative Law Review* (winter and spring).
Bowlby, J. (1953) *Child Care and the Growth of Love* (London: Penguin).
Briggs, N. (1974) *Women in Apprenticeship: Why Not*, Manpower Research Monograph No. 33 (Washington: US Department of Labor).
Bruley, S. (1980) *Women's Organisations in the UK: A Short History* (London: National Council of Voluntary Organisations).

Byrne, P. and Lovenduski, J. (1978) 'The Equal Opportunities Commission', *Women's Studies International Quarterly*, vol. 1 (1978) no. 2.

Byrne, P. and Lovenduski, J. (1978) 'Sex Equality and the Law in Britain', *British Journal of Law and Society*, vol. 5 (1978) no. 2.

Bryner, G. (1981) 'Congress, Courts and Agencies: Equal Employment and the Limits of Policy Implementation', *Political Science Quarterly* (fall 1981).

Cain, G. (1976) 'The Challenge of Segmented Labor Market Theories in Orthodox Theory', *Journal of Economic Literature* (December).

Callender, C. (1978) 'The Development of the Sex Discrimination Act 1971–1975', unpublished dissertation submitted at Bristol University (October).

Campbell, T. (1980) 'Earnings Differences Between Men and Women in Federal Government Employment', PhD dissertation submitted at University of Chicago.

Cary, E. and Peratis, K. W. (1977) *Women and the Law* (New York: National Text Book Co./ACLU).

Chafe, W. H. (1977) *Women and Equality: Changing Patterns in American Culture* (Oxford: OUP).

Chester, N. (1979) 'Fringe Bodies, Quangos and all that', *Public Administration*, vol. 57 (spring 1979).

Chiplin, B. and Sloane, P. J. (1976) *Sex Discrimination in the Labour Market* (London: Macmillan).

Coates, K. and Silburn, R. (1970) *Poverty, the Forgotten Englishman* (London: Penguin).

Col, J. M. (1979) 'Women's Support Networks: Strategies for Development', unpublished paper presented at IPSA Round Table, Essex, August 1979.

Commonwealth Club of California members' report (1978) 'Are Present Laws Effectively Ending Employment Discrimination Against Women and Minorities?', *Transaction A*, 1978.

Coote, A. (1978) 'Equality and the Curse of the Quango', *New Statesman* (December).

Coote, A. (1979) *Equal at Work?* (London: Collins).

Coote, A. and Gill, T. (1977) *Women's Rights: A Practical Guide*, 2nd ed. (London: Penguin).

Coote, A. and Hewitt, P. (1980) 'The Stance of Britain's Major Parties and Interest Groups', in P. Moss and N. Fonda (eds), *Work and the Family* (London: Temple Smith).

Coussins, J. (1977) *Amending the Equal Pay Act and Sex Discrimination Act* (National Council for Civil Liberties).

Coussins, J. (1976) *The Equality Report* (London: National Council for Civil Liberties).

Creighton, W. B. (1973) 'The Development of the Legal Status of Women in Employment in Great Britain', unpublished PhD thesis submitted at University of Cambridge, December 1973 (London: Mansell, 1979).

Creighton, W. B. (1976) 'Enforcing the Sex Discrimination Act', *Industrial Law Journal*, vol. 5 (1976) no. 1.

Crossman, R. (1978) *The Diaries of a Cabinet Minister*, Vol. III (London: Hamish Hamilton/Jonathan Cape/Book Club Associates).

Davies, L. (1981) 'Wider Opportunities for Women', unpublished paper presented at Conference on Women in the Labour Market at School for Advanced Urban Studies, Bristol (June 1981).

Davies, R. (1975) *Women and Work* (London: Arrow).

Dahl, R. (1967) *Pluralist Democracy in the United States* (New York: Rand McNally).

Dickens, L. (1979) 'Unfair Dismissal Applications and the IT System', *Industrial Relations Journal*, vol. 9, no. 4 (winter 1979).

Drewry, G. and Brock, J. (1983) *The Impact of Women on the House of Lords*, Studies in Public Policy No. 112 (Glasgow: University Strathclyde).

Dunleavy, P. and Hope, K. (1974) *Social Mobility* (Nuffield College).

Edelman, M. (1964) *The Symbolic Uses of Politics* (Illinois: University of Illinois Press).

Ellickson, K. P. (1976) 'The President's Commission on the Status of Women: Its Formation, Functioning and Contribution', unpublished paper, 1976, available from Walter P. Reuther Library, Wayne State University, Detroit, Michigan.

Elshtain, J. B. (1974) 'Moral Woman and Immoral Man: a Consideration of the Public–Private Split and its Political Ramifications', *Politics and Society*, vol. 4 (1974) no. 4.

Faulkener, M. (1969) *The British Federation of Business and Professional Women: An Appreciation* (London).

Finer, S. E. (1966) *Anonymous Empire* (London: Pall Mall).

Finer, S. E. (1970) *Comparative Government*, especially part 2 (London: Penguin).

Fogarty, M., Allen, A., Allen, I. and Walters, P. (1972) *Women in Top Jobs* (London: PEP/Allen & Unwin).

Fogarty, M., Rapoport, R. and Rapoport, R. N. (1971) *Sex, Career and Family* (London: Allen & Unwin).

Fredman, S. (1983) 'Equal Pay for Work of Equal Value: The Government's Draft Proposals', *Law Society's Gazette*, 27.4.83.

Freeman, J. (1975) *The Politics of Women's Liberation* (New York: David McKay & Co.).

Friedan, B. (1963) *The Feminine Mystique* (London: Penguin).

Friedan, B. (1977) *It Changed My Life* (New York: Dell).

Garrett, J. (1980) *Managing the Civil Service* (Heinemann).

Gates, M. (1976) 'Occupational Segregation and the Law', *Signs* (spring 1976), vol. 1, no. 3, part 2.

Gelb, J. and Palley, M. L. (1979) 'Women and Interest Group Policies: A Comparative Analysis of Federal Decision Making', *Journal of Politics*, vol. 41 (1979).

Gibson, A. 'Women in the Trade Unions: Present and Future Policy on Equal Opportunities', unpublished paper presented at PSA Women and Politics Group Conference, London (September 1980).

Glucklich, P., Hall, C. R. J., Povall, M. and Snell, M. W. (1976) 'Equal Pay Experience in 25 Firms', *Department of Employment Gazette* (December 1976).

Goodin, R. E. (1982) 'Banana Time in British Politics', *Political Studies*, vol. xxx, no. 1, March 1982.

Gramsci, A. (1972) *The Modern Prince and Other Writings* (New York: New World Paperbacks).

Gregory, J. (1982) 'Equal Pay and Sex Discrimination: Why Women are Giving up the Fight', *Feminist Review*, no. 10 (February 1982).

Greenwald, C. S. (1977) *Group Power: Lobbying and Public Policy* (New York: Praeger).

Griffith, J. A. G. (1974) *Parliamentary Scrutiny of Government Bills* (London: Allen & Unwin).

Griffith, J. A. G. (1977) *The Politics of the Judiciary* (London: Fontana/Collins).

Hakim, C. (1979) *Occupational Segregation: A comparative study of the degree and pattern of men and women's work in Britain, the United States and other countries* — Research Paper No. 9 Department of Employment (November 1979).

Heclo, H. (1978) 'Issue Networks and the Executive Establishment', in A. King (ed.) *The New American System* (Washington: American Enterprise Institute).

Heclo, H. (1977) *A Government of Strangers* (Washington: The Brookings Institution).

Heinemann, B. W. (1972) *The Politics of the Powerless* (London and Oxford: Institute of Race Relations/OUP).

Hewitt, P. (1975) *Rights for Women* (London: National Council for Civil Liberties).

Hewitt, P. (1979) *Income Tax and Sex Discrimination* (London: NCCL).

Hodder-Williams, R. (1980) *The Politics of the Supreme Court* (London: Allen & Unwin).

Holland, P. (1979) *Quango Quango Quango* (London: Adam Smith Institute).

Hood, C. (1978) 'Keeping the Centre Small: Explorations of Agency Type', *Political Studies*, vol. 25, no. 1 (March 1978).

Hood, C. (1980) 'The Politics of Quangocide', presented at Annual Conference of Political Studies Association, Exeter (April 1980).

Hood, C. (1979) 'The World of Quasi-Government: Central Non-Departmental Bodies and Government Growth', presented at Annual Conference of the Public Administration Committee, York (September 1979).

Hoskyns, C. and three other members of Rights of Women (1980) 'The EEC and Women – a Case Study of British and European Legislation on Equal Pay', unpublished paper presented at PSA Women and Politics Group Conference (September 1980).

Huidtfeldt, K., Jorgensen, K. and Nielson, R. (eds) (1982) *Strategies for Integrating Women into the Labour Market* (European Women's Studies in Social Science, No. 1) (Copenhagen: Women's Research Centre in Social Science).

Hunt, A. (1968) *Survey of Women's Employment* (London: HMSO).

Hunt, A. (1975) *Management Attitudes and Practices Towards Women at Work* (London: HMSO).

Huntingdon, S. P. (1965) 'The Marasmus of the ICC', in T. Rourke (ed.) *Bureaucratic Power in National Politics* (Boston: Little, Brown & Co.).

Incomes Data Service, Brief 114 (1977) (London: Unwin Brothers Ltd).

Incomes Data Services (1983) *Job Evaluation Review* (London: IDS Job Pay Unit, 1983).

Jaquette, J. (1974) *Women in Politics* (New York: J. Wiley & Sons).

Jain, H. C. and Sloane, P. J. (1978) 'Race, Sex and Minority Group Discrimination Legislation in North America and Britain', *Industrial Relations Journal*, vol. 9 (1978) no. 2.

Jeffreys, J. (1946) *The Story of the Engineers* (London: Lawrence and Wishart).

Jephcott, P., Seear, N. and Smith, J. (1961) *Married Women Working* (London: Allen & Unwin).

Johnson, N. (1977) *In Search of the Constitution* (Oxford: Pergamon Press).

Johnson, N. (1979) 'Quangos and the Structure of British Government', *Public Administration*, vol. 57 (winter 1979).

King, A. (1973) 'Ideas, Institutions and the Policies of Governments. A Comparative Analysis', parts I and II, *British Journal of Political Science*, vol. 2, parts 3 and 4.

King, A. (ed.) (1978) *The New American Political System* (Washington: American Enterprise Institute).

King, J. (1975) *Sex Differences and Society*, Manpower Paper No. 10 (London: HMSO).

Kohlmeier, L. M. (1969) *The Regulators, Watchdog Agencies and the Public Interest* (New York: Harper & Row, 1969).

Kreps, J. (ed.) (1976) *Women and the American Economy* (New Jersey: Prentice-Hall).

Lees, J. D. (1970) *The Political System of the United States* (London: Faber).

Lester, A. and Bindman, G. (1972) *Race and Law* (London: Penguin).

Lewis, J. (ed.) (1983) *Women's Welfare/Women's Rights* (London: Croom Helm).

Lewis, P. (1982) 'The Role of ACAS Conciliators in Unfair Dismissal Cases', *Industrial Relations Journal*, vol. 13, no. 3 (autumn 1982).

Lipset, S. M. (1953) *The First New Nation* (New York: Basic Books Inc.).

Lloyd, C. (ed.) (1975) *Sex, Discrimination and the Division of Labor* (New York: Columbia University Press).

Lowi, T. (1964) 'American Business, Public Policy Case Studies and Political Theory', *World Politics*, vol. 6.

Lowi, T. (1975) 'What Political Scientists Don't Need to Ask about Policy Analysis', in S. Nagel (ed.) *Policy Studies and the Social Sciences* (Lexington: D. C. Heath & Co.).

Lowi, T. (1978) 'Public Policy and Bureaucracy in the United States and France', in D. Ashford (ed.) *Comparing Public Policies* (Beverley Hills: Sage).

Lukes, S. (1974) *Power: A Radical View* (London: Macmillan).

Mackie, L. and Patullo, P. (1977) *Women at Work* (London: Tavistock).

Maidment, R. A. (1981) 'The US Supreme Court and Affirmative Action: The Cases of Bakke, Weber and Fullilove', *Journal of American Studies* vol. 15, no. 3 (December).

Marshall, M. and Aldred, C. (1976/77) *The Equal Pay and Sex Discrimination Acts Report from Scotland* (Aberdeen: People's Press, undated *c.* 1976/77).

Mitchell, J. and Oakley, A. (eds) (1976) *The Rights and Wrongs of Women* (London: Penguin).

Moroney, J. R. (1979) 'Do Women Earn Less Under Capitalism?', *The Economic Journal*, 89 (September).

Moss, P. and Fonda, N. (eds) (1980) *Work and the Family* (London: Temple Smith).

Moynihan, D. P. (1970) *SSRC Newsletter No. 10.*

Murgatroyd, L. (1976) 'What have been the Main Determinants of Male/Female Wage Differentials in the British Economy During the Period 1961–74'. Unpublished dissertation submitted at Cambridge University, 1976.

Nagel, S. (ed.) (1975) *Policy Studies and the Social Sciences* (Lexington: D. C. Heath & Co.).

Neustadt, R. (1960) *Presidential Power: The Politics of Leadership* (New York: John Wiley & Sons).

Novarra, V. (1976) 'Right on Sister! Impressions of the Movement for Equal Opportunity in North America'. Unpublished; available at the Women's Research and Resources Centre (London).

O'Neill, W. (1969) *The Woman Movement: Feminism in the United States and England* (London: Allen & Unwin).

Orfield, G. (1975) *Congressional Power: Congress and Social Change* (New York: Harcourt Brace Jovanovich).

O'Sullivan, J. and Gallick, R. (1976) *Workers and Allies: Female Participation in the American Trade Union Movement 1824–1976* (Washington: Smithsonian Institution Press).

Outer Circle Policy Unit (1979) *What's Wrong with Quangos?* (London: July 1979).

Panitch, L. (1977) 'The Development of Corporatism in Liberal Democracies', *Comparative Political Studies*, April 1977, p. 66.

Pannick, D. (1981) 'The Burden of Proof in Discrimination Cases', *New Law Journal*, 27.8.81.

Pannick, D. (1982) 'Indirect Discrimination under the Sex Discrimination Act', pts I and II, *New Law Journal*, 16.9.82 and 23.9.82.

Parker, J. (1975) *Social Policy and Citizenship* (London: Macmillan).

Pifer, A. (1976) *Women Working: Toward a New Society* (Report of President, Annual Report, 1976, of Carnegie Corporation).

Player, M. A. (1976) *Federal Law of Employment Discrimination* (St Paul, Minnesota: West Publishing Co., May 1976).

Pleck, J. et al. (1980) 'Conflicts between Work and Family Life', *Monthly Labor Review* (Washington: Department of Labor) March.

Potter, A. (1957) 'The Equal Pay Campaign Committee: A Case-study of a Pressure Group', *Political Studies*, vol. 5, no. 1 (February 1957).

Pym, B. (1974) *Pressure Groups and the Permissive Society* (London: David & Charles).

Rabinovitch, D. (1976) 'The Bias in the Government's Anti-Bias Agency', *Fortune* (December 1976).

Randall, V. (1982) *Women and Politics* (London: Macmillan).

Ratner, R. J. (ed.) (1980) *Equal Employment Policy for Women. Strategies for Implementation in the United States, Canada and Western Europe* (Philadelphia: Temple University Press).

Rendel, M. (1968) *Equality for Women* (London: Fabian Research Series).

Rendel, M. (1976) 'Law as an Instrument of Oppression or Reform', *Sociological Review Monograph, 23.*

Rendel, M. (1978) 'Legislating for Equal Pay and Opportunity for Women in Britain' *Signs*, vol. 3, no. 4 (summer 1978).

Richards, M. A. (1976) 'The Sex Discrimination Act – Equality for Women?', *Industrial Law Journal*, vol. 5, (1976) no. 1.

Richards, P. (1970) *Parliament and Conscience* (London: Allen & Unwin).

Richardson, J. J. and Jordan, A. G. *Governing Under Pressure* (London: Martin Robertson, 1979).

Rights of Women, Europe (1983) *Women's Rights and the EEC: A Guide for Women in the UK* (London: Rights of Women, Europe).

Robarts, S. with Coote, A. and Ball, E. (1981) *Positive Action for Women* (London: NCCL) .

Robinson, D. A. (1974) 'Two Movements in Pursuit of Equal Employment Opportunity', *Signs*, vol. 4, no. 3 (spring 1974).

Rogaly, J. (1977) *Grunwick* (London: Penguin).

Rose, E. and Associates (1969) *Colour and Citizenship. A Report on British Race Relations* (London and Oxford: Institute of Race Relations/OUP).

Rose, R. (ed.) (1976) *The Dynamics of Public Policy: A Comparative Analysis* (Beverly Hills: Sage).

Rose, R. and Suleiman, E. N. (eds) (1980) *Presidents and Prime Ministers*, especially Chapter 8 (Washington: American Enterprise Institute).

Ross, S. C. (1973) *The Rights of Women. The Basic A.C.L.U. Guide to a Woman's Rights* (New York: Discus Books/Avon).

Routh, G. (1965) *Occupation and Pay in Great Britain 1906–1960* (Cambridge: CUP).

Rowbotham, S., Segal, L. and Wainwright, H. (1979) *Beyond the Fragments* (London: Merlin Press).

Rowbotham, S. (1972) 'The Beginning of Women's Liberation in Britain', in M. Wandor (ed.) *The Body Politic* (London: Stage I).

Scarman, Lord Justice (1979) 'The Public Administration and the Courts', *Public Administration*, vol. 57 (spring 1979).

Sachs, A. and Wilson, J. H. (1978) *Sexism and the Law* (London: Martin Robertson).

Scheingold, S. (1974) *The Politics of Rights* (New Haven: Yale University Press).

Schattschneider, E. E. (1960) *The Semi-Sovereign People* (New York: Holt, Rinehart & Winston).

Scorer, C. and Sedley, A. (1983) *Amending the Equality Laws* (London: NCCL).

Seear, N. (1968) *Royal Commission on the Trade Unions and Employers' Associations* Research Paper 11 (London: HMSO).

Seear, N., Roberts, V. and Brock, J. (1964) *A Career for Women in Industry* (London School of Economics).

Sen, A. (1977) 'On Weights and Measures: Informational Constraints in Social Welfare Analysis', *Econometrica*, vol. 45, (1977) no. 7.

Shapiro, M. (1978) 'The Supreme Court: From Warren to Burger', in A. King (ed.) *The New American Political System* (Washington: American Enterprise Institute).

Sharr, J. (1967) 'Equality of Opportunity and Beyond', in J. Pennock and J. Chapman (eds), *NOMOS IX: Equality* (New York: Atherton Press).

Simpson, P. (1975) 'International Women's Year: an update. The Impact of Mexico City', *Civil Rights Digest* (Washington: US Commission on Civil Rights, Fall 1975).

Smith, B. L. R. and Hague, D. C. (1971) *The Dilemma of Accountability in Modern Government* (London: Macmillan).

Smith, B. C. (1976) *Policy Making in British Government* (London: Martin Robertson).

Smuts, R. W. (1971) *Women and Work in America* (New York: Schocken Books).

Snell, M. (1979) 'The Equal Pay and Sex Discrimination Acts: Their Impact in the Workplace' *Feminist Review*, (1979) no. 1.

Snell, M., Glucklich, P. and Povall, M. (1981) *Equal Pay and Opportunities: A Study of the Implementation and Effects of the Equal Pay and Sex Discrimination Acts in 26 Organisations* (London: Department of Employment).

Sundquist, J. L. (1968) *Politics and Policy* (Washington: Brookings Institution).

Thurow, L. (1975) *Generating Inequality* (London: Macmillan).

Vallance, E. (1979) *Women in the House* (London: Athlone Press).

Vile, M. J. C. (1970) *Politics in the USA* (London: Hutchinson).

Walker, J. (1969) 'Diffusions of Innovations Among the American States', *American Political Science Review*, vol. 63, no. 3 (September 1969).

Walkland, S. A. (1968) *The Legislative Process in Great Britain* (London: Allen & Unwin).

Walkland, S. and Ryle, M. (1977) *The Commons in the Seventies* (London: Fontana).

Wallace, P. A. (ed.) (1976) *Equal Employment Opportunity and the A T & T Case* (Boston: MIT).

Wallington, P. and McBride, J. (1976) *Civil Liberties and a Bill of Rights* (London: Cobden Trust).

Watson, D. (1977) 'Welfare Rights and Human Rights', *Journal of Social Policy*, vol. 6 (1977) no. 1.

Webb, B. (1919) *The Wages of Men and Women. Should They Be Equal?* (London: Fabian Society/Allen & Unwin).

Wolff, J. (1977) 'Women in Organisations', in S. Clegg and D. Dunkerly (eds), *Critical Issues in Organisations* (London: Routledge & Kegan Paul).

Index

242